This study explores the ways in which two spiritual teachers, one Christian (Teilhard de Chardin) and one Hindu (Rāmānuja) have seen the world as inherently divine, and have presented this insight theologically through their use of a symbol, the 'body of the divine' (the body of Christ/Brahman). Hunt Overzee shows how both thinkers understood reality in terms of consciousness, and believed that salvation/release is realised through attaining the Lord. The book makes a significant contribution to comparative theology, and explores the wide-ranging implications of a religious symbol whose potency is perennial, cross-cultural, and of continuing contemporary importance.

THE BODY DIVINE

CAMBRIDGE STUDIES IN RELIGIOUS TRADITIONS

Edited by John Clayton (University of Lancaster), Steven Collins (University of Chicago) and Nicholas de Lange (University of Cambridge)

1. *Religion and the individual: a Jewish perspective*
   Louis Jacobs
2. *The body divine: the symbol of the body in the works of Teilhard de Chardin and Rāmānuja*
   Anne Hunt Overzee

THE BODY DIVINE

The symbol of the body in the works of Teilhard de Chardin and Rāmānuja

ANNE HUNT OVERZEE

The right of the University of Cambridge to print and sell all manner of books was granted by Henry VIII in 1534. The University has printed and published continuously since 1584.

CAMBRIDGE UNIVERSITY PRESS

Cambridge
New York Port Chester
Melbourne Sydney

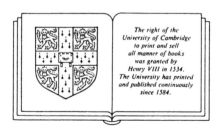

CAMBRIDGE UNIVERSITY PRESS
Cambridge, New York, Melbourne, Madrid, Cape Town, Singapore, São Paulo

Cambridge University Press
The Edinburgh Building, Cambridge CB2 8RU, UK

Published in the United States of America by Cambridge University Press, New York

www.cambridge.org
Information on this title: www.cambridge.org/9780521385169

First published 1992
This digitally printed version 2007

A catalogue record for this publication is available from the British Library

Library of Congress Cataloguing in Publication data

Hunt Overzee, Anne.
The body divine: the symbol of the body in the works of Teilhard de Chardin and
Rāmānuja/Anne Hunt Overzee.
p. cm. – (Cambridge studies in religious traditions: 2)
ISBN 0 521 38516 4
1. Body, Human – Religious aspects – History. 2. Teilhard de Chardin, Pierre.
3. Rāmānuja, 1017–1137. I. Title. II. Series.
BL604.B64094 1992
291.2′2 – dc20 91-11363 CIP

ISBN 978-0-521-38516-9 hardback
ISBN 978-0-521-04669-5 paperback

To Klaas, and all who want to 'see'

God is an intelligible sphere whose centre is everywhere and whose circumference is nowhere.

(Corpus Hermeticum)

Nature is an infinite sphere whose centre is everywhere, whose circumference is nowhere.

(Pascal)

All are but parts of one tremendous whole, whose body nature is and God the soul.

(Pope)

Contents

Preface

This book represents an exploration of the relationship between how we view the world and how we view the divine. And it focuses on the way the symbol of the divine body functions as a model of consciousness in the worldviews of two thinkers who speak within the context of mainstream Christianity and Hinduism respectively.

It is a revised form of my doctoral thesis, the research for which I undertook at Lancaster University. I am indebted to Professor Ninian Smart and Dr Patrick Sherry for their thoughtful guidance and encouragement throughout my time in Lancaster. I would also like to acknowledge the financial support I received from the Department of Education and Science in the form of a Major State Scholarship, and from the Spalding Trusts, who made an invaluable contribution towards my last year's research.

There are others without whom the book would not be as it now stands. My deepest thanks go to Freda Matchett for her valued friendship and scholarly advice, and to Augustine Thottakara, CMI for his laughter and help with Sanskrit. Caroline Mackenzie has truly inspired me with her letters from the Rāmānuja temple town of Melkote in India, and her beautiful illustration of the cosmic Lord. My parents, Wynnell and Paul Hunt, provided tremendous support at the proof-reading stages. Alex Wright of Cambridge University Press encouraged me at a critical stage, in my attempts to place this study in a broader context. Alyson Twyman supplied ingenious organisational and typing skills which transformed my drafts into thesis and book format. And my husband Klaas offered me love and encouragement throughout.

The structure of the book is quite simple. In Part 1 I look at the 'lineages' of the divine body in the religious traditions of Teilhard de Chardin and Rāmānuja respectively, and show how each thinker understood and used the divine body within the context of his own theological understanding. In Part II I bring my findings together and explore the structures of consciousness the divine body symbol reveals in the writings of both Rāmānuja and Teilhard, and the functions these structures serve in their respective worldviews.

Abbreviations

Teilhard de Chardin

AE	*Activation of Energy*
CE	*Christianity and Evolution*
HE	*Human Energy*
HM	*The Heart of Matter*
HU	*Hymn of the Universe*
LLZ	*Letters to Léontine Zanta*
MD	*Le Milieu divin*
MM	*The Making of a Mind*
PM	*The Phenomenon of Man*
SC	*Science and Christ*
TF	*Toward the Future*
WTW	*Writings in Time of War*

Rāmānuja

GB(S)	*Gītābhāṣya*, trans. M. R. Sampatkumaran
GB(VB)	*Gītābhāṣya*, trans. J. A. B. van Buitenen
GM	*Granthamālā* (complete works)
SB(T)	*Śrībhāṣya*, trans. G. Thibaut
VS(R)	*Vedārthasaṃgraha*, trans. S. S. Raghavachar
VS(VB)	*Vedārthasaṃgraha*, trans. J. A. B. van Buitenen

Introduction

> Worldmaking as we know it always starts from worlds already on hand: the making is really a re-making.
>
> (Nelson Goodman)

This book is about worldmaking. It is concerned with two very different men who sought, in their own ways, to create new worlds, new ways of seeing things. They were both deeply committed to their respective religious traditions and worked within the frameworks of those existing worldviews[1] to revision their sense of the divine in relation to the cosmos. Rāmānuja (*c.* 1017–1137)[2] was a religious teacher in the Śrīvaiṣṇava community in South India. Teilhard de Chardin (1881–1955)[3] was a French Jesuit priest, who, as a palaeontologist, travelled extensively throughout his life. Both men drew upon symbols to model their worldmaking, symbols which have a rich heritage in their respective traditions. The symbols they chose, however, were fundamentally similar. For both of them the worlds they perceived were symbolised by 'the body of the divine'.

The question arises, 'What did Rāmānuja and Teilhard de Chardin understand by "the body of the divine"?' And in order to begin looking for answers to this question I spend more time at the beginning of the book 'locating'[4] the divine body symbol in the specific religious contexts of Rāmānuja and Teilhard. After all, religious experience does not arise in a vacuum,[5] and the very term 'body of the divine' has a wealth of associations, memories and meanings, some of which apply to the Hindu tradition of Rāmānuja, and some to the Roman Catholic tradition of Teilhard de Chardin. To explore the ways in which these two thinkers 'saw' things we need to start with the religious alphabets they used to describe their experiences.

It may occasion surprise that many religious beliefs and doctrines are formulated in metaphorical and symbolic language. Thus part of the task of one seeking to understand religious thought-systems is to study the symbolism inherent in discursive material. Such a study broadens out immediately to involve psychological questions ('Where does this metaphor come from, and why?') and questions about religious practice ('Why does this symbol prove valuable to this group of people, and how does it work?'). Immediately, therefore, the enquiry has become an inter-disciplinary quest for understanding. In seeking to understand what 'the body of the divine' meant to Teilhard de Chardin and Rāmānuja, I have been involved in relating their use of symbolic language to their theological[6] worldviews, and also to their didactic purposes.

It is interesting to find that when describing something symbolic it appears necessary to use symbolic language,[7] that is, language which is not direct but suggestive and evocative. But by analysing the function of the term 'the divine body' and responding to it as it is expressed in the writings of Teilhard de Chardin and Rāmānuja respectively, it is possible to cut through this problem: it is not just a question of describing 'the divine body' but of exploring how it 'works'. When I go on, for example, to look at 'the divine body' in the context of religious practice, the question I am seeking to address is basically, 'How do Rāmānuja and Teilhard de Chardin understand the divine body to function in the religious traditions they represent?'

One indication of how 'the divine body' functions in these particular Christian and Hindu traditions is to be found in the roles each of these two theologians adopt in relation to their respective traditions. Both were innovative teachers within mainstream traditions, with a strong sense of spiritual purpose. Rāmānuja integrated classical teachings with popular beliefs and practices in highly sophisticated systematised theological works. He argued that non-Vedic texts support and elucidate the Vedic tradition, and he evolved an inclusive methodology which developed into what is now regarded as one of the main schools of Vedānta, namely, *viśiṣṭādvaita* or differentiated non-dualism. His role as theological innovator is expressed in the way he draws upon a powerful symbol, the body of Brahman, to help him integrate the spiritual path of devotional love (*bhakti*) with Vedic tradition.

Teilhard de Chardin's influence in Christian theology is arguably less significant than Rāmānuja's in Hinduism. However, he represents an authentic tradition which, from the earliest times in

Christian history, has sought to integrate traditional and popular belief with current thinking. He was, like Rāmānuja, a theological innovator, even though for most of his life he was not allowed to teach or write about his theological ideas. He sought to expand current conceptions of Christ and even of human life, to measure up to contemporary understandings of the cosmos.[8] In this endeavour he used Pauline symbolism and that of the early Greek Fathers to create a synthesis of Christian doctrine and modern evolutionary theory. In particular he drew upon the symbol of the body of Christ.

From what we know of Rāmānuja it is clear that he worked as a religious teacher (*ācārya*) within the Śrīvaiṣṇava religious community (*sampradāya*) at Śrīrangam. His lineage was through Yāmuna, who was a person of considerable stature spiritually and intellectually. In this tradition, such a teacher who is both experienced in the religious life and learned in terms of Vedāntic knowledge – in practice these two cannot be separated – actually brings the received tradition (*śruti*: literally 'that which is heard') to fulfilment in the hearts and minds of people. The fact that Rāmānuja wrote so systematically about aspects of knowledge of Brahman[9] (*Brahmajñāna*) suggests that he was aware of his responsibilities as Yāmuna's successor as spiritual guide and teacher. In the opening words of one of his major works, the *Vedārthasaṃgraha*, he writes:

> The crown of the Vedas, i.e. the Upaniṣads, which lays down the good of the whole world, enshrines this truth: a seeker, after first acquiring a true understanding of the individual self and the Supreme, and equipped with the performance of the duties pertaining to his station in life, must devote himself to the meditation, worship and adoring salutation of the blessed feet of the supreme Person. This done with immeasurable joy leads to the attainment of the Supreme.[10]

This extract shows us the spiritual purpose underlying Rāmānuja's philosophical and theological writings. In the context of the Vedāntic notion of *ācārya*, we may, perhaps, conclude that he saw himself as a transmitter of given truths, and as one whose task was to assist in their realisation. We shall see in the following chapters that the 'body of Brahman' was inherited and developed by him as a tool for self-realisation.

Teilhard de Chardin's self-understanding was fundamentally related to his priestly vocation. He believed that his task was to participate in Christ's work of universal salvation.[11] He saw himself as a kind of apostle or evangelist in a secular world. Through his job as palaeontologist he sought to integrate a devotional Catholic outlook and experience of the religious life with contemporary scientific research and neo-humanistic[12] philosophy. He speaks in his writings of teaching people how to 'see'[13] the divine presence within the world. He, in fact, equates this perception with knowledge of God. He writes:

> I would wish, through my meditations, speech and the practice of my whole life, to disclose and preach the bonds of continuity which make the Cosmos, with which we are involved, a milieu divinized through the Incarnation, divinizing through Communion, and divinizable through our co-operation.[14]

Teilhard clearly believes he has a specific vocation to make known the universal Christ, perceived as a divine milieu.[15] It is in trying to communicate his particular vision that he draws upon New Testament references to the body of Christ and interprets them from within a new philosophical framework. In the succeeding chapters we shall see how he uses the 'body of Christ' to reveal his vision of a divinised world.

So the symbol 'the divine body' speaks of worlds 'already on hand'. It discloses Rāmānuja's and Teilhard's own worldviews, and it uncovers sacred ways of 'knowing' and 'seeing' which belong to the original visions of the traditions which they espoused. To explore this symbol is to engage in religious interpretation which, like any other form of interpretation, involves listening to what is being said, identifying patterns of meaning, and translating these for a given audience. I am interested in the inherent structure of the divine body symbol, and the form this takes in the writings of Teilhard de Chardin and Rāmānuja respectively.

Paul Ricœur speaks of the theologian as a hermeneut, whose task is to interpret the multivalent, rich metaphors arising from the symbolic bases of tradition so that the symbols may 'speak' once again to our existential situation.[16] Certainly this can be one aspect of a theologian's task, but in today's pluralistic world, many who work with metaphors and symbols in this way would not align themselves with a confessional stance in the way that a theologian does. An anthropologist, philosopher, or historian of religion has much to contribute to the task of interpreting traditional metaphors. Perhaps such an undertaking requires the collaboration of people from different disciplines, representing a variety of approaches which together could provide 'multivalent', 'rich' interpretations of symbols for today.

Eliade once suggested that dialogue between peoples of different cultural backgrounds needs to be conducted in a language which is 'capable of expressing human realities and spiritual values', not, he argued, in the 'empirical and utilitarian language of today'.[17] In our contemporary multi-cultural society, and particularly in those communities where inter-religious encounter is not a luxury for the specialists but a necessity for mutual co-operation, there is a real need for languages which communicate directly between people. The language of symbolism is, perhaps, of particular value in this context, where the interpreting and revisioning of symbols can be explored together and thus 'lived' into existence.

The tools which I use to explore the divine body symbol in Rāmānuja and Teilhard de Chardin are those of any 'hermeneut' or interpreter. The tool of listening and reading with an open mind is a prerequisite for the job. This ensures that the approach is relatively value-free because judgements are suspended while the world of the believer is consciously entered and explored.[18] This does not mean the interpreter has no feelings, no beliefs of his or her own. It signifies rather an ability to see things through another's eyes as well as your own.[19] This involves knowing where you yourself 'stand', and then listening until something resonates and you can feel a response to what is being said by another. At this point there is a possibility of empathy, from which understanding can arise.

An ability to see ideas as pictures or patterns which can then be presented as 'wholes' to others is also important. This requires a sense of structure and relationship between things being communicated. A phenomenological or systematic approach is not enough to really grasp what is being communicated by the symbol or idea as a whole, which needs to be taken on board and allowed to find its own 'shape' inside a person. It can then be expressed through a personal sense of its own inherent 'character'.

Obviously there is the need for critical evaluation and reflection in the ongoing task of creating meaning. It is necessary to be able to step back and view the material from a position of non-involvement. But often this comes later, since the attraction towards a thinker, an idea or a symbol is usually quite strong. However, the attraction is necessary for establishing interest and contact in the first place, so both involvement and non-involvement are necessary on the part of the hermeneut. Ninian Smart refers to 'a kind of passion for evocative dispassion' in discussing the approach of a student of Religious Studies to his or her subject.[20] I would say that the person seeking to interpret religious symbols needs to feel both 'passion' and 'evocative dispassion', and to be able to integrate the qualities of the right and left hemispheres of the brain in order to engage fully in the task.

In my exploration of the divine body symbol in Teilhard and Rāmānuja I have used these tools of listening and then identifying the patterns or 'wholes' of meaning, as part of the process of relating these back to the historical traditions out of which they arose, and to the theological worldviews of their creators. This locates the symbol in its religious and philosophical context while enabling the symbol's own structure to provide the framework for theological and reflective enquiry.

Having done this I have also chosen to relate the divine body symbols one to another in order to see if there are any overlaps of structure or form. At the outset I expected little in the way of correspondence between the two, since the religious worlds of Teilhard de Chardin and Rāmānuja could hardly be more contrasting. I chose to undertake this task of relating the divine body symbols one to another not as an exercise to compare disparate symbols and thinkers, but rather to explore a new way of looking at the encounter between, in this case, Śrīvaiṣṇavism and Roman Catholicism, or between Christian and Hindu expressions of truth.

I make no apology, therefore, for focusing more on the similarities, the overlaps of meaning, in the encounter. My objective is not to 'compare and contrast', as I have said, but to allow the symbol's in this case inherent integrative structure of wholeness to continue 'working'.[21] Chapter 8 begins to show the context in which this symbol could be encouraged to make its presence felt today, although really this is the subject of a book in its own right, and deserves to be addressed by specialists from many different fields. This relates, as I see it, to the final task of the hermeneut: enabling the symbol to 'speak' once again to our contemporary situation.

The original Greek word, *symbolon*, came to denote the veiling and unveiling of hidden things or of secrets.[22] In the Pythagorean Neo-Platonic tradition, for example, symbols were methods of instruction in the form of symbolic modes of speech. They guarded secret things 'in an enigmatic form', revealing their truths 'unambiguously' to those able to perceive them.[23] For the purposes of this book I shall look on them as functions of the human power to relate things one to another in a way that is not always obvious, and to structure reality. They are able to teach us how to see things according to the patterns of associations and experiences they embody.

Throughout the book I shall continually be talking of the divine body as a metaphor. This is not in any way to belittle its value. Rather it is to recognise its disclosive and evocative character. I am drawing upon the network of association and nuance connected with each thinker's experiences and concepts of the 'divine' and the 'body', in order to allow us to be challenged to see the world through their eyes and to respond to what they disclose to us.

This metaphorical language stems from symbolic tradition. Symbols are strange creatures. They represent things to us, indicate things to us, associate things one to another in a way that is meaningful to us, and evoke reactions in us. They 'speak' to us in a 'language' which communicates to our whole being, not just to our intellect, and reveal 'secrets' to us about the way things are. It has been said that we, as humans, are symbolic beings: we create symbols in order to function as perceiving, thinking people.[24] The fact remains that symbols are important to us, particularly in terms of our self-understanding.

If symbols stand for, represent or denote something other than themselves, and religious symbols function in relation to things divine, then we can be sure that 'the divine body' when viewed as a symbol 'hides' and 'reveals' knowledge that is regarded as sacred. And as religious concepts often involve reference to spiritual transformation,[25] so religious symbols often provide the means to attain that transformation. It is through appropriating for ourselves a new way of seeing the world in the light of our sense of the divine that the divine body symbol can really be said to 'work' for us.

PART I

CHAPTER I

The background to the divine body in Teilhard de Chardin

Teilhard de Chardin's vision[1] of the body of Christ is communicated to us in his writings. However, his Christological insights are not presented systematically; they are to be found in a variety of contexts, amidst ideas on a wide range of subjects. It could be argued that if we were to extrapolate all these reflections and put them together we would find Teilhard's vision. But it is not that simple. You cannot reconstruct visions like jigsaws; they come entire and complete. One of the ways in which such completeness is communicated to us is through metaphorical language. Teilhard drew upon an ancient Christian metaphor to communicate his vision: that of 'Christ's body'. As a way of approaching Teilhard's vision I shall look, first of all, at the origins of this metaphor, and at some of the ideas which helped Teilhard revision the 'body of Christ' for the twentieth century.

THE NEW TESTAMENT

The major source for Teilhard de Chardin's Christology is the New Testament, and in particular, St Paul.[2] One of the most commonly cited references in the New Testament quoted by Teilhard is Colossians 1:17b, 'in him all things hold together',[3] and the one he stated to be his 'fundamental article' of belief.[4] 'Christ is all', he writes, 'or nothing',[5] when referring to the relationship between Christ and the cosmos.[6]

The setting of Colossians 1:17b provides a useful background to Teilhard's claim that Christ is everything to the world about us:

For in him all things were created, in heaven and on earth, visible and invisible, whether thrones or dominions or principalities or authorities – all things were created through him and for him. He is before all things, and in him all things hold together... For in him all the fullness of God was pleased to dwell, and through him to reconcile to himself all things, whether on earth or in heaven, making peace by the blood of his cross.[7]

Clearly this passage claims Christ's creative power and authority over and within all the dimensions of reality. It also links Christ with the goal or fulfilment of that reality: 'all things were created for him'. Of Christ himself, it is stated that he is also 'before' all things, that they hold together 'in' him, and that the 'fullness' of God is 'in' him for the purpose of reconciling all things to him. This is a very explicit statement about the relationship between Christ and 'all things'. He is their source, goal and means of unity and reconciliation.

Teilhard views this fundamental relationship between Christ and matter as a physical reality. In other words, it is a relationship the effects of which are able to be perceived and studied in the world about us. For him, one of the main effects of the relationship is a unity[8] which can be seen as a constituent aspect of all forms of matter:

Physically speaking, there is only one dynamism in the present world, that which gathers all things to Christ. Christ is the centre to which all the successfully realised, living, *elect* portions of the cosmos make their way, in whom each finds its being. In him, 'the plenitude of the universe', *omnia creantur* because *omnia uniuntur* – all things are created because all things are made one.[9]

It is in the context of this 'bonding' of things to one another in Christ that the cosmic[10] dimensions of Teilhard's Christ are disclosed. He envisages an infinite network of inter-related layers of life which comprise both the object of scientific research and the subject of Christology. In accepting and building on contemporary understandings of the cosmos, he is developing a dialectical relationship which began in the Early Church: between Christology and cosmology.

In the New Testament, it is the term 'body of Christ' which stands for a vision and experience of all things holding together in Christ. In Pauline usage the term is used metaphorically, usually to denote a local group of Christians constituting Christ's body (*sōma*) by being 'in Christ'. It can also refer to Christ as the body of which they are the limbs. And 'the Church' (*ecclēsia*) is also Christ's body, with Christ (or the Messiah) as its head. It is the presence and transcendence of Christ, however, which is the prior necessity for the existence of a community of believers. Christ is, as it were, the believers' environment.[11] Through living 'in' him, the harmony and unity of a body is realised.

This 'bonding' together in Christ is portrayed in the New Testament as being of eschatological significance. Consider, for example, the following claim: 'In [Christ] all the fullness of God was pleased to dwell, and through him to reconcile to himself all things...' (Colossians 1:19–20). It is in God's fullness (*plērōma*) that everything 'holds together': all is 'reconciled' in Christ's 'fullness' of God: 'For in him dwells all the fullness of the Godhead bodily; and in him you are made full [i.e. filled].'[12] The *plērōma* becomes an important term for Teilhard, indicating the consummation of the whole universe in Christ as its 'Omega Point'.

The body of Christ comprises, then, those who have not 'conformed' to this world (Romans 12:2) but to the image[13] of the Son (Romans 8:29). Since the verb 'to conform' (*summorphousthai*) can also mean 'to assimilate', we can say that those who conform to Christ become him in some way; they become part of his body.

The writer of the Epistle to the Romans views this body in terms of the physical world and its 'redemption' or fulfilment:

> For creation watches with eager expectation for the revealing/unveiling of the sons of God. For creation was not subjected to error willingly, but in hope, on account of the one who subjected it; because even creation itself will be freed from its bondage to decay and corruption, into the freedom[14] of the glory of the children of God. For we know that the whole of creation has been groaning in labour together until now; and not only that, but we ourselves, having the first-fruits of the spirit, groan inwardly as we eagerly look for the redemption of our body.[15]

When Teilhard refers to Christ as in some sense physically linking all things, this theme of the transformation of the created world into the body of Christ lies at the basis of his thought.[16]

The question of how such a transformation takes place is answered in part by the Johannine theme of the mutual indwelling of the Father, Son and believers.[17] This is discussed slightly differently in Ephesians:

> I bow my knees before the Father, from whom every family in heaven and on earth is named, that according to the riches of his glory he may grant you to be strengthened with might through his Spirit in the inner man, and that Christ may dwell in your hearts through faith; that you, being rooted

and grounded in love, may have power to comprehend[18] with all the saints what is the breadth and length and height and depth, and to know the love of Christ which surpasses knowledge, that you may be filled with all the fullness of God.[19]

The key to the transformational process described in this passage is the Holy Spirit, Christ dwelling in the heart. Through faith this presence is concretised in the energy of love. Teilhard presents the spirit in terms of the 'within' of things which he ascribes to consciousness. He relates spiritual growth to an increase in the energy of love, and to the power to perceive more clearly. In other words, spiritual growth requires a transformation of consciousness. He refers constantly to learning how to 'see' the 'milieu' around and within us of Christ's presence. Such 'seeing' signifies growth in Christ–consciousness.

Here the emphasis is not so much on Christ as the believer's 'environment' as his or her inner 'ground'. Teilhard speaks of being rooted in Christ and coming to know and love him as a personal Centre. This interpretation of knowing Christ ties in with his view of mysticism as 'physicalism'. For him, 'comprehending' the 'breadth and length and height and depth' has experiential value, and directly corresponds to being 'filled with all the fullness of God'. He clarifies his position in 'Mon univers' (1924):

I have, in fact, become convinced that men include two irreconcilable types of minds: the physicalists (who are 'mystics') and the juridicists. For the former, the whole beauty of life consists in being organically structured; and in consequence Christ, being pre-eminently attractive, must radiate physically ... The physicalists ... will see in the word mystical the expression of a hyper-physical (super-substantial) relationship – stronger, and in consequence more respectful of embodied individualities, than that which operates between the cells of one and the same animate organism ... I am a physicalist by instinct: and that is why it is impossible for me to read St. Paul without seeing the universal and cosmic domination of the Incarnate Word emerging from his words with dazzling clarity.[20]

Teilhard is making an important theological point here about the unity of Christ and the whole of the natural world. It is only because of this unity that Christ is inseparable from every life-form: he radiates through all things in virtue of being part of the 'conforming' or structuring process which makes them what they are. He is their inner 'form'. Hence his Christology is realistic:[21] Christ is 'all', since without him there would be no cosmos.[22]

THE GREEK FATHERS OF THE CHURCH

Although little is known about the theological reading Teilhard de Chardin selected for personal choice, it is obvious that in addition to biblical studies, his theological formation as a Jesuit would have included study of the Church Fathers. There are several themes in Patristic thought which reappear in Teilhard's own writings, and almost certainly influenced them. Origen (*c.* CE 185–*c.* CE 254), for example, clearly describes the universe in organic terms, 'informed'[23] by God:

Although the whole world is arranged in diverse parts and functions, we must not suppose that its condition is one of discord and self-contradiction; but as our one body is composed of many members and is held together by one soul, so we should, I think, accept the opinion that the universe is, as it were, an immense organism held together by the power and reason of God as one soul.[24]

The 'body' simile is not new (for example, it occurs in 1 Corinthians 12:12–31), but here Origen is suggesting that the 'opinion' or worldview that the universe is an organism be accepted. He understands this immense organism to be 'held together' by the 'power and reason' of God's 'soul'.

Christ is, for Origen, conceived as Logos and Wisdom, the creative function of God and the one in whom creation is restored and redeemed. His mediatorial role[25] is exemplified in Origen's interpretation of Revelation 22:13: Christ is the Alpha and the Omega, the first and the last, the beginning and the end:

God the Logos is the Alpha, the beginning and the cause of all things, the one who is first not in time but in honour... To him glory and honour are offered. Let it be said that, since he provides an end for the things created from him, he is the Omega at the consummation of the ages. He is first and then he is last, not in relation to time, but because he provides a beginning and an end. Here are understood the extremities of the letters, which are the beginning and the end and include the others in between.[26]

It is this eschatological emphasis which Teilhard considered so important for his evolutionary Christology. Christ–Omega becomes a central concept for him, referring to the power of Christ to unite all things by drawing them to himself and forward to their fulfilment in God (the pleroma). Lyons makes the point that this view is equivalent to Origen's concept of *apokatastasis*, or 'the restoration of a transformed creation to God through Christ'.[27] Remember that this emphasis was drawn from the New Testament themes of the cosmic dimension of Christ's body and the unitive function of Christ creating and redeeming creation.[28]

To Irenaeus' (*c.* CE 130–*c.* 254)[29] mind, humanity has its own place in the process of redemption. He believed that mankind becomes 'deified'[30] as it develops in holiness: 'It was necessary that man should first be created, then that he should grow up, then that he should become adult man, then that he should multiply, then gain in strength, then attain glory, and having attained glory, that he should have the vision of his master.'[31] This development takes place through the grace of God rather than by individual effort. As Dai Sil Kim points out in her paper 'Irenaeus of Lyons and Teilhard de Chardin: a Comparative Study of "Recapitulation" and "Omega"', deification is, after all, the natural conclusion of Irenaeus' doctrine of humanity whose image is found, from the beginning, in Christ.[32] Teilhard's use of the term 'divinisation' rather than 'deification' precludes the confusion over 'man becoming God'. As he sees it, men and women become 'informed' by God as by a 'living flame'; correspondingly, they embody Christ, and 'become' him.

For both Irenaeus and Teilhard de Chardin, it is through the Eucharist that such an integration of the individual and Christ takes place. Irenaeus views the Eucharistic elements as in some sense containing the risen Christ.[33] The Eucharist is a sacrament, participation in which enables the individual to be united with Christ through matter. For Teilhard, it is the means by which the universe is divinised. Teilhard develops Irenaeus' position to suggest that participating in the Eucharist is an opportunity for the Christian to help build Christ's body. This relationship between Christ and believers, and between the elements of the natural world and those specifically used for the Eucharist, is fundamental to Teilhard's vision. He sees the Mass as a process of realising, that is, making real, the divine 'form' of Christ.

Teilhard never infers, however, that Christ is 'the same' as we are. Teilhard draws upon Athanasius' (*c.* CE 296–373) defence against Arianism to maintain the uniqueness of Christ's function as the creative Word of God. As well as being the beginning or 'Alpha' of life, he is also 'Omega', the fulfilment and completion of all in God. Athanasius argues for clarity in distinguishing Christ from the beginner of a series:

If then the Lord is in such sense created as a 'beginning' of all things, it would follow that He and all other things together make up the unity of creation, and He neither differs from all others, though He become the beginning of all, nor is He Lord of them, though older in point of time... He who is before all is not a beginning of all, but is other than all; but if other than all (in which 'all' the beginning of all is included), it follows that He is other than the creatures.[34]

Teilhard maintains that Christ is both unique as Omega (i.e. the Word which is before and beyond all) and incarnate within each 'thing' in the universe as its 'Centre' of consciousness. He speaks of Christ being in the world as a universal 'Element', uniting all centres, all life, in himself.

Another aspect of Athanasius' work, and one which is familiar to a student of Teilhard, is that of redemption through divinisation. Using the Patristic categories of Christ's human and divine natures, he claimed that it is through Christ's human nature, transformed and divinised, that man is redeemed: 'For therefore did he assume the body originate and human that having renewed it as its Framer, He might deify it in Himself, and thus might introduce us all into the kingdom after his likeness.'[35] In other words, what is assumed by Christ is sanctified and becomes the means of salvation for others.

Teilhard de Chardin was, of course, deliberately using language to overcome the dualism inherent in the Chalcedonian formulations. But when he speaks of the spiritual power of matter as a divine milieu, he is making a similar claim: that it is the divine in relation to the material world which is the basis for any notion of salvation.

It is important to recognise that Teilhard's vision of Christ as inseparable from the world, and of all life becoming progressively more complete through becoming informed by and transformed into him, is essentially in the mainstream of New Testament theology and the tradition of the Greek Fathers. A cosmic dimension to Christ properly belongs to early eschatological formulations. Teilhard's struggle to relate Christ's 'nature' to contemporary scientific and humanistic worldviews was not new, and his adoption of an evolutionary model is not as revolutionary as it is sometimes believed to be.

ST THOMAS AQUINAS (*c.* 1225–74)

A major figure in the formative studies of Teilhard de Chardin would have been Thomas Aquinas. St Thomas, the Dominican philosopher and theologian, had been reaffirmed as the model for Catholic scholasticism by Pope Leo XIII's encyclical *Aeterni Patris* (1879), and made the patron saint of all Catholic universities (1880). Pius XI had reasserted Aquinas' authority as a teacher of the Church, and considerable attention was given to him by Catholic intellectuals at the beginning of the century. In addition to studies during his scholasticate, Teilhard de Chardin encountered Aquinas through his friend Pierre Rousselot (1878–1915), whose doctoral thesis of 1908 was entitled *The Intellectualism of St Thomas.*[36]

One of Aquinas' main theses is that man can discover God's existence, together with his eternity, simplicity, providence and creative power, through his own natural reason. Aquinas adopts the Aristotelian theory that there is an essential likeness between the knower and the known. He distinguishes, however, between the material objects of sense-perception and the 'forms' perceived by the intelligence or mind. Man, for Aquinas, possesses intellectual and corporeal faculties, and all objects of knowledge pertain to one or other of these categories.

Knowing God, however, is the one exception. One cannot know the form of God, since his essence is unknowable. Instead, the individual has recourse to material objects, which are the effects of a divine cause:

> Our natural knowledge begins with sensation, and therefore can be led as far as sensible things can take us. Through these effects, which do not equal the virtue of their cause, we cannot know the full power of God or, consequently, see his essence. Nevertheless they are his effects and dependent on their cause. We can be led by them so far as to know of his existence and some necessary attributes. He is the first universal cause surpassing all his effects, and we can know his relationship to creatures and their difference from him.[37]

Rousselot's first doctoral thesis, *The Intellectualism of St Thomas*,[38] argued for a fresh understanding of the intellect in Aquinas. According to Rousselot, it is the faculty of the real, the divine, through which the individual comes to know God. He explains:

> I understand by *intellectualism* the doctrine which places the supreme value

and intensity of life in an act of intellect, that sees in this act the radical and essential good, and regards all things else as good only in so far as they participate in it... Intelligence, for St Thomas, is the faculty of the real, but it is the faculty of the real only because it is the faculty of the Divine... The coincidence of spiritual Reality and of Idea indicates that the acquisition of the supreme Reality formally takes place by means of intellect, and that the destiny of the universe is linked up with the noblest act of mind, the vision of God. Now all religion centres around the beatific vision...[39]

This interpretation of Aquinas, in which man can contemplate God through the use of his intellect, represented a challenge to traditional scholasticism. Rousselot maintained that an intuitive approach to God is both possible and necessary for knowledge of the divine, and that the human intellect is the means by which this is achieved.

Teilhard de Chardin develops Aquinas' basic thesis that knowledge of God can come through natural reason, to argue that human consciousness is, in itself, spirit (i.e. divine) and thereby both the supernatural and natural means of knowing God. In other words, human consciousness has the potential to develop the ability to perceive Christ's presence (*le milieu divin*). It is, Teilhard would agree, the human mind which functions as the faculty of the divine: human self-consciousness leads to knowledge and vision of the Lord. In this respect, his view is similar to Rousselot's understanding of the intellect as the faculty of divine knowledge.

In presenting Christ as the personal Centre of human consciousness, and its elemental Form, Teilhard is using consciousness analogously as the model of divine knowledge, in true Thomist style. The difference is that for Teilhard, consciousness is the structure of reality: human knowledge of God may be understood analogously, but it has an experiential basis. Christ 'in-forms' human consciousness and brings it, together with himself, to completion in God.[40] In practical terms this means that Teilhard understands the human powers of reflection to be crucial to the transformative process by which Christ is realised in the world.

Aquinas had claimed that knowing, like sensing, was a mutual exchange. The mind cannot know without things to know, and for things to be intelligible they must be drawn into the sphere of the mind. In knowing something, both the mind and the form of the thing known are realised together. Teilhard approached the question differently, but he made a similar claim: that Christ, as the Centre of all centres, is being realised simultaneously with the world's divinisation: as the 'form' of knowledge (or consciousness), Christ is completed through his 'in-formation' of human minds.

JOHN NEWMAN (1801–90)

We know that Teilhard de Chardin read Newman from the references he makes to him. 'Plus je lis Newman, plus je sens une parenté (combien humble, sans doute!) entre son esprit et le mien', he wrote in 1916.[41] He made notes from Newman's writings,[42] and refers in particular to his *Essay on the Development of Christian Doctrine*[43] and his *Apologia*,[44] describing the latter as one of those books '(the only sort that should be written!...) in which a life is laid bare'.[45] We also know that Fr Henri Bremond wrote a book about Newman[46] which Teilhard would almost certainly have come across.

Perhaps it was Newman's particular blend of intellectual clarity and solidity combined with his concern for the inner life of the 'ordinary' Christian which appealed to him. No doubt Teilhard, who would have been familiar with that strand of French philosophy which focused on the intuitive powers of the human heart, namely, the movement represented by Pascal,[47] would have found Newman's writings accessible and refreshingly 'modern'.

When discussing Newman's influence on Loisy (one of the key thinkers of the Modernist movement), Gabriel Daly points out that Newman suggested an evolutionary framework to facilitate a marriage between historical method and an epistemology based on a relative, evolutionary understanding of truth.[48] This could have applied to Newman's influence on Teilhard, and certainly applies to those elements of thought they shared. Newman provided a vital link for Teilhard between contemporary theories of development and evolution, and traditional Catholic teachings: he argued for the validity of doctrinal development.[49] Using different elements of Christological understandings (such as Pauline concepts, together with those of the Church Fathers), Teilhard felt justified in formulating them in contemporary, evolutionary language. In his view, this represented not just a development of an idea, but a development in consciousness.

For Teilhard, this evolution of consciousness involves a progressive divinisation. It is interesting that Newman, following Athanasius, also believes in man's divinisation: for him, it refers to the relationship between Christ's humanity and individuals. In his book *Newman and the Gospel of Christ*, Roderick Strange comments that Newman notes Athanasius' claim that men's flesh is made 'Word' through God's Word who became 'flesh' (*Contra Arianos* 3.33).[50] He explains that Newman interpreted this to mean that God changes men in such a way that the term 'divinisation' is justified, although there is always an essential distinction between Godhead and manhood. Newman argues that those who believe share in the divine nature so fully that they are 'all but Divine, all that they can be made without violating the incommunicable majesty of the Most High'.[51]

When discussing man's share in the divine nature of Christ, Newman makes an interesting comment: it is 'mystical fellowship' he explains, with the Father, Son and Holy Spirit. In a letter to Samuel Wilberforce (1835) he uses 'physical' as a synonym for 'mystical': this renewal of the individual is 'the indwelling of the Holy Spirit in the soul as in a Temple', and it has 'a physical or (as we term it) a mystical influence on the soul uniting it to Christ'.[52]

It may be that Newman was the source of Teilhard's understanding of mystics as 'physicalists'[53] who can perceive the organic inter-relationships structuring reality. Certainly both referred to a substantial unity between Christ and humanity.

NINETEENTH-CENTURY GERMAN PROTESTANTISM

While discussing Newman's views on the relationship between Christ and believers, it is worth remembering that in contemporary Protestant circles, this featured prominently in theological debate. Teilhard de Chardin may not have been aware of developments in, for example, nineteenth-century German theology,[54] but in the context of the background to his understanding of the body of Christ, and the context of influences on the Modernist[55] movement,[56] it is pertinent to examine ideas which prefigure those we are considering.

Drawing upon an idea from Hegel, and in response to Schleiermacher's 'prototype' and Strauss' *Life of Jesus*, Richard Rothe (1799–1867)[57] developed a concept of Christ as the 'Central Individual', whose progressive incarnation involved man's evolution as 'Second Adam'. In his *Dogmatik*, Rothe uses the concept of Christ as Centre (Central Individual), organically related to all 'world-spheres' (i.e. individuals), uniting all things, and manifesting through them the 'cosmic being' of God:

And thus one necessarily arrives at the idea of a Central Individual, who is such for every particular world-sphere, insofar as He is the absolute and real unity of the individuals of all the particular world-spheres, as they are organically integrated with one another. This Central Individual is also the original of the first creature-sphere, and at the same time the absolute, in that He is the organic compound of all the creature-spheres. All the prophecies that we for our part have made about Him refer to such a 'first-born of all creation' in a remarkable way. For since there is brought about in each particular individual's sphere of creation a genuine being of God, a genuine cosmic being of God, and therefore also a genuine self-revelation of God, so, through this total Central Individual, the whole cosmic being of God, and hence also the whole cosmic self-revelation of God, is mediated.[58]

Rothe refers to Colossians 1:15 in his exposition of the idea of a morally based universe centred on Christ, to whom and in whom all things are related. Christ's determining power is actualised, in an archetypal sense, in each individual's life.[59] The fruits of the spiritual life unconsciously converge in the person's acknowledging Christ as his or her centre,[60] or in other words, Christ is a tangible focus for an evolving universe. In soteriological terms Christ is also referred to as 'Second Adam', the one who brings redemption to the whole cosmos, and in whom Christians are transformed as they participate in the maturing process of Christ.

We do not know whether Teilhard himself read Rothe or encountered his thought through someone else,[61] but it is clear that his understanding of Christ as Centre and his use of the term 'sphere' for matter in relation to its inner dimension are strikingly similar to Rothe's Christological formulation.[62]

MODERNISM

What is commonly referred to as the doctrine of the 'mystical body of Christ' was, as we can see, already receiving new formulations in Protestant and Catholic thought of the nineteenth century. The emphasis, to be developed by Teilhard de Chardin, was placed on the summation of all things through unification in Christ. And this process was understood in terms of a physical relationship between Christ and individuals. Teilhard saw this as a substantial bond holding together the cosmos in relationship to its very core or Centre.

The fact that he chose to reflect upon his understanding of Christ in scientific terms places Teilhard firmly in the context of French intellectualism and Catholic Modernism.[63] Whether we choose, together with Maude Petre, to associate Teilhard de Chardin with Modernism[64] or not, it is evident that the circles in which he moved were influenced by the ideas and effects of this current of change.[65]

In his article 'Roman Catholic Modernism', Bernard Reardon refers to the movement's aim of relating traditional Catholic teaching to current thought, especially philosophy, history and social theory.[66] Modernism crystallised a concern with an increasing split between traditional scholasticism and secular research in a variety of disciplines offering new interpretations of the nature of human existence. Those individuals associated with the movement, such as Alfred Firmin Loisy (1857–1940), George Tyrrell (1861–1909), Friedrich von Hügel (1852–1925), Lucien Laberthonnière (1860–1932) and Edouard Le Roy (1870–1954),[67] attempted to relate their scholarship in historical criticism and philosophy to biblical exegesis and theology.

The implications for Christian doctrine, and in particular Christology and the understanding of revelation, were considerable. Basically, there was a general trend interpreting God's revelation to humankind in terms of self-awareness. Loisy argued, for example, that revelation is both the manifestation of God to man and the consciousness man has of his relationship with God.[68] Ecclesiastical formulas are then no longer statements of absolute truth, but incomplete expressions of that relationship.

Tyrrell's view was similar: man's language about God can only be analogous; the value of doctrine lies in its practical application in every area of life. Revelation is a direct experience, a spiritual vision.[69] As such it can be expressed in language which evokes a response of faith and recognition: 'Were it not already written in the depths of our being, where the spirit is rooted in God, we could not recognize it.'[70] Jesus spoke in transcendental terms of God, Tyrrell pointed out, because that was the prevailing thought-form of the day. But if his language was of transcendence, nevertheless his life, teaching and spirit implied the 'truth of immanence'.[71]

It is in the context of this ferment of ideas about the status of the Bible, the search for a 'historical Jesus' and the nature of revelation and its function in the ordinary lives of men and women that Teilhard de Chardin can best be visualised. As a scientist, whose research in geology and palaeontology began in the early 1900s, he was also aware of contemporary scientific theories. Bergson's concept of 'creative evolution', for example, offered a new interpretation of the Darwinian theory of evolution, and one which was held to be incompatible with the traditional Catholic doctrine of creation. It is in the light of these conflicting ideas, and the resulting papal encyclical, *Pascendi dominici gregis* (1907), issued by Pius X[72] against those new ideas, that Teilhard de Chardin's own writings, subsequent exile (1926)[73] and imposed silence (on theological issues) become more comprehensible.

HENRI BERGSON (1859–1941)

Teilhard's depiction of Christ in physical terms was also influenced by contemporary thinkers such as Bergson, who was concerned with issues relating science to religion. We know that Teilhard thought very highly of Bergson.[74] And in his autobiographical *Le Cœur de la matière*, he refers specifically to the influence of Bergson's *L'Evolution créatrice* (1907).[75]

Bergson depicted reality as developing or evolving through an antecedent cause, a 'push' from behind. This *élan vital* holds all things together so that there appears to be one reality, one whole. It was this creative inner impulse which featured in certain Modernist writings, and which Teilhard adopted for his theory of evolving consciousness. Bergson explains:

> As the smallest grain of dust is bound up with our entire solar system, drawn along with it in that individual movement of descent which is materiality itself, so all organised beings from the humblest to the highest... do but evidence a single impulsion, the inverse of the movement of matter, and itself indivisible. All the living hold together and all yield to the same tremendous push.[76]

Teilhard's Omega Point was a teleological point beyond and ahead, rather than behind, but the causal function of his view of Christ bears resemblance to Bergson's *élan vital* (in spite of the latter's lack of religious formulation). This evolutionary theory affected Teilhard's reformulation of certain aspects of Christian doctrine, and in particular, that of creation. And such reformulations align him with those French thinkers whose views were classified as Modernist, although, as we have seen, Teilhard's main sources were primarily biblical.

Teilhard's uniqueness lay in reforming doctrine in the light of current thought in the fields of biology, for example, and physics. There is a progression in life from plant through animal to man, he argued (along with Bergson and others), and – this is where he parts company from most – this evolution of consciousness is a progressive growth of a divine reality: the body of Christ. When we look at Teilhard's descriptions of this reality, we can almost hear an echo of Bergson:

> Now the more we fix our attention on this continuity of life, the more we see that organic evolution resembles the evolution of consciousness... From this point of view, not only does consciousness appear as the motive principle of evolution, but also, among conscious beings themselves, man comes to occupy a privileged place... If our analysis is correct, it is consciousness, or rather supra-consciousness, that is at the origin of life.[77]

His theory of evolving consciousness provided the vital link Teilhard needed to reconcile his religious and scientific concerns. He adopted Bergson's evolutionary model of life and revolutionised the concept of Christ as the Incarnate Word by putting this within a 'phenomenological' framework. Christ is seen as Bergson's 'supra-consciousness' (Teilhard uses the term 'Super-Person'), the source and fulfilment of life on earth.

PIERRE ROUSSELOT (1878–1915)

I have already referred to Rousselot's influence on Teilhard de Chardin in the interpretation of Aquinas (pp. 18–19 above). They were together during their scholasticate in Jersey, at Ore Place (Hastings) for their theological formation, and afterwards in Paris.[78] These were important points in their lives, and the influence was mutual. In addition, their individual influences would have overlapped. They both drew upon St Paul for their understanding of Christ, for example, and both had a cosmic conception of the body of Christ.[79]

Rousselot's interpretation of Aquinas' *intellectus* as the intuitive mind,[80] becoming more aware of its own nature and movement, was important because it was preparing a way for a synthesis between traditional Catholic thought and the new thinking represented by Bergson, for example, and Blondel. It was Teilhard who attempted such a synthesis by relating human activity to passivity and interior states of being, and by relating the phenomenological world of our senses to the divine milieu of the body of Christ.

In attempting this synthesis it may well be that Teilhard drew considerably on the reflections of his friend. In particular, Rousselot's second doctoral thesis, in which he explored the different attempts made in the Middle Ages to relate love of self to love of God, was perhaps more significant for him. For Rousselot, as for Teilhard, the 'problem of love' was fundamental:

That which is referred to here as 'the problem of love' could, in abstract terms, be formulated in the following way: is it possible to have love that is not egoistic? And, if it is possible, what is the relationship between this pure altruistic love and love of self, which appears to be at the basis of all natural inclinations? The problem of love is, therefore, analogous to that of knowledge. On the one hand, one asks oneself if and how a being can have consciousness of that which is other than itself; and on the other hand, whether a being's desire can lead to that which is not truly good for it; in both cases, an affirmative response seems more and more difficult as one studies more deeply the notion of consciousness and the notion of desire.[81]

Teilhard de Chardin, writing to Victor Fontoynont, reformulates the same question: 'Cannot the object, the actual matter of our human passions be transfigured, transformed into the Absolute, the definitive, the divine?' He suggests to Fontoynont that it can, and that the one evolves into the other. He uses the term 'cosmic Christ' to explain how he understands Christ to be the natural term of every human desire. Christ, he believes, gathers together every impulse and movement by atoms, cells and souls at the conscious Centre of his Person and Heart. Thus, for him, it is possible to love Christ passionately through loving the universe.[82]

MAURICE BLONDEL (1861–1949)

A third contemporary figure whose thought was undoubtedly seminal to Teilhard's development of ideas was Maurice Blondel. A controversial French philosopher, Blondel sought to locate an analysis of human existence in the study of 'action'.[83] By 'action' Blondel meant more than a simple act. He referred to the dynamism of life itself, including 'all the conditions, immanent and transcendent, interior and superior, that contribute to the gestation, birth and expansion of the free act'.[84] The main thesis of his argument, outlined in *L'Action: le problème des causes secondes et le pur agir*,[85] is that only action synthesises the innumerable inherent contradictions of human thought and feeling; it creates a unique unity of knowing, willing and being:

Man's need is to equal himself, so that nothing of what he is may remain foreign or contrary to his will, and nothing of what he wills may remain inaccessible or be denied to his being. To act is to seek this harmony of knowing, willing and being, and either to contribute to its production or to imperil it. Action is the dual movement which carries being to the end to which it tends as to a new perfection, and which reintegrates the final into the efficient cause. In the plenitude of the mediating role it is a return from the absolute to the absolute... The role of action is therefore to develop being and to constitute it...[86]

It is through human action that Blondel understood the divine or absolute to be espoused, this being a response to God's initiative and power. In explaining this, he drew upon Leibniz' idea of a *vinculum substantiale*,[87] an unseen bond which unites and transforms the natural elements as in the Eucharist:

The *Vinculum* is, as a matter of fact, not only a physical nature, a metaphysical essence, an immanent finality; it is also, without prejudice to all that, the supreme magnet, which attracts and unites from above, step by step, the total hierarchy of distinct and consolidated beings; it is that without which, or rather He without whom 'everything that has been made would become again as nothing'... By substituting the *Vinculum ipsius Christi* for the natural being of bread and wine, Transubstantiation accordingly appears to us to act, under the veils of mystery, as a prelude to the final assimilation, to the supreme incorporation of everything which belongs to the Incarnate Word...[88]

In Teilhard's writings Christ (or Christ–Omega) is this *vinculum substantiale*, the universal 'binding' *in quo omnia constant* (Colossians 1:17b). And the form this 'binding' takes is portrayed in Eucharistic terms:[89] the world is divinised, filled, with the pleromising presence of God by Christ, its active[90] Centre.

When referring to the spiritualising activity of Christ, Blondel had coined a term which Teilhard was to take up and develop: 'pan-Christism'.[91] He advocated inclusion of all aspects of life in the transforming power of Christ. Indeed, he added, creation anticipates and needs Christ, in whom all things exist as the 'firstborn'. On the other hand, Blondel was anxious to guard against what he called 'the dangers of immanentism'. Christ as *vinculum* does not hold things together in a 'transnaturalising clasp' but in an embrace which respects their nature. The more Christ is viewed as an innate presence, he explains, the more important it is to stress the centrality of transcendence and grace for the 'plan towards deification'.[92]

Blondel was rather pointedly warning against the absolutisation of scientific concepts to explain Christ's role, or of 'the luxury of symbols' which are, he said, in reality, 'deficient and misleading'.[93] He was not in favour of a 'purely physical supernaturalism',[94] which is perhaps how he understood Teilhard's rather ebullient, poetic turns of phrase.[95] But Teilhard was, in fact, arguing rather for a limitless supernaturalism, informing and pervading the most ordinary of actions and things; not restricting Christ to the 'purely physical'.[96]

'True pan-Christism sharply disassociates itself from anything having to do with physicism[97] and pantheism', Blondel had declared.[98] And Teilhard was to defend himself in no uncertain terms: as Omega, Christ draws us on, differentiating rather than fusing consciousness, and impelling the Christian to action rather than inducing him or her to a false sense of 'oneness' with all things.[99] It is only gradually, to the eyes of the believer, that a 'mystical ambience' appears, in which all things consist and converge:[100] 'If we had to give a more exact name to the mystical Milieu we would say that it is a Flesh', wrote Teilhard. He goes on to explain that the world is increasingly experienced as being warm and active by the believer, who is gradually transformed into him who animates it.[101]

I have shown in this chapter how Teilhard's vision of Christ was based upon a tradition going back to the earliest formulations of Christian experience. References to 'Christ's body' have been associated with the experience of living in relationship with Christ from the time of the Early Church onwards. Such expressive metaphorical language seems to be crucial to communicating an important part of Christian experience.

The Greek Fathers associate 'Christ's body' with the organic transformation through which the whole world is 'redeemed' or brought to completion in God. They speak of the whole of humanity being divinised (or deified) as part of that response. Perhaps the correlation between individual experience and the accompanying sense of being part of a collective process relates to the transformation of perception which signifies life 'in' Christ.

Teilhard de Chardin was working with this primary experience and traditional understanding. He revisioned 'the body of Christ' for himself and his times, using tools drawn from contemporary sources, both Christian and non-Christian. Clearly one such tool was evolutionary theory; another was philosophical science. It could be said that the breadth of Teilhard's vision could not be encompassed by existing theological language. He needed to create his own synthesis of traditional symbolism and contemporary thought to express his own worldview centred on a cosmic Christ.

CHAPTER 2

The background to the divine body in Rāmānuja

When we turn to Rāmānuja, we are entering another world altogether from the one inhabited by Teilhard de Chardin. Rāmānuja lived in India during the eleventh century CE, and the influences upon his thought were derived from the spiritual traditions he valued and incorporated within the authoritative lineage of Śrīvaiṣṇavism.[1]

Rāmānuja was a *Vedāntin*: he worked within the long-established oral tradition of providing expository commentaries on those religious texts believed to be part of Vedic knowledge or *śruti* (literally 'that which is heard').[2] He would have been trained in the knowledge of the *Upaniṣads*, and one of his major works was a commentary on the *Brahma-sūtras* (or *Vedānta-sūtras*, as they are sometimes called). All his work was based on the teachings of earlier spiritual teachers, so that in one sense it was purely traditional. Ramakrishnananda, a biographer of Rāmānuja, makes the point very strongly:

> We should not think that Rāmānuja developed any new philosophy, and he makes no claim of originality. He was the culmination of the movement that started from the Vedas and was nourished by the Āḻvārs, Nāthamuni and Yāmunacharya... In his exposition of the Vedānta, he claims merely to follow the doctrines of Bodhayana, Tanka, Dramida, Guhadeva, Kapardin and Bharuci.[3]

Rāmānuja's originality lay in his method, which integrated popular spirituality with the rather rigid structures of accepted Vedāntic tradition. He found a way of doing this while working as teacher (*ācārya*) in a Śrīvaiṣṇava religious community (*sampradāya*). He is recorded as being general manager (*śrīkāryam*) of the important Viṣṇu temple at Śrīrangam.[4] His teachings are found in commentaries on key texts such as the *Brahma-sūtras* and the *Bhagavad-gītā*;[5] in a major philosophical treatise, the *Vedārthasaṃgraha*; and in several smaller works on temple ritual and devotional practice.[6] Stylistically, several works are in the form of debates with contemporary teachers or schools of thought.[7] The sections dealing with the body of Brahman are scattered throughout his writings as a key theme appearing in different contexts.

Perhaps one of the most exciting features of Rāmānuja's depiction of the body of Brahman is that he brings together different elements from very different sources to communicate his spiritual vision. This reflects his own experience, which was broad: as a Tamil brahmin (he was a member of a sub-caste of Tamil brahmins) he was well versed in Vedic scholarship; his first teacher, Yādava Prakāśa, was probably an adherent of the Bhedābheda school;[8] and he chose to be initiated into a Śrīvaiṣṇava community.

It is important at this initial stage to look at some of the major influences on Rāmānuja's understanding of the body of Brahman. But beforehand, we need to be clear about Rāmānuja's attitude to his different sources: he sees *śruti* as divine truth, supported by the different texts classified as *smṛti* (literally 'that which is remembered'). Together these form one inclusive body of knowledge.[9]

THE *VEDAS*

The original four *Vedas* (literally 'knowledge') form the infrastructure of the Vedāntic corpus, which includes Rāmānuja's works. Dating from the time of the Aryan invasions of India (between 1500 and 900 BCE), they represent the sacred word (*vāc*) given by the divinely inspired seers (*ṛṣis*). The subject matter, mostly instructional for performing brahminical rites of sacrifice, provides valuable material on the Vedic perception of the world. One theme which Rāmānuja uses and develops is that of *puruṣa*, the primordial divine-human person whose being symbolises the inter-relatedness of all life, and whose sacrifice brings about its creation and continued preservation:

> A thousand heads hath Purusha, a thousand eyes, a thousand feet.
> On every side pervading earth he fills a space ten fingers wide.
> This Purusha is all that yet hath been and all that is to be;
> The Lord of Immortality which waxes greater still by food.
> So mighty is his greatness; yea, greater than this is Purusha.
> All creatures are one-fourth of him, three-fourths eternal life in heaven...
> When Gods prepared the sacrifice with Purusha as their offering,
> Its oil was spring, the holy gift was autumn; summer was the wood...[10]

This, together with other poetic passages, relies heavily upon the use of metaphor to create an immediacy and directness of effect. *Puruṣa* has 'a thousand heads, a thousand eyes', we are told, and the presence of an all-knowing and all-seeing person is communicated powerfully to the hearer or reader. Using images of daily life (body language, food), the author discloses a heightened perception of reality in terms of divine presence.[11]

The picture is built up through multiple metaphors of a Person who symbolises the whole of reality: three-quarters of him comprise 'eternal life' and one-quarter, all living creatures. He both contains all things and transcends them. He is correspondingly vast ('on every side pervading earth') and tiny ('ten fingers wide'): the traditional size of a human heart. His self-offering is bound up with the seasonal changes, with time; yet he is greater even than that. This paradoxical quality and micro–macro parallelism recurs in Rāmānuja's references to the Highest Person or *puruṣottama*, suggesting that there is an important link between the Vedic *puruṣa* and Rāmānuja's concept of Brahman as *puruṣottama*. For Rāmānuja, Brahman is none other than *puruṣa*, or *puruṣottama*.

The *Ṛg-veda* also refers to *puruṣa* as Prajāpati, Lord of Creation. It is *puruṣa* (the 'first of this creation') who controls 'this world in highest heaven'.[12] A weaving image depicts the process: *puruṣa* 'extends' and 'unbinds' the threads drawn from the sacrifice, from the 'seat of worship' to the 'vault of heaven'. For Rāmānuja the creation, preservation and reabsorption of the world take place through Brahman, referred to as *puruṣottama*. Just as *puruṣa* is, in the *Ṛg-veda*, a symbol of unity, integrating the physical world with the gods, so *puruṣottama* serves, for Rāmānuja, to affirm the inter-relatedness of all things. It is in this context that the divine body assumes importance as Rāmānuja's major symbol for the integration of the divine and the world.

The relationship between *puruṣa* and the seers or *ṛṣis* is presented in the *Ṛg-veda* as horses' reins pulling a chariot. The *ṛṣis* are seen to take control for *puruṣa*, while remaining subject to him: 'Viewing the path of those of old, the sages have taken up the reins like chariot-drivers.'[13] As I have shown, Rāmānuja claims ultimate authority for the body of 'transcendent knowledge' which is based on the *Vedas*. The *ṛṣis*, who have 'attained the direct vision of the supreme Brahman', can be said to control the imparting of sacred knowledge through their words, spoken to the self or *ātman* in the heart of the hearer. Rāmānuja identifies *puruṣottama* as the inner Ruler (*antaryāmin*) within the *ātman* of each person.[14]

THE *BRĀHMAṆAS*

The *Brāhmaṇas*, as commentaries on the *Vedas* (written about 850 BCE onwards), elucidate the Vedic theory of sacrificial ritual. There are several references to *puruṣa* which provide a link between the *Vedas* and the *Upaniṣads*, and these were of considerable importance to Rāmānuja.

One theme which emerges from these passages is *puruṣa*'s association with light. He is referred to as 'that man in yonder orb' (i.e. the sun);[15] as Vivasvant, the Radiant One; the 'gold man' (in the altar); and 'this man in the right eye'.[16] These powerful metaphors reveal to the hearer or reader *puruṣa*'s presence and pervasiveness.[17]

It is also interesting to note that in the *Śatapatha-brāhmaṇa*, *puruṣa* is often referred to as Prajāpati (Lord of Creation), also identified as Agni (Fire) and Savitṛi, the 'golden deity' whose radiance illumines the atmosphere and all regions of the earth. In one sense this is hardly surprising, since the context is the sacrificial ritual, but still it is worth noting that *puruṣa*'s power is linked with human actions, and especially sacrificial ones.[18]

In chapter 10 of the *Śatapatha-brāhmaṇa*, the nature of the sacrifice required of the individual is explained. It involves meditating on *puruṣa* as self (*ātman*):

> Let him meditate on the Self which is made up of intelligence, and endowed with a body of spirit, with a form of light, and with an ethereal nature, which changes its shape at will, is swift as thought, of true resolve, and true purpose, which consists of all sweet odours and tastes, which holds sway over all the regions and pervades this whole universe, which is speechless and indifferent; – even as a grain of rice, or a grain of barley, or a grain of millet, or the smallest granule of millet, so is this golden Puruṣa in the heart; even as a smokeless light, it is greater than the sky... greater than all existing things; – that self of the spirit (breath) is my self: on passing away from hence I shall obtain that self. Verily, whosoever has this trust, for him there is no uncertainty.[19]

The similarity with Rāmānuja's teaching on *upāsana*, which is a form of devotional meditation, is quite striking: in identifying Brahman as the Supreme Self (*paramātman*), Rāmānuja claims that release (*mokṣa*) is attained through meditating on the Lord as one's true Self. It is this practice of meditation which leads, finally, to a vision of the Highest Person (*puruṣottama*), the Lord of all, seated within all things and in the human heart. In this vision the world is seen as the body of Brahman.

THE *VIṢṆU-PURĀṆA*

This *smṛti* text may well have been handed on to Rāmānuja by his predecessors at Śrīrangam.[20] It extols the praises of Viṣṇu, sometimes identified as *puruṣottama* (or *paramapuruṣa*), the Highest Person.[21]

In the *Viṣṇu-purāṇa* Brahman is identified as Viṣṇu. The teachings on meditation focus on two forms[22] of Brahman: the perishable and the imperishable.[23] The world is the 'perishable' form of Brahman; it is his 'body': 'Thou art earth, water, fire, air, ether, mind, crude matter and primeval soul: all this elementary creation, with or without visible form, is thy body.'[24] The 'imperishable' form of the divine corresponds to Viṣṇu's *vibhūti*[25] or manifestation of power.[26]

The devotee seeking release (*mokṣa*) is told to meditate on Viṣṇu under both aspects ('perishable' and 'imperishable'), progressing to the highest state. His meditation thus becomes a form of self-purification, a preparation for beholding the Lord. The text explains that just as fire, blazing in the wind, burns dry grass, so Viṣṇu, seated in the heart, 'consumes' the impurities of the sage.[27]

The *Viṣṇu-purāṇa* has specific instructions on meditation: first, the devotee meditates on the universal 'perishable' form of the Lord, and then on the 'imperishable' form – 'that imperceptible, shapeless form of Brahmā, which is called by the wise, "That which is"'.[28] The devotee visualises Viṣṇu in increasing simplicity of form. The retention of the mental image aids concentration, and can lead to a higher state of awareness.

The initial visualisation is rich in detail, and this is subsequently simplified to exclude, for example, legs and arms:

> Viṣṇu ... [has] a pleased and lovely countenance, with eyes like the leaf of the lotus, smooth cheeks, and a broad and brilliant forehead; ears of equal size, the lobes of which are decorated with splendid pendants; a painted neck, and a broad breast, on which shines the Śrīvatsa mark; a belly falling in graceful folds, with a deep-seated navel; eight long arms, or else four; and firm and well-knit thighs and legs, with well-formed feet and toes.[29]

Rāmānuja, through also treating of the divine as Viṣṇu,[30] is making an important claim: Brahman is personal.[31] He goes further: *upāsana* or devotional meditation is the practical way to attain the Supreme Person. This is because the Lord is none other than the Highest Person (*puruṣottama*), the Self of all. In this context it is important to note that Rāmānuja's language when referring to the body of Brahman is strongly reminiscent of the *Viṣṇu-purāṇa*.[32]

THE *ĀḺVĀRS*

The *Āḻvārs* were Tamil sages who worshipped Kṛṣṇa, and they were alive between the sixth and the tenth centuries. They have been associated with about ninety-five temples in South India, and represent a movement of popular devotionalism. Twelve people in particular are recognised as being representative of this movement. It is claimed that Nāthamuni, the grandfather and predecessor of Yāmuna, Rāmānuja's spiritual guru, rediscovered the famous *Tiruvāymoḻi* of Nammāḻvār, one of the twelve. This is a very significant claim, clearly associating Nāthamuni with Nammāḻvār and his 'Tamil *Veda*'.[33]

There are other links between Rāmānuja and the *Āḻvārs*. Śrīvaiṣṇavas claim that Nāthamuni performed the huge task of gathering together the hymns and songs of the *Āḻvārs* in the *Nālāyirativiyappirapantam* ('Corpus of the Four Thousand' (stanzas)) or the *Prabandham*, as it is commonly known. It is also claimed that he set the *Prabandham* to music. The other important link is that Rāmānuja's centre at Śrīrangam was the second most important temple of the *Āḻvārs*, who called the place 'Araṇkam'.[34] It is highly likely, therefore, that the *Āḻvār* songs were sung by the Vaiṣṇavite devotees at Śrīrangam during Rāmānuja's time there.

Supporting these external links is the fact that Śrīvaiṣṇavas today claim descent from the *Āḻvārs*.[35] Nāthamuni, for example, who had such links with the *Āḻvārs*, is traditionally recognised as being the initiator of the Vaiṣṇava lineage. Yāmuna is said to have died with three wishes for Rāmānuja to fulfil, one of which was to give honour to Nammāḻvār. So it was that the *Āḻvār* connection was handed down to Rāmānuja.[36]

I am struck by the similarity of concern in many of the *Āḻvār* songs and Rāmānuja's writings, namely, 'to see the body of the Lord'. The *Āḻvār* poet, often assuming a female role, praises the beauty of the physical world and expresses longing to be united with the invisible

Lord whose beauty transcends that of his creation. In Nammāḻvār's *Tiruvāymoḻi* there is an example of this:

> You dwell in heaven
>   stand on the sacred mountain
>   sleep on the ocean
>   roll around the earth
> Yet hidden everywhere
>   you grow
>   invisibly:
> moving within
>   numberless outer worlds
> playing with my heart
>   yet not showing your body
> will you always play hide and seek?[37]

The distinction between the beauty of the physical world and that of the Lord is important, separating this religious form of expression from pure nature mysticism. It foreshadows the doctrinal distinction, in Rāmānuja, for example, between *saguṇa* and *nirguṇa* Brahman: Brahman in both his manifest and unevolved states. In the *Āḻvār* songs, Nammālvār illustrates the theme of the Lord's pervasive presence within the world:

> Touching the ground she cries out it is Vāmana's earth.
> Saluting the heavens she cries out it is Vaikuṇṭha.
> She points to her tears and says it is the Ocean of God...
> Showing the sun she says He is the body of Śrīdhara...
> Pointing to the rain she says that that is the residence of Nārāyaṇa...[38]

He also points to the Lord's unsurpassable glory:

> O Māl, Supremest Light, speaking truly the lotus is not equal to Thine eyes or feet or hands. Even the purified (burnished) gold cannot equal the effulgence of Thy divine body. To praise Thee with analogies drawn from the world, being mere words will express faults alone...[39]

It is clear from these extracts that poetic style and the use of metaphor become tools for Nammāḻvār not only to express religious emotion, but to communicate a very particular perception of the divine. Song becomes a meditation on the presence of the Lord, and devotion the fruit of its practice in the heart. Such technique is not absent from Rāmānuja's own writings, and especially the more devotional works such as the *Gītābhāṣya* and the *Śaraṇāgati-gadya*.[40]

The concern in Nammāḻvār and Rāmānuja with 'seeing the body of the Lord' is an important link between the *Āḻvārs* and subsequent Vaiṣṇava theology. It is an epistemological link: 'seeing' is equated with 'knowing' the Lord, and perceiving his 'body' refers, ultimately, to an inner transformation. In Vedāntic terms this is expressed as *tat tvam asi* ('that art thou'). Rāmānuja interprets this as realising the true nature of one's self or *ātman*.

This relates to yet another theme in the *Āḻvār* corpus which recurs in Rāmānuja: referring to the Lord as *antaryāmin* or 'inner Ruler'.[41] Certain of the *Āḻvār* songs refer to the Lord dwelling in the devotee's heart as *antaryāmin*. Rāmānuja uses this idea[42] and associates it with the idea of Brahman as the Self of the world.

THE *PĀÑCARĀTRA* TRADITION

The *Pāñcarātra* tradition is one of the two *Āgamas* underlying Śrīvaiṣṇavism (the other being *Vaikhānasa*). Taken literally, the name means 'five nights'. There are various hypotheses about its meaning, but it came to refer to the five types of knowledge recognised in the *Pāñcarātra* system. The *Pāñcarātra* literature comprises over two hundred *saṃhitās* or *tantras* written sometime between the writing of the Nārāyaṇīya section of the *Mahābhārata* and the eighth century CE. Originating in the North, the tradition spread to the South, where the oldest, *Īśvara-saṃhitā* (probably written before 840 CE), was referred to by Yāmuna as the 'Fifth Veda'.[43]

It appears likely that the *Pāñcarātra* tradition (also *smṛti*) was handed down to Rāmānuja as part of the Śrīvaiṣṇava heritage. Nāthamuni's father, Īśvara Muni, is traditionally understood to have been a *Pāñcarātrika*.[44] Also, Yāmuna wrote a work defending the orthodoxy of the *Pāñcarātra Āgama* (called *Āgama-prāmāṇya*) in which he referred to it as *Ekāyana Śākhā* (one of the branches of the *Veda*). This illustrates his desire to integrate *Pāñcarātra* with existing Śrīvaiṣṇavism. We know from his own references to certain texts[45] that Rāmānuja was not unaware of this tradition, and in the light of his predecessors' involvement it seems probable that he himself would be familiar with, and favourable towards, this movement.

One of the southern texts, the *Upendra-saṃhitā*, advocates leading a virtuous life in Śrīrangam, which supports the idea of a *Pāñcarātra* link with Śrīrangam (suggested by the fact that Nāthamuni's father was a *Pāñcarātrika*). Another factor in assessing the position of the *Pāñcarātra* tradition in Rāmānuja's background is the fact that the *Viṣṇu-purāṇa* and the *Āḻvārs*, which we know had some influence on him, both reveal *Pāñcarātra* influences.

We know that Rāmānuja instigated some kind of temple reform, and it is possible that Carman is right in suggesting that he replaced *Vaikhānasa* rites with *Pāñcarātra* ones.[46] In any case, it seems to be mainly in the context of religious practice that Rāmānuja drew from *Pāñcarātra* sources, to judge by the use he made of certain terms.

There are some features of the *Pāñcarātra* tradition which are of relevance to Rāmānuja's understanding of the body of Brahman. For example, Rāmānuja refers to the Pāñcarātra concept of the *ṣaḍguṇas* or six qualities of the Lord. In *Pāñcarātra* literature these are clearly listed as knowledge (*jñāna*); lordship (*aiśvarya*); potency (*śakti*); strength (*bala*); virility (*vīrya*); and splendour (*tejas*).[47] Rāmānuja, however, refers to them collectively, and often in the context of the *rūpa* or form of Brahman which is to be visualised, meditated upon and worshipped.[48] *Jñāna* does receive more detailed attention, being understood by Rāmānuja in its *Pāñcarātra* sense as the 'essence' (or 'essential property') as well as 'attribute' of the divine.[49] It is this knowledge, which Rāmānuja equates with consciousness, that ultimately characterises Brahman and the self (*ātman*).[50]

For Rāmānuja, attaining this ultimate knowledge involves devotional meditation or *upāsana*. In the *Pāñcarātra* tradition, *upāsana* is associated with an iconic representation (the *arcā* form of the divine). The *Lakṣmī-tantra* refers, in its *yoga-pāda*, to what it calls *śakti-upāsana* in terms of *ārādhanā* ('ritual worship of the Lord'). Such a link between meditation practice and a focused image of the divine[51] also features in Rāmānuja's teachings, where the disciple is encouraged to visualise and then integrate the divine 'form' into his or her consciousness, thus 'attaining' the Lord.

There is one final point for consideration, and it concerns Rāmānuja's use of terminology. Firstly, the description of the self as *kṣetrajña* (literally 'knower of the field') is to be found in *Pāñcarātra* texts,[52] and may, therefore, have had some bearing on Rāmānuja's use of the term. Secondly, the term *antaryāmin* is found in *Pāñcarātra* literature, where it refers to one of the five *prakāras* or forms of the divine.[53] However, Rāmānuja's usage of the term suggests that whatever his source, he is keen to place it in an Upaniṣadic context.[54]

THE *UPANIṢADS*

The *Upaniṣads* are a loose-knit body of spiritual teaching handed down through generations as one of the most revered sources of Indian religious thought. It is estimated that there are over two hundred *Upaniṣads*, of which some ten to seventeen are considered to be the principal ones. Their origins are unknown, but they are classified as *śruti*, the *vedānta* (the end or goal of the *Veda*), coming as they do at the end of the Vedic period. The word *upaniṣad* comes from *upa* ('near'), *ni* ('down') and *sad* ('to sit'), possibly referring to the way knowledge was transmitted from guru to disciple ('sitting at his feet'). It came to refer to a mystery, a secret (*rahasyam*), given only to the initiated.

As *ācārya* or spiritual teacher, Rāmānuja's task would have been to interpret and elucidate the *Upaniṣads*, *Brahma-sūtras* (which summarise the Upaniṣadic teachings) and the *Bhagavad-gītā*. Of these, the *Upaniṣads*, being *śruti*, were the most important. Given this, it is interesting that Rāmānuja never wrote a commentary specifically on the *Upaniṣads*, although as others have pointed out, his *Śrībhāṣya* and *Vedārthasaṃgraha* summarise his interpretation of them.[55]

It is in the *Antaryāmī-brāhmaṇa* of the *Bṛhad-āraṇyaka Upaniṣad*[56] that Brahman is referred to as inner Ruler (*antaryāmin*). The question is asked, for example, 'Do you know... that thread[57] by which this world, the other world and all beings are held together?' This later becomes: 'Do you know... that inner Controller [*antaryāmin*] who controls this world and the next and all things from within?' The point is that 'He who knows that thread... and that inner Controller, indeed knows Brahman, he knows the worlds, he knows the gods, he knows the *Vedas*, he knows beings, he knows the self, he knows everything.' The sage Yājñavalkya explains:

> He who dwells in the earth, yet is within the earth, whom the earth does not know, whose body the earth is, who controls the earth from within, he is your self, the inner controller, the immortal...
>
> He who dwells in all beings, yet is within all beings, whom no beings know, whose body is all beings, who controls all beings from within, he is your self, the inner controller, the immortal...
>
> He who dwells in the understanding, yet is within the understanding, whom the understanding does not know, whose body the understanding is, who controls the understanding from within, he is your self, the inner controller, the immortal.[58]

Theologically, this understanding of Brahman as the Self, controlling all things from within, is crucial for Rāmānuja's self–body doctrine (*śarīra-śarīrī-bhāva*).[59] It is because Brahman is Self that all things are his body; through realising that he is 'my' Self I can come to see the world as belonging to him, as part of him; and it is through meditating on him as Self, says Rāmānuja, that this realisation occurs.[60]

Another Upaniṣadic text of major importance for Rāmānuja is the *sadvidyā*,[61] as it is called, in *Chāndogya Upaniṣad* 6. This deals with the relationship between the individual self and Brahman which, Rāmānuja says (in contradiction to the *advaitins* or non-dualists), is one of union yet differentiation. The form of the Upaniṣadic teaching is a conversation between Śvetaketu and his father about the fundamental nature of reality, *sat* (being), which multiplies in union with the three elements and develops names and forms. The conversation concludes with the father's words: 'That which is the subtle essence (root), this whole world has for its self. That is the true. That is the self. That art thou (*tat tvam asi*), Śvetaketu.'[62]

Rāmānuja refers to this text at the beginning of his *Vedārtha-saṃgraha*, refuting thereby the advaitic conception of reality. He interprets *adeśa* ('command') in terms of that which gives the command,[63] and the ensuing dialogue, therefore, in terms of knowing Brahman as Self (who gives the command); of knowing his proper form (of knowledge, bliss and perfection); and his infinite number of perfections. It is he whom, as cause, Śvetaketu is being taught to know. It is Brahman, Rāmānuja maintains, that all things, through their relation to him, denote as their inner Ruler (*antaryāmin*) and cause. He is the fundamental object of knowledge.[64] The famous statement *tat tvam asi* ('that art thou') refers, Rāmānuja goes on to explain, to Brahman in both instances.[65]

These two Upaniṣadic texts have been dealt with in some detail because they are important for understanding Rāmānuja's presentation of the divine body. It is Brahman as Self in relation to the world, his body, which provides the context for his thought, and it is through maintaining the unity of all things through their differences (*viśiṣṭādvaita*) that he evolves a method of textual exegesis using the principle of co-ordinate predication. Using this principle, things can have different names and yet refer, ultimately, to the same thing.

One final word must be mentioned about the Upaniṣadic understanding of *puruṣa*: there is continuity with the Vedic use of the term, but in addition there is a new emphasis on *puruṣa* or *ātman* within the heart.[66] (Indeed at times, there seems to be no clear-cut distinction between the use of *puruṣa*, 'Brahman' and *ātman*.) This new concentration on the divine within the heart is taken and developed by Rāmānuja for teaching how to meditate on the Self (i.e. Brahman) in order to attain the Lord. His fundamental soteriological theme is drawn, it would seem, from the most orthodox of sources: the *Upaniṣads* themselves. His language illustrates this.[67]

THE *BHAGAVAD-GĪTĀ*

Rāmānuja's focus upon the heart was also influenced by his understanding of the *Bhagavad-gītā* (literally 'Song of the Lord'). The *Gītā*, as it is called, epitomises a devotional approach to the divine. It represents a unique *bhakti* tradition which Rāmānuja draws upon and integrates with other sources to communicate knowledge of Brahman (*brahmajñāna*).

There are different estimated datings for the *Bhagavad-gītā*, although most scholars accept that it was not written before the fifth century BCE since it shows familiarity with certain Upaniṣadic and Buddhist ideas. The war in question is understood to refer to the Great War (between the Kauravas and Pāṇḍavas), which is dated variously between 3101 and 1300 BCE.[68] The author, traditionally believed to be Lord Kṛṣṇa himself, is unknown, although the legendary Vyāsa is associated with the complete *Mahābhārata*, of which the *Gītā* is one small part.

It is difficult to estimate the extent of the *Gītā*'s influence on Rāmānuja.[69] As part of the *Mahābhārata* epic it is clearly *smṛti*; yet Rāmānuja as *Vedāntin* and theologian of the Vedāntic school would have had to defend and test his interpretation of the *Gītā* along with certain *śruti* texts. His commentary on the *Gītā*, his *Gītābhāṣya*, demonstrates his assimilation of *Gītā* ideas and in particular, his espousal of the practice of *bhakti-yoga*. This becomes, for Rāmānuja, the only complete way to attain release (*mokṣa*), integrating as it does the paths of knowledge (*jñāna*) and action (*karma*). So there is a degree of tension between the use of the *Gītā* as *smṛti* to support *śruti*, and the major influence of *bhakti* upon Rāmānuja's soteriology.

One reason for supposing that Rāmānuja was in fact deeply influenced by the *Gītā* is the fact that Yāmuna, his revered guru, was clearly persuaded that the work was worthy of a commentary (*Gītārthasaṃgraha*). Rāmānuja's own *Gītābhāṣya* is dedicated to Yāmuna, to whom he admits indebtedness and whom he quotes.[70] It may be that Rāmānuja's method of using *smṛti* to support *śruti* still holds good for the *Gītā* but that in addition he adopts Yāmuna's prescription for release (*mokṣa*) in terms of *bhakti* and makes this a major theme in his spiritual teachings.

The most illuminating *Gītā* text on the integrative discipline of *bhakti* or *bhakti-yoga*[71] is, perhaps, in chapter 18 (18.57–66).[72] Here, Kṛṣṇa tells Arjuna to surrender inwardly all that he does to the Lord, who is to be treated as his goal (*upeya*),[73] and meditated upon constantly. Through Arjuna taking refuge in the Lord in this way, Kṛṣṇa's grace will bring him supreme peace. The mysterious and secret truth, Kṛṣṇa explains, is that he (Arjuna) is beloved by the Lord and will be helped to find him. Kṛṣṇa's final word (the famous *caramaśloka*)[74] is the advice to turn to the Lord, free from care, for deliverance.

Often, it is when explaining his own view of *bhakti-yoga*[75] as meditation and devotional worship (which Rāmānuja equates with knowledge of the divine), and when describing its visualising and perceptive content that Rāmānuja refers to what is called his *śarīra-śarīrī-bhāva* or body–self doctrine.[76]

There are certain key terms in Rāmānuja's works which reflect the *Bhagavad-gītā*. They elucidate the general theme of *bhakti* by referring to the relationship between the divine and the individual or the world. Generally speaking, Rāmānuja uses these *Gītā* references to back up quotes from the *Upaniṣads* or the *Vedas* which substantiate his points.

One such term found in the *Gītā* is 'the Highest Person' (*puruṣottama*). The fifteenth chapter is traditionally called 'the Yoga of Puruṣottama': it teaches the essential nature of the Highest Person.[77] This chapter contains the 'secret of all secrets', which is encapsulated in śloka 19: 'Whoever, being free from delusion, understands Me thus to be the Highest Person, he knows all and (thereby) worships Me, O Arjuna (Bharata), in every way.'[78]

Another important term for the divine in the *Gītā* which Rāmānuja uses is the Knower or *kṣetrajña*. He uses it in conjunction with *kṣetra* (field) to distinguish between the self and the body (see chapter thirteen of the *Gītā*). Having made this distinction, Kṛṣṇa tells Arjuna that he is the 'Knower of the field in all fields' and that true knowledge is that of 'the field and its knower'.[79] Rāmānuja develops this by equating the Lord as Knower with inner Ruler (*antaryāmin*) and Supreme Self (*paramātman*). All things, he elucidates, comprise the Lord's *kṣetra* or body.[80]

YĀMUNA

In concluding this brief look at the background to Rāmānuja's understanding of the body of Brahman, it is fitting that we should turn to Yāmuna (or Āḷavandar),[81] whose position as Rāmānuja's guru makes him perhaps the single most important influence. In addition to being his predecessor at Śrīrangam, Yāmuna was, as fourth in the line of Śrīvaiṣṇava *ācāryas*, Rāmānuja's spiritual 'father'. His works[82] bear comparison with those of Rāmānuja, who, supporting traditional claims for their relationship (although they never actually met), himself acknowledges Yāmuna's influence.[83]

I have already indicated Yāmuna's interest in the *Gītā*. He specifically advocated *bhakti-yoga* as the means to *mokṣa*: '[Release is] to be attained by means of the discipline of an un-divided and absolute loving devotion (*aikāntika-ātyantika-bhakti-yoga*) on the part of one whose mind has been purified by both (*karma* and *jñāna yoga*).'[84] It was this *sādhana* or spiritual practice that Yāmuna transmitted to Rāmānuja,[85] as he in turn had received it from Nāthamuni.[86]

As well as transmitting the *sādhana* of *bhakti-yoga* to Rāmānuja, Yāmuna had a theological influence. His descriptions of Brahman as the Supreme Self (*paramātman*), for example, are echoed in Rāmānuja's references to Brahman as the Self of the universe, who has 'all conscious and unconscious beings' as his body.[87] Yāmuna clearly speaks of the Lord of the manifest universe, who has 'immutable consciousness' as his essential form (*svarūpa*), is 'qualified' by his perfections, and possesses all the different classes of beings which are produced and governed by him.[88] He is none other, he writes, than a particular Person who is an ocean of auspicious qualities.[89]

In his *Ātmā-siddhi*, Yāmuna defines the self (*ātman*) in terms of its essential form (*svarūpa*), which comprises consciousness: 'But others declare (the *ātman* to be) this self-luminous one... that manifests its own essential form (*svarūpa*) without beginning and end; this one... is none other than that which has consciousness as its sole essential attribute (*bodha-eka-svabhāvam eva*).'[90]

In an important succeeding paragraph, Yāmuna elucidates the relationship between the Supreme Self (*paramātman*) and the individual self (*ātman*). There is both difference and non-difference between the two, he explains: the *ātman* is different in that it is the attribute or quality of the Lord,[91] but the same in that the relation is that of a whole to its parts;[92] between an object and its dependent (as a property cannot exist without its possessor); or between an accessory and its principal[93] (even a master and slave). These metaphors recur in Rāmānuja[94] and it seems possible, as Neevel points out, that Rāmānuja's whole viśiṣṭādvaitic (differentiated non-dualistic) approach stems from this proposition of Yāmuna's.[95] Clearly it was he who began to refer to the divine body in relational terms,[96] and hence profoundly influenced Rāmānuja's understanding of the world as the body of Brahman.

CHAPTER 3

The body of Christ in the writings of Teilhard de Chardin

When Teilhard de Chardin refers to the body of Christ, it is clear that for him the term has very specific meaning. The body of Christ is not just a theological concept to Teilhard, or a spiritual reality experienced only in times of prayer and at Mass. He speaks expressively of Christ's body as a kind of aura radiating out from everything, and clearly it is an integral part of his own perception of the world. But how does this relate to the findings of his scientific research? How does Teilhard integrate his faith and commitment to science in his vision of the world? In this chapter I want to explore the relationship between Teilhard's understanding of the body of Christ and his worldview as a whole.

Teilhard did not write systematically about theological issues, but there are threads running through his works which intertwine to produce a consistent theological description of his vision. And the body of Christ has great significance in his vision – and in its theological representation. In a short, undated paper (probably written in 1919) entitled 'What Exactly is the Human Body?',[1] Teilhard gives us a useful definition:

> The Body... is the very Universality of things, in so far as they are centred on an animating spirit, in so far as they influence that spirit, [and] also in so far as they are influenced and sustained by it. For a soul to have a body is to be *enkekosmismenē* (rooted in the cosmos).[2]

This provides a framework to investigate Teilhard's use of the term 'body of Christ'. I shall alter the sequence of the definition to read: (i) the body is centred on an animating spirit; (ii) the body influences that spirit; (iii) the body is itself influenced and sustained by (that spirit); (iv) the body is the very universality of things; (v) for a soul to have a body is to be *enkekosmismenē* (rooted in the cosmos).

(i) THE BODY IS CENTRED ON AN ANIMATING SPIRIT

Teilhard's use of the term 'spirit' is quite specific: he is referring to God as Holy Spirit in relation to the cosmos.[3] By that I mean that he interprets God's spirit as the primary form of energy ('psychic energy') known to us:

Spirit is neither a surimposition nor an accessory in the Cosmos – but it represents quite simply that superior state effected in and around us by the primary, indefinable thing that we call, for want of a better term, 'the stuff of the Universe'. Nothing more; and also nothing less. Spirit is neither a meta- nor an epi-phenomenon; it is *the* Phenomenon.[4]

The spirit of God is recognised as the primary category of life, 'the stuff of the universe'.[5] It is this energy which is creating our world in the divine image and simultaneously 'forming' Christ: a process Teilhard calls *Christogenesis*. Thus 'spirit' refers both to the divine creative power and also to the activity through which things become 'Christified'.[6] Traditionally, the Holy Spirit refers to the former, and the latter is designated by the term 'matter'. Teilhard is claiming right from the outset that 'spirit' and 'matter' are interrelated states of being:

Taken as a whole, in its temporal and spatial totality, life represents the goal of a *transformation* of great breadth, in the course of which what we call 'matter' (in the most comprehensive sense of the word), turns about, furls in on itself, *interiorizes* – the operation covering, so far as we are concerned, the whole history of the earth. The phenomenon of spirit is not therefore a sort of brief flash in the night; it reveals a gradual and systematic passage from the unconscious to the conscious, and from the conscious to the self-conscious. It is a cosmic *change of state*.[7]

This cosmic 'change of state' is an evolution of spirit through which matter becomes increasingly 'conscious'. The universe, Teilhard says, is orientated to spirit[8] and produces spirit, or rather the 'spiritualization' of conscious being.[9] Spirit has what Teilhard calls 'the organic characteristic' of 'a supremely complicated corporeal system':[10] the greater the spiritual or psychic development, the more complex the organic 'body'. The reason for this, he says, is that it is the *act of uniting* disparate elements which comprises spirit.[11] To create, he is fond of saying, is to unite.[12]

In this context it becomes easier to grasp the significance of Teilhard's adjective 'animating' in the term 'animating spirit'.

Clearly, God as spirit is life's inherent creativity and power to unite. And in Teilhard's view, the degree of conscious life – we might say 'spiritual life' – depends upon the extent of unification.[13]

To speak of 'degrees' of conscious life is to imply stages of consciousness. And for Teilhard the whole universe is evolving through this inter-relationship between spirit and the process of unification. He speaks of this as the relationship between the 'centricity' (i.e. spiritual 'power') of a thing and its 'complexity' (i.e. corporeal process):

Centricity (soul) [is] itself a function of a certain degree of complexity (body, and more particularly, brain). This *co-efficient of centro-complexity* (or, what comes to the same thing, consciousness) is the true and absolute measure of being in the beings that surround us.[14]

This is a complicated idea to grasp: that consciousness is spirit in relation to matter, or the 'stuff of life' in the process of evolving towards its own completion. Teilhard sees consciousness, therefore, as the primary term ('spirit' being misleading since it is used in contradistinction to matter), appropriate theologically to denote God in relation to the world or the 'Holy Spirit'. Consciousness is both the *telos* (as Christ-consciousness) and the form or structure of life on earth: 'Consciousness is, in other words, a universal, molecular property, and the molecular state of the world manifests a pluralized state of possibility for universal consciousness.'[15] It is in the context of consciousness, then, that he uses the term 'animating spirit'. Spirit is the (divine) basis of our reality and the power which creates and sustains us as corporeal beings in the physical universe. We, along with the earth, are evolving spirit; we are 'conscious'.

It is clear, therefore, that the 'dimensions' of the spirit are none other than those of our evolving universe.[16] This is obvious from Teilhard's definition of consciousness as centre in relation to complexity ('spirit' and 'matter'), and from the claim that the universe is experiencing a progressive spiritualisation. Teilhard discusses the evolution of the cosmos in terms of levels of consciousness,[17] each exhibiting a particular structure of spiritualisation:[18] at the most basic level or 'sphere' (the geosphere), matter is unconscious and 'stable' because the centricity is fragmented. At the next level (the biosphere), matter is conscious and increasingly complex; its centricity is marked by the 'phylum' through which it passes to become polycellular. And at the highest level (the noosphere), the centres are 'hominised' (personal) and capable of self-conscious thought and action. Organic complexity develops, he argues, in relation to a greater degree of unification or centricity. This characterises a higher level of spiritualisation.[19]

Towards the end of his life Teilhard wrote that 'spirit' as understood by philosophers and theologians was seen by him to be a direct extension of a universal 'physico-chemism'.[20] He meant by this that the most basic energy of life is spiritual and, furthermore, evolving a divine self-consciousness. This has implications, of course, for his Christology.

Teilhard sees Christ as the physical centre of the cosmos, the source of all creation and unity. As spirit he has the power to attract all things to himself and the means, through his humanity[21] – his 'elemental' nature – to actualise the fulfilment of the world. In him, all things find their spiritual consistence.[22] He represents the 'fullness' of God's spirit attaining self-consciousness in the world.[23]

I think Teilhard's use of the term 'centre' warrants further exploration at this juncture. It is one of several metaphors which have considerable importance for Teilhard's understanding of the body of Christ. It is a linking factor between his theological and scientific perspectives. The context in which the term is used is, as I have already indicated (p. 47 above), the evolution of consciousness. In 'L'Atomisme de l'esprit' he refers to consciousness in terms of a being 'folding back and concentrating upon itself', and as seeing or thinking in terms of acting (or being acted upon) as a 'centre of convergence' for things radiating around us. To be conscious, he says, is to be internally centred.[24]

It is the centre of a thing which gives it consistence and hence organic reality. Consciousness and complexity, he explains, are two aspects of the one reality, a centre, which represents viewpoints inside or outside oneself respectively.[25] Being centred is the fundamental characteristic of 'being'. And each thing or person in the universe, each 'element of consciousness', belongs to a level or 'sphere' which represents a stage in the process of spiritualisation.

On a larger scale, the universe itself, being centro-complex,[26] is structured concentrically,[27] and undergoing a cosmic process of concentration[28] and unification.[29] As each sphere converges more and more upon itself, it becomes increasingly interiorised and conscious (or, in the noosphere, self-conscious) until it reaches a 'critical threshold' and breaks through to a deeper level of consciousness and centration. For the future Teilhard envisaged a form of 'monocentrism': all things, he said, will become self-conscious and centred upon a single consciousness, 'Omega'.[30]

This theory of centration is very interesting. It allows for both the natural organic form (complexity) and the inner structure (spirit) of a thing. It includes the 'point' at which energy is created and the 'ambience' of surrounding elements.[31] One could say that the centre represents the totality of its constituent elements, its depth measured in exact proportion to the size of its sphere. Teilhard expresses this in his own way:

> [the centricity of an object] represents... a *magnitude* that is essentially *variable, proportionate to the number of elements and interconnections* contained in each cosmic particle under consideration. *A centre is the more simple and profound, the greater the density and the wider the radius of the sphere in which it is formed.*[32]

Teilhard envisaged the development of consciousness comprising the evolving of centres or 'centre-spheres'. This he termed 'centrogenesis'.[33] The world, he says, is following an irreversible pattern or law of universal concentration,[34] or recurrence.[35] And, Teilhard theorised, it is itself forming one final 'Centre of centres'[36] which acts as the magnetic point of attraction for all existing centres: Omega Point.[37] This is a 'super-centre', a pole of convergence which unifies and synthesises all things.[38]

For Teilhard, this universal personal Centre is Christ or Christ–Omega. The risen Christ, he says, is within each soul (as the Centre of all centres) seeking for fulfilment.[39] The language he uses to speak of Christ depends upon his audience. In his more scientific works, he speaks of Omega, Omega Point, a 'super-centre' of cosmic unification; but in his personal and spiritual works, he speaks of Christ or Christ–Omega, and in particular, of the 'Heart' of the world. In his spiritual autobiography, entitled 'The Heart of Matter', Teilhard explains how we are drawn to the centre of our universe:

> We are awoken by the first rays of a universal centre of convergence and attraction, in which the bonds that make us one whole reach the upper limit of their complexity and then tend to merge into the magnetic force that pulls our *ego* ever more rapidly into what lies ahead. This is the miraculous effect that is specific to the Centric, which does not dissolve nor subordinate the elements it brings together, but personalizes them. And this because its way of absorbing them is constantly to 'centrify' them more and

more. We may, indeed, say that at these high latitudes of the Universe Totalization reduces the Multiple to the One by synthesis, and so acts as a liberating agent. In other words, Matter becomes Spirit at just the same pace as love begins to spread universally.[40]

In other words, centring is a process of becoming more and more personal, corresponding to an intensification and radiation of love.

For Teilhard this process which we all undergo is one in which Christ is being completed. Each individual is part of this: 'I do not think there is any better, or even any other natural centre of coherence for the whole of things than the human personality', he said in 1936.[41] He spoke of humankind as 'the leading shoot of evolution',[42] representing the humanity of Christ.

Christ is also 'above' creation, he added, waiting for its consummation. As Omega he is the transcendent[43] Point, drawing the world towards its own self-fulfilment in God:[44]

Christ himself does not act as a dead or passive point of convergence, but as a centre of radiation for the energies which lead the universe back to God through his humanity... Christ reveals himself in each reality around us... and shines like *an ultimate determinant*, like a centre, one might almost say like a universal Element.[45]

Teilhard does not speak of Christ's 'divinity', because this may suggest a separation from, rather than relationship with, the world. Rather he speaks of Christ in his role as Centre, as universal Element and as the Form of all forms.[46] It is Christ, he claims, who represents the cosmic 'principle of superindividuation', bringing each being to perfection by 'universalising' or 'cosmising' him or her.[47]

When Teilhard speaks in this way, he is once again ascribing a divine core or centre to the material universe. Referring to Christ as Form, for example, he alludes to the biblical notion of humankind, 'formed' in the image of God. The process by which humanity is thus 'formed' is through the penetrating[48] and formative[49] influence of Christ as Centre, he explains. Thus Teilhard speaks of Christ as the Form of the world:

If the universe is regarded in relation to its term (the total Christ, *in casu*), it is not in fact an aggregate, but an organic whole of a higher entitative order than that of the elements considered in isolation. The universe's own particular form, therefore, must be impressed upon each monad by some determination higher in order than the degree of being found in the monads separately. That is the function of the universal element X... In *our* universe X is the penetrating influence of Christ-*w*, of Christ – '*Forma-Mundi*'.[50]

In this sense Christ is the universal structure or form both of the cosmos, and of each individual element within the cosmos. He is the personal blueprint for life or consciousness at whatever level of existence: 'Truly, Christ acts upon us *as a Form*, and the amount of souls that are ready (for him) is matter, which takes shape internally (substantially) in him.'[51] It is important to remember that Teilhard saw Christ's universalising presence as essentially personal. He sometimes refers to him as the 'Form of the Incarnate Word'.[52] It is Christ's personal influence which brings the world to completion. There is, therefore, a simultaneous universalising and personalising of all things, because they are fulfilled through their integration into him: 'The whole history of the universe... is the history of the progressive information of the universe by Christ.'[53]

It is clear from this contextualising of Teilhard's use of 'centre' and 'spirit' that his method is to integrate the physical universe into his vision of Christ. He consistently presents matter as intrinsically 'spiritual', and the universe in terms of its 'centre'. He describes the world in terms of its 'heart', Christ, who is its 'animating spirit'. He refers to the cosmos as a body, a 'flesh':

> if every collective soul is born in *our* world through the instrumentality of a body, then Christ can consummate our unity in the Centre *that stands firm above us* – the Centre, that is, which is his Spirit – only if he first encloses us in a material network *underlying* our 'esse corporeum'. If he is to be the soul of our souls, he must be the flesh of our flesh.[54]

(ii) THE BODY INFLUENCES THAT SPIRIT

Teilhard is making quite a remarkable claim here: there can be no spiritual being without matter; there can be no Christ without the cosmos:[55]

> In fact, the purely spiritual is as unthinkable as the purely material. It is the same, in a sense, as the fact that no geometric point exists, rather there are as many structurally different points as there are methods of producing them from the various shapes (centre of a sphere, apex of a cone... etc.) – so every spirit takes its reality and nature from a particular type of universal synthesis.[56]

Spirit, he maintains, presupposes and structurally integrates matter.[57] In order for the world to exist, a 'shape' is necessary; in this sense Christ is the world's 'personal, convergent structure'.[58] On the analogy of the geometric point, Christ's 'centredness' can be as various as the organic beings in existence. In fact, Teilhard points out that there are many centres – many souls – of which Christ is their core or Centre of centres.

It is important to clarify this: Teilhard envisions Christ as continually incarnating in direct correspondence to the evolution of the universe. Not only that, but the role of individual souls in the world is crucial to this incarnation process. To him man (i.e. humankind) is, above all, supremely capable of reflection[59] and can be seen, existentially, as a multitude of points or centres of vision and action, each co-extensive with the entire universe.[60] It is through us, therefore, that the disparate elements of the world are integrated:

> It is we who, through our own activity, must industriously assemble the widely scattered elements. The labour of seaweed as it concentrates in its tissues the substances scattered, in infinitesimal quantities, throughout the vast layers of the ocean; the industry of bees as they make honey from the juices broadcast in so many flowers – these are but pale images of the ceaseless working-over that all the forces of the universe undergo in us in order to become spirit.[61]

So collectively we are 'making Christ' in our lives.[62] This is a participation in and an extension of one creative and salvific process. The goal of humankind is to 'attain Heaven by bringing Earth to its fulfilment'.[63] As a 'monad' of the universe, each person can become 'a function of a cosmic stream',[64] divinising the cosmos[65] and 'completing' God through completing the universe.[66]

Our role, then, is that of Christ's: to divinise the world. To do this, each person needs to develop himself or herself and extend the 'radius' of his or her activity. 'To grow and to fulfil oneself to the utmost – that is the law immanent in being', Teilhard wrote to his cousin, Marguerite Teillard-Chambon in 1916.[67] Personal growth and fulfilment are found, argues Teilhard, through a 'universalising' process: each individual must abandon a narrow sense of self, 'and extend himself, intellectually and emotionally, to the dimensions of the universe'.[68]

The human task of divinising matter corresponds to what Teilhard calls 'the arising of God'.[69] Teilhard explains that God, as 'eternal Being in itself', is everywhere in process of 'formation' for us.[70] In this sense Christ is continuously being incarnated in the world, structuring and unifying all that by virtue of being created is implicated in the divine process: 'Through his Incarnation he entered not only into mankind but also into the universe that bears mankind ... Christ has a *cosmic body* that extends throughout the whole universe.'[71]

It is humankind, therefore, which, as the evolutionary spearhead of creation, most influences the spirit. We all complete the spirit, in that through humankind Christ is completed. In loving the world we are loving God, and transforming energy (more particularly, material energy) into spirit. At the same time our sense and understanding of God develops.[72] Christ emerges as a new consciousness in us, personalised yet universal. You could say that in humankind the world becomes self-aware. And correspondingly, for human eyes (imbued with an increasing awareness of Christ's presence) the world becomes a divine milieu.[73]

The phrase (*le*) *milieu divin*, which is used frequently by Teilhard, is synonymous with 'the body of Christ'[74] and denotes the world seen in its inner, divine perspective. The spiritual path which cultivates this power of perception will be the subject of another chapter. It is important not to misunderstand what Teilhard means by *milieu*: he is not suggesting an indiscriminate merging of things. Rather is he referring to the way in which individual worlds (i.e. individual people)[75] are integrated[76] through Christ, their common Centre. So unification signifies, for him, mutual differentiation.

Teilhard describes, in his spiritual writings, how the divine milieu is generated in the 'utmost depths of human consciousness'[77] through the fusing of the energies of divine grace and humankind.[78] The human ego, he explains, ex-centrates and integrates with the common, Christic centre.[79] This process of human divinisation which he calls a milieu is, we learn, none other than the Kingdom of God seen and described from within:[80] 'The mystical (i.e. divine) milieu is *not a completed zone*, ... it is a complex element, made up of *divinized created being*, in which, as time goes on, the immortal distillation of the universe is gradually assembled.'[81]

Teilhard refers to the Kingdom of God as the divine milieu or as the body of Christ: the three are, to all intents and purposes, synonymous. It is hardly surprising, therefore, to find that he uses similar terms for both Christ and the divine milieu. The latter is, he says, the 'Sphere of the world ... a Centre[82] in process of centration upon itself'.[83] In Teilhard's words the divine milieu is a 'pan-christifying' as well as a 'pan-humanising' element.[84]

Teilhard's understanding of the relationship between humankind and the cosmos is now clear: we are all responsible[85] for bringing ourselves and our world to its proper completion in God as the body of Christ. It is our duty, Teilhard maintains, to transform our egos and transmute life's energies into love.[86] 'By its nature', he wrote (in 1941), 'love is the only synthesizing energy whose differentiating action can super-personalize us.'[87] By that he means that the human being, as one small element ('atom') of the universe, learns to love all things (the world) through loving their common centre, hence intensifying and extending the radius of that centre's influence.[88]

To summarise the main point of this section: matter influences spirit in the sense that it is the 'matrix of spirit'. Only through the evolution of matter can spirit be actualised. It is in man in particular that spirit or consciousness is transformed and 'embodied' as Christ; Christ who, as Omega, is the goal of the universe. And it is in relation to Christ that the universe assumes the form of a divine milieu, a personal world.[89]

(iii) THE BODY IS ITSELF INFLUENCED AND SUSTAINED BY (THAT SPIRIT)

The third area we have to consider in our exploration of Teilhard's understanding of the body of Christ is his claim that all material things are influenced and sustained by the spirit: in other words, that spirit or consciousness affects, even determines, the material states characterising the evolution of the cosmos. We have already looked at what Teilhard means by spirit, namely, the divine psychic energy which manifests itself in varying degrees as centricity or the inner structure of things. Having argued that matter is essential for the development of spirit, he goes on to claim that all material things are ontologically dependent upon spirit.

Here we are brought straight to the concept of the universe as one body, the body of Christ. The whole world, says Teilhard, in all its complexity and diversity, is somehow united and supported by the influence of 'a distinct centre of super-personality'.[90] In 'L'Energie humaine', for example, Teilhard refers to Christ as 'a true pole of psychic convergence', an assimilative super-centre which perfects all persons by uniting with them. In this sense he is a 'cosmic point', Omega, ahead in time and space.[91]

This demonstrates the physical dimension of Teilhard's understanding of the body of Christ. In an early paper, 'La Vie cosmique' (1916), he had written: 'The mystical body of Christ should, in fact, be conceived as a physical reality, *in the strongest sense the words can bear.*'[92] Even then, he portrayed Christ as a physical 'Centre of centres', the Centre of the world. In some of his works, Teilhard uses the metaphor of Christ's 'kingship' in connection with this: it is his 'kingship' or kingly rule which extends throughout the cosmos as the inner dynamic and structure of things, impelling them forward and upward towards their transcendent goal.[93] This suggests that the qualities of Christ radiate throughout the cosmos, imbuing even the most mundane things with a divine charisma.

When we read Teilhard's more personal, devotional writings, we can sense the personal experience which contributed largely to the formation of his understanding of the world's inner unity in Christ. 'La Messe sur le Monde', for example,[94] demonstrates an almost overwhelming sense of adoration and awe before the power and 'majesty' of Christ – the 'dazzling centre' of matter:

> Glorious Lord Christ: the divine influence secretly diffused and active in the depths of matter, and the dazzling centre where all the innumerable fibres of the multiple meet; power as implacable as the world and as warm as life; you whose forehead is of the whiteness of snow, whose eyes are of fire, and whose feet are brighter than molten gold; you whose hands imprison the stars; you who are the first and the last, the living and the dead and the risen again; you who gather into your exuberant unity every beauty, every affinity, every energy, every mode of existence; it is you to whom my being cried out with a desire as vast as the universe, 'In truth you are my Lord and my God!'[95]

As the 'dazzling centre' of matter, Christ is described in different terms, depending upon the context. He is the 'pole of psychic convergence', the 'Centre of centres', and the 'glorious Lord', who gathers into his 'exuberant unity' all that is beautiful, all that exists. But whatever the context, whatever the terminology, Teilhard consistently makes the same point: that it is Christ who unites and binds the world together as his body because he is its centre and heart.[96] Ultimately, when Teilhard speaks of the world being influenced and sustained by an animating spirit, he is referring to Christ.

This is seen most clearly when he speaks of the 'properties' of Christ. In a paper he wrote in 1943, entitled 'Super-humanité – Super-Christ – Super-charité: de nouvelles dimensions pour l'avenir',[97] he talks of Christ's universal power in terms of his relationship to the cosmos. St Paul's language becomes startlingly real, he argues, if the risen Christ is perceived as the world's goal.[98] He then assumes the character of a Person whose greatness can only be glimpsed in relation to the ever-extending boundaries of the physical universe. Indeed, Christ's 'properties' are to be understood in terms of the universe:

In the first place, he is physically and literally, *He who fills all things*: at no instant in the world, is there any element of the world that has moved, that moves, that ever shall move, outside the directive flood he pours into them. Space and duration are filled by him.
Again physically and literally, he is he who *consummates*: the plenitude of the world being finally effected only in the final synthesis... And since he, Christ, is the organic principle of this harmonising process, the whole universe is *ipso facto* stamped with his character, shaped according to his direction, and animated by his form.
Finally, and once more physically and literally, since all the structural lines of the world converge upon him and are knitted together in him, it is he who *gives its consistence* to the entire edifice of matter and spirit.[99]

This, perhaps more than any other text, illustrates Teilhard's vision of the world as dependent upon Christ: he 'fills' all things (nothing can exist without him);[100] he 'consummates' all things (everything depends upon him for fulfilment);[101] and he gives 'consistence' to or in-forms all things.[102] Initially Teilhard spoke of all things finding their definitive consistence in an 'ultimate Element'.[103] Later he explicitly identified this with the cosmic influence or nature of Christ,[104] calling the sphere in which Christ operates the 'universal Element'. He meant by this the cosmic dimension of Christ. It is through Christ, he said, that the universe develops. He is the 'principle'[105] through which the cosmos evolves. As 'universal Element' Christ's properties are the following: he makes the transcendent immediate and present; he unifies all things by a process of differentiation; he enables a completion to take place of what is already in existence; and he paradoxically allows us to become released from the world through our involvement in it.[106]

The implication of Teilhard's claim is that Christ is co-extensive with the universe.[107] To be the consistence and consummation of all things he must, says Teilhard, become 'co-extensive with the physical expanse of time and space'.[108] And to 'reign' as 'king', Christ must 'sur-animate' the world.[109] It is in him that personality 'expands (or rather centres itself) till it becomes universal'.[110] In him the world 'lives, moves and has its being'.

The idea that Christ and the world are co-extensive is related to Teilhard's concept of the centre, which denotes both the point and that which surrounds it (see above, p. 49). According to him, every element and event in the world, being centred to some degree, is 'in reality co-extensive (in its preparatory stages, in its inclusion in the general frame-work, and in its completion) *with the totality* of Space-Time'.[111] Christ, as the Element of all elements, is, therefore, co-extensive with all things. The extent of his cosmic influence expresses the infinite extensions of his incarnation.[112]

In the context of Christ's universality, how does Teilhard envisage the relationship between Christ and the individual? Perhaps the fundamental point he makes is that the individual is pervaded by grace.[113] Through grace and the individual's will and effort, each person is responsible for his or her own growth towards a deeper participation in the sanctification of the universe; hence a deeper participation in the life or consciousness of Christ. So commitment to Christ involves commitment to the universe.

Seen in this light, the concepts of morality and sanctity advocated by the Christian tradition represent for him an organic extension of the spiritualisation of the cosmos.[114] In living out the fundamental Christian virtues,[115] individuals are contributing to the 'progressive unification' of all things, which is the building of the body of Christ.[116] 'Moral effort', wrote Teilhard in 1917, '*is the continuation in our souls of the same dynamic effort* that gave us *our bodies.*'[117]

To look at morality apart from Christ's grace is, for Teilhard, meaningless. What we call morality is, to him, a part of our human nature,[118] and a function of our relationship with him. In a sense it is an extension of Christ's grace – a sign of his 'animating spirit' within us. And to become fully ourselves we need to acknowledge and consolidate our links with the universe, since only then are we enabling Christ's presence to fill us. For Teilhard, therefore, morality is cultivated through contact with the world, not through separation from it. When talking about purity, for example, Teilhard says, '[it] does not lie in separation from, but in a deeper penetration into the universe'. He concludes, 'it lies in a chaste contact with that which is "the same in all"'.[119]

Contact with that which is 'the same in all' is the prerequisite for spiritual development. Teilhard speaks of an 'immersion' in matter, and of the 'morphogenic' influence of Christ within matter. Christ's 'imprint' is to be found in all:

> By Baptism in cosmic matter and the sacramental water we are more Christ than we are ourselves – and it is precisely in virtue of this predominance in us of Christ that we can hope one day to be fully ourselves.
>
> So much, then, for the physical intensity of grace. As for the scope of its

'morphogenic' influence, it is boundless ... To enable himself to unite us to him through the highest part of our souls, he has had to undertake the task of making us win through in our entirety, even in our bodies. In consequence, his directing and informing influence runs through the whole range of human works, of material determinisms and cosmic evolutions.[120]

Immersion in the world is not genuine, however, if there is an absence of love. Love he sees as a power;[121] the basic energy[122] which divinises all things. He refers to it as the transformed affinity of material elements into an interiorised 'radial' (i.e. centre-to-centre) attraction.[123] The human problem, points out Teilhard astutely, is to learn to love a multitude.[124] The only way to do this, he continues, is through identifying with the shared Centre, Christ.

(iv) THE BODY IS THE VERY UNIVERSALITY OF THINGS

The human task of learning to love a multitude – the cosmos – involves a sharing in Christ's universal 'nature',[125] Teilhard explains. It represents the transformative and integrative function of Christ:

Between the Word on one side, and the Man–Jesus on the other, a sort of 'third Christic nature' (if I may use so bold a phrase) emerges – constantly to be found in the writings of St. Paul: it is the nature of the total and totalizing Christ, in whom the individual human element born of Mary is subject to the transforming influence of the Resurrection, and so raised not merely to the state of cosmic element (an element, one might say, of what makes up the whole cosmic milieu or curvature) but to that of ultimate psychic centre of universal concentration.

To this, Teilhard adds a footnote:

Each element in the universe ... is both physically and metaphysically an elementary centre in relation to the totality of time and space. In Christ, however, this co-extension of co-existence has become co-extension of sovereignty.[126]

So when Teilhard speaks of the 'universality of things', he is referring to their physical nature.[127] And when he speaks of Christ as universal Element, he is referring to his cosmic nature.[128] Confusingly, these are really one and the same thing, seen from different perspectives! Our 'physical' world and Christ's body are one and the same: Christ's life incorporates the life of the cosmos,[129] which is experienced as 'the mystical Milieu'.[130]

I would like to clarify further what Teilhard is suggesting when he refers to the universe as Christ's 'body'. Obviously he is expressing the divine immensity and pervasiveness[131] of the world's own 'animating spirit' and 'form'. Christ's body is that process which con-centrates the stuff of the universe.[132] In the same way that matter and spirit are, for Teilhard, interdependent, so Christ's body is inevitably cosmic as well as personal. It is complex because centred.[133] It can be compared, says Teilhard, to a sphere and its centre.[134] The totality of the world is present in its centre, just as the centre's influence pervades the entire sphere. Given that the universe comprises many individual centres of consciousness, this means that the totality of the world is partially reflected in each of these centres,[135] and that their mutual interaction affects the 'building' of the whole Christ.

I think it is unquestionably the case that Teilhard's personal experience influenced this theological perspective. The way he experienced things can be glimpsed in his *Pensées*, for example. In one text[136] he speaks of seeing the world as translucent and illumined from within. The light he attributes to the 'mighty radiance' born of the synthesis, in Jesus Christ, of all the elements of the world. The more complete and naturally fulfilled beings are, he explains, the 'closer' and 'more perceptible' their radiance. Correspondingly, the more perceptible this radiance is, the more clearly the particular objects it bathes 'stand out', and the deeper their roots are.

Clearly Teilhard could himself perceive the spiritual 'consistence' (what he sometimes calls the 'concentricity')[137] of objects and living beings around him. He believed this to be a natural extension of a common human faculty: to experience the joy that comes from an awareness of 'fullness' or completeness. He maintained that everyone has the potential to perceive an inner dimension to life and to the things around them, and this experience can result in a sense of fulfilment and joy: an inner security. Teilhard calls this the 'Pleromic Sense'.[138] As a Christian, he interprets this experience as the mysterious attraction and beauty of Christ, who is worthy, therefore, of worship:

> You, Jesus, are the epitome and the crown of all perfection, human and cosmic. No flash of beauty, no enchantment of goodness, no element of force, but finds in you its ultimate refinement and consummation... The unique fragrance of the glory and wonder of your being has so effectively drawn from the earth and synthesized all the most exquisite savours that the earth contains... that now we can find them... in you...[139]

You the centre at which all things meet and which stretches out over all things so as to draw them back into itself: I love you for the extensions of your body and soul to the farthest corners of creation through grace, through life, and through matter... I love you as a world, as *this* world which has captivated my heart.[140]

Perceiving the 'concentricity' or concentrated being of things means, for Teilhard, becoming aware of their divine 'fullness', their Christic nature. The inner radiance thus perceived is, he explains, the 'corona' (i.e. crown) of Christ which signifies their inner form and Christ's cosmic nature (see p. 58 above). This is the *locus* of the transformation through which life takes on form (the Word becomes flesh). In 'Le Prêtre' (1918), Teilhard refers to Christ's 'personal and sacramental Body' being enveloped in 'a "corona" of living dust as vast as the world'.[141] Later he speaks of this corona as 'the seat of the encompassing and unifying activity of the Incarnate Word'.[142] This corona, he goes on to say, is the 'universal physical element' of Christ.[143]

Christ's body concerns this elemental radiance. A universal yet personal light 'haloes' each one of us and extends to the furthest reaches of the universe. This aura is both common to all and peculiar to each. Christ, in this context, is 'a magnification, a transformation... of the *aura* that surrounds every human monad'.[144] The body of Christ is, therefore, perceptible and describable in visual terms: it is the inner radiance, the spiritual life and 'consistence' of the world, which both illumines from within and envelops all as a unifying 'crown' of glory.

When referring to the perceived presence of Christ in the world in this context, Teilhard uses a specific term: he speaks of the 'Diaphany' (i.e. of light). In a letter to Léontine Zanta he illustrates what he means by the term 'Diaphany' by speaking of the universal Christ illuminating the 'unique and higher substance of things' in order to act through them, drawing them towards their common goal. He comments that the more he advances in life, the more he thinks that true wisdom lies in 'being able to discern – and then migrate to – this divine milieu, which is so mixed up with things, and yet so superior to them'.[145]

I noted earlier that Teilhard refers to the body of Christ, the Kingdom of God and the divine milieu synonymously (p. 53 above). In this context we could explain this by saying that the form or the inner life of each and every thing is both unique and shared. It comprises a universal 'Christic' presence. This is experienced as light or radiance. As a person develops spiritually, she or he begins to see the world as consisting of this light, and it begins to appear as one whole, as a (divine) milieu. Thus Christ's presence within the individual correlates to his presence within the world, and this is experienced as one unity: the milieu of Christ.

For Teilhard, perceiving this divine milieu is to perceive the glory of Christ's physical and universal presence. It was this vision of Christ which was the inspiration and *raison d'être* for his work: 'The Diaphany of the divine at the heart of a glowing universe, as I have experienced it through contact with the Earth – the divine radiating from the depths of blazing matter; this it is that I shall try to disclose and communicate.'[146]

He interprets this milieu as God becoming 'Christified',[147] creating and integrating all things into himself. On the one hand the universe is becoming more personalised through convergence upon its Centre, and on the other, Christ is becoming increasingly universalised through evolution.[148] What appear to be two discontinuous processes are parts of one organic movement through which the universe and Christ are mutually completed, one through the other. This cosmogenesis, or 'Christogenesis', as Teilhard calls it, is a vast transformation of the universe effected by and through all things and peoples in so far as they consciously and unconsciously adhere to that mysterious milieu within and around them which presses them forward to Christ–Omega.

(v) FOR A SOUL TO HAVE A BODY IS TO BE 'ENKEKOSMISMENĒ' (ROOTED IN THE COSMOS)

Teilhard's understanding of 'the Incarnation' relates to his perception of the universal dimensions of our humanity. Each individual, being by definition 'centred', partakes of the life and influence of the world's Centre and reflects, in part, that totality (see pp. 56–7 above). It is in this sense that each person is 'rooted in the cosmos':

> My own body is not these cells or those cells that *belong exclusively* to me: it is *what*, in these cells *and* in the rest of the world feels my influence and reacts against me. *My* matter is not a *part* of the universe that I possess *totaliter*; it is the *totality* of the Universe possessed by me *partialiter*.
>
> Thus the limited, tangible fragments that in common usage we call…

bodies, are *not complete* beings. They are only the nucleus of such beings, their organisational centre. In each case, the real extension of these bodies coincides with the full dimensions of the universe.[149]

The human body partially represents the cosmic body. As Teilhard puts it in 'Esquisse d'un univers personnel', the human body 'represents the mesh of the cosmos'.[150] One implication of this is that not only is the world's creation synonymous with the 'enfleshment' of Christ, but also the 'salvation' of one individual is in some sense linked to that of the whole.[151] And the redemption of the world involves the fulfilment of Christ in God.

All this raises questions about what it is to be embodied. Teilhard de Chardin was not alone in raising these questions, as we know from the correspondence of Maurice Blondel. In a letter to Auguste Valensin of 1919 he claims that the general understanding of the body, and even the scientific one, is deficient. He argues that the 'action' of our presence is boundless; that we act *in toto* as we 'undergo, direct and make specific within ourselves' the action of the Whole. There is thus a universal interpenetration: 'We are literally made up of one another, without ceasing to be this *ineffable individuum*.'[152]

Teilhard's concept of body provides a framework for an entire cosmology, synthesising both his understanding of matter in terms of spirit and his evolutionary theory. For him, each person as a conscious centre provides one perspective of the world which is his or her body: 'We are countless centres', he writes, 'of one and the same sphere.'[153] The world is really 'world centred on Mary' plus 'world centred on John', and so on.[154] 'Since each element is strictly co-extensive with all the others', concludes Teilhard, 'it is really a *microcosm*.'[155]

Given that each individual is co-extensive with the totality that comprises his or her milieu, then each person, as a centre, contains and reflects that totality. The task of that individual is to integrate those elements which are particularly 'his' or 'hers'. To the extent that these elements are integrated, the person concerned is centred in Christ. The wholeness of the individual is measured by his or her degree of integration. In addition, the world is 'realised' (made real) through that person to the extent that she or he is integrated or centred. It is in this sense that Jesus Christ becomes for Teilhard a transformative power of unification and integration in the cosmos. It is his 'animating spirit' which shapes our world, his body.

CHAPTER 4

The body of Brahman in the writings of Rāmānuja

In this chapter I shall begin to explore Rāmānuja's use of the term *śarīra-śarīrin* (body–self) to refer to the relationship between all conscious and non-conscious beings (which for simplicity's sake, I shall henceforth refer to as 'the world') and Brahman. There is one definition of 'body' (*śarīra*) in his *Śrībhāṣya* (his main commentary on the *Brahma-sūtras*) which can assist in this enquiry:

> Therefore the definition should be considered in this way: that substance [is] the body of a conscious being which can be controlled and supported [by that conscious being] for its own purpose in all circumstances, and which has the essential form of being its accessory.[1]

Thus, a body (i) belongs to a conscious being; (ii) is controlled and supported by that being; (iii) serves to further that being's purpose in all circumstances; and (iv) its proper or essential form is accessory to that being.

These four points will serve as guidelines for our enquiry, since Rāmānuja's argument develops from this definition into a claim that the world (i.e. all conscious and non-conscious beings) comprises the body of Brahman: 'Since everything [is] in all circumstances controlled and supported by the Supreme Person, and always has the nature of being his subordinate, then all conscious and non-conscious beings [are] his body.'[2] This claim, which summarises Rāmānuja's *śarīra-śarīrī-bhava* or body–self doctrine, can now be investigated in more depth.

(i) THE BODY BELONGS TO A CONSCIOUS BEING

Firstly we need to understand what Rāmānuja means by referring to Brahman as a 'conscious being', before going on to consider how the world may be said to belong to him. In Chapter 2 I showed how the divine was, from an early date, conceived in terms of Person (pp. 31, 33; 40 above) and later referred to as the Highest Person (pp. 34, 42 above). In depicting Brahman as the Highest Person (*puruṣottama*), Rāmānuja is affirming the authenticity of his tradition.

He does this by beginning his *Śrībhāṣya* with the claim that the word 'Brahman' denotes *puruṣottama*.[3] The implication of this is that the entire Vedāntic enquiry, the desire to know Brahman (*Brahmajijñāsā*), concerns the Highest Person (*puruṣottama*) as its object. He develops this claim in the following section of the text by interpreting the divine 'that', from which the world proceeds, as:

> that highest Person who is the ruler of all; whose nature is antagonistic to all evil; whose purposes come true; who possesses infinite auspicious qualities, such as knowledge, blessedness, and so on; who is omniscient, omnipotent, supremely merciful; from whom the creation, subsistence, and reabsorption of this world proceed – he is Brahman.[4]

Here Rāmānuja clearly states that the supreme reality is to be viewed as the Person[5] through whom the world is actualised, whose nature is 'antagonistic to all evil', and who is characterised by perfections (omniscience, omnipotence, supreme mercy).

Elsewhere he identifies the Highest Person as the Supreme Self (*paramātman*), developing the Upaniṣadic and *Gītā* theme of Brahman as the self or *ātman* of all things. When discussing chapter 15: 17–19 of the *Gītā*, for example, he writes:

> But the Highest Person is other than the bound and freed selves denoted by the words 'destructible' and 'indestructible'. That is, He constitutes an entirely different entity. He is described in all the *Śruti* texts as the Supreme Self...[6] Whoever, being free from delusion, understands the Highest Person as Myself thus, in the manner already stated, that is, understands Me to be of a different kind from the destructible and indestructible *puruṣas*, on account of My being endowed with the power to pervade, support and rule and such other faculties – he knows all. That is, he knows all that has to be known as the means for attaining Me.[7]

In this passage Rāmānuja makes it clear that although the term *puruṣottama* refers to the inner Self of all things, nevertheless, strictly speaking, it primarily denotes Him who 'possesses greatness, of essential nature as well as of qualities, in unlimited fulness'.[8] He also explains that although understood to be *puruṣottama*, Brahman is to be sought as the intimate *paramātman*,[9] the Supreme Self.

This *Gītābhāṣya* passage introduces the central theme in Rāmānuja of seeking to attain the Supreme Person. This, for him, is the highest soteriological goal, equated with release (*mokṣa*).[10] The method he advocates is a form of *bhakti-yoga* (literally 'bringing together in loving devotion') integrating the *bhakti* of the *Gītā* with the interior contemplation of the *Upaniṣads*[11] and a practice of meditation similar to that referred to in earlier texts, such as the *Brāhmaṇas*, the *Viṣṇu-purāṇa* and *Pāñcarātra* texts.[12] More specifically, he speaks about knowing the Lord in terms of sharing in love (*bhakti*)[13] and the experience of devotional meditation (*upāsana*).[14] He teaches the way to attain such knowledge by describing a committed practice of meditation focusing on the divine form (*divya rūpa*)[15] of the Lord as the object of visualisation. This, when part of a totally committed life-style and daily practice, leads finally, he says, to the vision and knowledge of the Lord.[16]

I choose to explain a little of Rāmānuja's soteriological teaching at this point because it is the appropriate context for understanding a crucial aspect of his depiction of Brahman as 'conscious being'. I am referring now to his references to the divine form (*divya rūpa* or *rupavatva*). At one level Rāmānuja uses this term to refer to Brahman's 'form', which transcends his 'body' (comprising the world). This distinction is important: whereas Brahman's body is analogous to a human person's body, in its dependence upon a self, his form is depicted in terms of transcendence and self-sufficiency.

The Lord's form serves an altogether different purpose, for Rāmānuja, from that of his body. It inspires *bhakti* in his devotees through manifesting the beauty of the Lord:

> He who exists within the orb of the sun, whose splendour is like an impressive mountain of burning gold, whose brilliance is of a hundred thousand suns, whose eyes are pure and long like the petals of a lotus or a translucent stalk, rising out of deep waters, [and] opening out in the sun's rays, whose forehead has well-matched eyebrows, whose nose [is shapely] ...and who has a pair of graceful feet like full-blown lotuses...he has attracted the eyes and thought of all by his manifold and wondrous beauties. The nectar of his beauty completely fills all animate and inanimate beings...The endless space between the [four] cardinal points is perfumed by the fragrance of his holiness.[17]

This descriptive passage may fruitfully be compared with earlier references to *puruṣa*.[18] Allusions to seeing ('gloriously visible'), the 'orb of the sun' and 'rays of thousands of suns' are reminiscent of light symbolism in the *Brāhmaṇas*, as is the reference to 'molten gold'.[19] The vivid description of the Supreme Person which follows (abbreviated here) is remarkably similar to that of Viṣṇu in the *Viṣṇu-purāṇa*,[20] and to that of the Lord in the *Bhagavad-gītā*.[21] As in these earlier passages, the anthropomorphic imagery is counteracted by images of transcendence: the Lord's all-pervading 'nectar of comeliness' and 'fragrance of holiness' indwell and pervade all things.

For Rāmānuja Brahman's form has specific functions. Firstly, it is this form that assumes a descent form (*avatāra*) to protect and help all devotees.[22] Secondly, it is the goal (*upeya*) itself as the 'form'[23] or 'abode'[24] attainable by the devotee. Thirdly, it is the means (*upāya*) to attain that goal, both as a manifestation of the Lord's grace and also as the object of meditation for aspirants.

The clearest exposition of these functions is given in Rāmānuja's *Gītābhāṣya*, chapter 11, where Arjuna attains a vision of Kṛṣṇa (an avatar of Viṣṇu). Here it is made clear that the universe is only fully seen by the devotee as the body of the Lord through realising the Lord's form. In other words, through the devotee's desire and meditation, the Lord's gift of grace ('the divine eye'[25]) enables the devotee to realise his or her own true form and 'see' the Lord's all-pervading form enveloping and indwelling all things, which then appear as his body.[26] When commenting on 11.15–18, Rāmānuja says:

> O Lord! I see in your body all the gods, as well as all the groups of various kinds of living beings...
>
> I see you everywhere – you who are of boundless form, with many arms, stomachs, mouths, and eyes...
>
> I see you who are a mass of light, resplendent everywhere, difficult to look at anywhere, effulgent like the brightness of the blazing fire and the sun...
>
> You the supreme abode of this universe, that is, what constitutes the supreme support of this universe is you alone...
>
> Of whatever nature, quality or dominion you are, you remain always with that same form. The protector of perpetual *dharma*... My conviction is that you are the eternal *puruṣa*.[27]

This teaching on the divine form of Brahman is profound. It encapsulates the heart of Rāmānuja's spiritual vision, and indicates the nature of transformation experienced by one deeply committed to the task of Self-realisation. It is not, for Rāmānuja, an undifferentiated experience, but one which integrates each facet of a person's worldview into a sense of divine and personal presence.

I think this is easier to comprehend when we remember Yāmuna's references to the self (*ātman*) in terms of consciousness and to the Lord's essential form (*svarūpa*) as consciousness (p. 43 above). Rāmānuja's descriptions of the divine form of the Lord refer to the Self-manifestation of his essential form. Thus to refer to Brahman as a 'conscious being' is to indicate his essential form as the Self of all beings.

Having considered briefly what Rāmānuja means by referring to Brahman as a 'conscious being', we can move on to consider how the world may be said to belong to him. For Rāmānuja the equation was simple: just as a body 'belongs' to a self, so the world 'belongs' to Brahman; just as the body depends upon a self for its life, energy, inspiration and co-ordination, so the world depends upon the Supreme Self for its very existence.

Rāmānuja explains this ontological dependence[28] by having recourse to the *Sāṃkhyan* doctrine of *satkāryavāda*, by which a substance or cause (*kāraṇa*) is transformed in time into a new form or effect (*kārya*), but not into a new substance. In this case, Brahman in his causal state is transformed into the world, his effected state, without changing his essential nature.[29] As *sat* (literally 'being'), Brahman is the material cause[30] of the universe; in his effected state, he is the operative (or 'efficient') cause,[31] guiding each new creation in its emergence and dissolution. The clearest exposition of this teaching is found in the *sadvidyā* discussion (see p. 40 above), when Rāmānuja interprets the *ārambhaṇādhikaraṇa* text about the relationship between the individual and Brahman. At the beginning of the *Vedārthasaṃgraha*, for example, he explains:

> Thus, the section of the *Upaniṣad* under consideration develops in detail the thought that the entire universe of *cit* and *acit* (conscious and non-conscious beings) has *sat* (being) as its material cause, its efficient cause, its ground, its controller and its Lord to which it is instrumental in value. This is done in the passage commencing with the text, 'All these creatures have *sat* as their source, abide in *sat* and are based on *sat*.' Secondly it proceeds through the principle of causality to the thought that the only truth about the universe is that it is animated by Brahman: 'All this is ensouled by this *sat*. That is the truth.'[32]

While explicating this doctrine of *satkāryavāda* Rāmānuja describes the world's dependence on Brahman in metaphorical terms as a (non-temporal) mode–mode-possessor relation.[33] The world 'belongs' to Brahman as his 'mode'. He illustrates this by referring to the way in which class characteristics are dependent upon particular examples for their meaning. In the same way, he says, individuals are dependent upon Brahman as their Self to enable them to be who they respectively are.

To grasp Rāmānuja's meaning here it is important to realise that he argues for the primacy of a substance over the classes or generic structures which inhere in them.[34] The attribute or mode only attains its status as such through its relation with the substance it modifies and these, he maintains, are inseparable.[35] You could say that the substance is modified by its attributes, but in the case of Brahman and the world, only part of Brahman is thus modified.[36]

There is another theory that Rāmānuja expounds to define the inseparability of, yet distinction between, Brahman and his 'mode', the world, and this he refers to as *sāmānādhikaraṇya* or 'co-ordinate predication' (see p. 40 above). He means by this 'the application of two terms to connote one meaning under the aspects of two modifications'.[37] His *sadvidyā* interpretation has precisely this sense: both 'that' (*tat*) and 'you' (*tvam*) refer to Brahman; the latter as 'mode' of the former. In other words, *tvam* refers to a spiritual being (in this case, Śvetaketu's true self) which denotes a 'mode' of Brahman. Rāmānuja concludes: 'As all [conscious] and [non-conscious] beings are thus mere modes of the highest Brahman, and have reality thereby only, the words denoting them are used in co-ordination with the terms denoting Brahman.'[38]

A body is a 'mode', since it serves 'as a distinctive feature for a certain substance', namely, a self. And a body can have no function apart from that self.[39] In this case, he adds, it is quite correct to co-ordinate (by a *sāmānādhikaraṇya* construction) selves with Brahman, and to declare them as his mode. Thus 'the sum-total of [conscious] and [non-conscious] entities [i.e. the world] is ensouled[40] by the Supreme Brahman inasmuch as it modifies him'.[41]

(ii) THE BODY IS CONTROLLED AND SUPPORTED BY THAT BEING

While considering how Rāmānuja understood the world to belong to Brahman, it is necessary to refer to another metaphor he used in this context. He spoke of Brahman and the world as 'support' and 'supported' (*ādhāra-ādheya*, or occasionally, *āśraya-ādheya*). To illustrate this relationship he refers to clay and pottery objects,[42] Brahman being likened to the basis or ground of all forms of life. He refers to the self (*ātman*) as the support (*ādhāra*) of the body, and to Brahman, the Supreme Self, as the support of all selves comprising his body: 'In the heart of all beings who constitute My body, I am seated as their Self (*ātman*), for to be the "Self" means that I am entirely their support (*ādhāra*), controller (*niyantṛ*), and master (*śeṣin*).'[43]

The nature of this support accords with Brahman's personal qualities,[44] as we can see from Rāmānuja's use of the terms 'Highest Person' (*puruṣottama*) and 'controller' (*niyantṛ*) in conjunction with *ādhāra*. By 'controller' he means 'personal, inner guide', as we learn from his customary choice of the term *antaryāmin* or 'inner Ruler' (see pp. 33; 37; 39 above).

Rāmānuja draws extensively upon the metaphor of the 'inner Ruler' to refer to the way in which the world is divinely guided from within. In his *Śrībhāṣya*, for example, he uses the traditional body simile of the chariot and the charioteer to explain the relation between unevolved matter (*pradhāna*) and Brahman. The chariot (the body) is guided and restrained by the charioteer (the self), the point being that only the person who can control the chariot arrives at his or her destination ('the abode of Viṣṇu').[45] It is in this sense that Rāmānuja uses the terms *niyantṛ* and *antaryāmin*: as the self, guiding and directing the body. He makes it clear that the Highest Person is the inner Ruler (*antaryāmin*) of all selves, indwelling and ruling them as the Supreme Self ruling his body: 'The highest Person, the inner Ruler and Self of all [is] the term and goal of the journey of the individual soul; for the activities of all the beings enumerated depend on the wishes of that highest Self.'[46]

In the description of Brahman as the world's inner Ruler, the theological significance of the self's inherent power and truth is underlined. It is Brahman as inner Ruler, therefore (i.e. the Self guiding all beings from within), who brings about meditation in the devotee, and it is he who is the proper subject of meditation.[47] Rāmānuja is depicting Brahman as the coherent thread linking and guiding all selves simply by being their individual and collective Self. As inner Ruler Brahman 'in-forms' the world with consciousness.[48]

In epistemological terms the traditional spiritual teaching that it is through knowing one's self (*ātman*) that Brahman can be known is endorsed and developed. When commenting on the *sadvidyā* (see pp. 67–8 above), Rāmānuja explains that it is through knowing the inner Ruler (or Self) of one's own self, and knowing him to be distinct from one's own self, that one attains *Brahmajñāna*:

> We maintain in the first place, that Brahman is the inner ruler, and of this inner ruler, the individual self is a mode, being his body. Thus by the term 'thou', only the highest Brahman characterized by the individual as his mode is designated and denoted. This truth must be apprehended as such without any qualification. This is the meaning of the text, 'Thou art that'. In the second place, the highest Self is other than the individual self, in which the Supreme abides as the inmost Self.[49]

Another way in which Rāmānuja maintains the distinction between the individual self (*ātman*) and Brahman, as well as inseparability, is to use another pair of metaphors for the relationship, namely, the 'knower' (*kṣetrajña*) and the 'field' (*kṣetra*). Brahman, he explains, is the knower, and individual selves are the field of his knowledge (see pp. 38; 42 above). To defend his use of these terms Rāmānuja points out[50] that the *Kāṇvas* rendering of the *Antaryāmī-brāhmaṇa* speaks of 'he who abides in knowledge' (as opposed to the *Mādhyandina* recension, which gives 'he who abides in the Self'). The true nature of the Self, he argues, is knowledge.[51]

In elucidating the way in which the 'field' is dependent upon the 'knower', Rāmānuja brings in the body–self model.[52] He represents the two pairs of metaphors on two levels simultaneously: the micro level, of individual self–body (knower–field) relation, and the macro level, of Brahman–world (Knower–field) relation. Consider this passage, in which Rāmānuja explains that Brahman is the Self and Knower of all beings:

> Know as Myself the *kṣetrajña* who is also the sole form of the knower in all bodies like those of gods and men. That is, know him as having Me as his Self. By the word 'also' (*api*) in, 'And... the *kṣetrajña* also', it is made out by implication that it has been taught, 'know the *kṣetra* (or the body) also to be Myself'. Just as the body, by reason of its having primarily the character of an attribute of the *kṣetrajña*, cannot exist independently of it, and hence can be denoted only through a grammatical equation with it, know that likewise both the *kṣetra* and the *kṣetrajña*, by reason of their having primarily the character of My attributes, cannot exist independently of Me and therefore can be denoted only by means of a grammatical equation with Me.[53]

In this passage, Rāmānuja is pointing out that all beings are divine ('Myself') in the sense that they cannot exist independently of Brahman, their Self. However, they are also limited in their experience. Rāmānuja illustrates this by referring to the human body, which is a circumscribed form for the self. The body, he explains, is a combination of elements which forms the support of consciousness (*cetanādhṛtiḥ*). It is a compound of different substances which enables the senses to function, and pleasure, pain or even the final bliss to be experienced. This support for the self he calls the *kṣetra*.[54]

Here Rāmānuja portrays the human body as the field (*kṣetra*) of consciousness (*cetana*) or knowledge (these are synonymous to him), circumscribed by karma or incompleted action or energy. The human self, however, is very different in that it is uncircumscribed, infinite and undivided. It supports the body, yet is independent of it. Having consciousness as its essential form (*svarūpa*), it is of the character of light (*jyotiḥ*). Rāmānuja goes on to explain that the goal of each devotee is precisely to distinguish the body/world from the self/Brahman; and to realise (in the sense of 'make real') the self's proper form, which is, in itself, Brahman-knowledge or -consciousness. This, he says, will enable the individual to attain release (*mokṣa*).[55]

The question of the world's 'control' and 'support' by Brahman is, as I have shown, linked to that of the body's 'control' and 'support' by a self. The nature of this support relates to Brahman's/the self's true nature as consciousness or knowledge (often described as light and bliss). The form of the control exercised over the world by Brahman and the body by the self determines the way in which guidance is understood in terms of 'knowing': it is comparable to the way in which a field (of experience) is dependent entirely upon its subject, its 'knower'. And Brahman, having knowledge (or consciousness) as his true nature, simply manifests that knowledge in the world. (Or from another perspective, the world, in becoming what it is, realises Brahman.)

Rāmānuja cleverly builds up a composite picture to communicate this core relationship at the heart of his worldview. He uses different pairs of metaphors and puts them together so that they all influence each other: support–supported (*ādhāra-ādheya*), controller–controlled (*niyantṛ-niyāmya*) and knower–field (*kṣetrajña-kṣetra*). These are put in the wider context of Brahman as the Supreme Self (*paramātman*) and inner Ruler or Guide (*antaryāmin*). We are given thereby a theological picture of the world known intimately by Brahman in the same way that each of us knows his or her own body. The world is supported and controlled by Brahman not as by an external power but through consciously or unconsciously manifesting Brahman himself, being inseparable from him.

(iii) THE BODY SERVES TO FURTHER THAT BEING'S PURPOSE IN ALL CIRCUMSTANCES

We can further understand what Rāmānuja means by saying that the world is supported and controlled by Brahman, if we look at his use of the term *vibhūti*. This can be translated in a general way as 'divine realm', its primary connotation being manifestation(s) of the Lord's rule. In the *Viṣṇu-purāna* the term is understood to refer to Viṣṇu's 'rule' or 'power' (p. 34 above), which is made manifest or expressed.

Rāmānuja refers to this in his *Śrībhāṣya* when, for example, he argues that the 'abode of heaven and earth' is the Supreme Self who is characterised by *bhuman* (literally 'fullness'). Rāmānuja explains that the meditating devotee can attain an intuition of that fullness (bliss), and begin to reach that state in which he cannot see anything apart from it:

> the whole aggregate of things is contained within the essence and *vibhūti* of Brahman. He, therefore, who has an intuitive knowledge of Brahman as qualified by its attributes and its *vibhūti*, which is also called *aiśvarya*, i.e. its lordly power – and consisting of supreme bliss, sees nothing else since there *is* nothing else apart from Brahman.[56]

In this extract, Rāmānuja is teaching that the devotee's goal involves seeing the 'nature' of Brahman in form(s) manifesting his rule (or power). His *vibhūti* is 'contained within' all things, and indeed *is* all things understood as manifestations of his glorious 'rule'.[57]

A development of the idea that the universe is, in some sense, the Lord's *vibhūti* is found in Rāmānuja's *Gītābhāṣya*, chapter 10, which is traditionally called *vibhūtiyoga*.[58] Basically, Rāmānuja interprets the text to mean that the Lord's *vibhūti* is the devotee's desired object of vision. Arjuna states that it is right for Kṛṣṇa to tell him about all the manifestations or creative qualities of the Lord's *vibhūti*.[59] Kṛṣṇa replies by pointing out that there are an endless number of such objects, each varying in its relative importance or eminence.[60]

It is interesting that Kṛṣṇa, in reply, speaks about the *objects* of the Lord's *vibhūti*, because this brings out the dual meaning of the term alluded to in the *Śrībhāṣya* passage above: it denotes both the Lord's

'Self-manifestation', and the objects or forms that manifestation takes. Applying the principle of *sāmānādhikaraṇya*, this is because all things denote Brahman as their primary meaning. Hence the objects of the Lord's *vibhūti* are endless: they are co-terminous with the universe and all created worlds.

Kṛṣṇa begins by teaching Arjuna about the most important object of the Lord's *vibhūti*, namely, the Highest Self. This is, in other words, Kṛṣṇa himself, the Lord, who is 'in the heart of all beings who constitute [his] body'.[61] This form of the Lord, the text explains, is the vision most greatly to be desired. It is the most supreme and sovereign of all. Kṛṣṇa goes on to illustrate this: he, Kṛṣṇa, is Viṣṇu among the Ādityas, the sun among all the heavenly bodies, the *sāmaveda* among the *vedas*, the mind (*manas*) among all the sense-organs, and consciousness in conscious beings. So the objects of the world, which are themselves *vibhūtis*, reveal, as Arjuna realises, the Lord's greatness, his power and his sovereignty. And yet, says Kṛṣṇa, they are but a fraction of the Lord's full glory.[62]

From these examples we can see that *vibhūti* means 'divine realm' in the sense of 'manifestation of the Lord's rule' and refers both to the Lord's nature and to examples of his greatness. As the Lord's body (i.e. belonging to Brahman and being controlled and supported by him), the world is the Lord's *vibhūti*, since through its dependence on him it reveals his purpose of Self-manifestation. Thus the world reveals Brahman as Supreme Person. The aspiring devotee is, therefore, encouraged to long for the vision in which the Lord is seen to pervade all things as their Self; in which nothing can be seen apart from his fullness, his bliss.

At this point it is necessary to remind ourselves of Rāmānuja's descriptions of Brahman's 'divine form' (see pp. 65–6 above). We saw earlier how the devotee, represented by Arjuna in the *Gītā*, was enabled by Kṛṣṇa to see the universe as the body of the Lord. Clearly, seeing the Lord's true form and seeing his *vibhūti* belong together: to see and know the Lord[63] is to see and know him in relation to the world.

This is a very important theological point: we, as human beings, are not able to see Brahman in his unevolved (*nirguṇa*) state: we can only see him in his evolved or manifest state. This means that realising our self (*ātman*) is to realise who we truly are in this world. We may experience Brahman in his transcendent, divine form, but while we still live, this cannot be separated from experiencing him in his world. Our vision and knowledge of Brahman is a transformed vision and knowledge of all we ordinarily see and know because all the objects of the world belong to his *vibhūti*, his divine realm.

To return to our original line of enquiry, it is now clear that Brahman 'controls' and 'supports' the world as part of the process of his Self-manifestation. And all objects in the world participate, consciously or unconsciously, in realising this 'purpose' by virtue of the fact that they share his essential nature.

Let us look more closely at what Rāmānuja means by the Lord's 'nature'. If you read his writings, you will find that he uses two distinct yet related words when referring to the nature of Brahman: *svarūpa* and *svabhāva*. And in order to understand what Rāmānuja means, we need to look at his usage of these two terms.

An example of this is found in a passage from the *Vedārthasaṃgraha*:

The Supreme Brahman is by nature such that his *svarūpa* is absolutely opposed to imperfections and is solely constituted by infinite knowledge and bliss. He is an ocean of noble qualities – unlimited, unsurpassed and immeasurable – which are proper to his *svabhāva*.[64]

Firstly we note that *svarūpa* and *svabhāva* both refer to Brahman's transcendence. This is important because Rāmānuja's use of the term 'body', if not balanced by terms such as these, might lead to a misunderstanding of Brahman's essential nature, which, we learn in the continuation of this passage, is unaffected by time and evolution. His guidance of the world, though from within, as inner Ruler (*antaryāmin*), does not imply involvement in the permutations and limitations of matter.

We can begin to grasp the difference as well as the continuity between the meanings of these two terms in the passage above. Brahman's *svarūpa* is 'absolutely opposed to imperfection' and solely constituted by 'infinite knowledge and bliss'; his *svabhāva* includes an 'ocean of noble qualities'. Knowledge and bliss are qualities, but the difference is that they belong to the five 'defining' attributes referred to in the *Upaniṣads*, which serve to inspire and develop *bhakti* in the devotees of the Lord.

If we turn to a passage in the *Śrībhāṣya*, we find this distinction developed. There seems to be a functional difference between Rāmānuja's use of the terms *svarūpa* and *svabhāva*. Here, Rāmānuja is discussing which qualities should be included in devotees' meditation on the Self in the heart:

Those... qualities which are 'equal to the thing', i.e. which are attributes determining the essential character of the thing, and therefore necessarily entering into the idea of the thing, must be included in all meditations, no less than the thing itself. To this class belong qualities such as true being, knowledge, bliss, purity, infinity, and so on... Such additional qualities, on the other hand, as for example compassion, which indeed cannot exist apart from the subject to which they belong, but are not necessary elements of the idea of Brahman, are to be included in those meditations only where they are specially mentioned.[65]

We can see that Rāmānuja is distinguishing here between those qualities which are 'equal to the thing' and those which are not 'necessary elements of the idea of Brahman'. Only the former are to be included in all visualisations and meditations on Brahman; the rest serve specific purposes and are to be included when particularly mentioned.

We learn that the qualities which Rāmānuja classifies as 'equal to the thing' are the Upaniṣadic 'defining attributes' (*kalyāṇaguṇas*): true being (*satya*), knowledge (*jñāna*), bliss (*ānanda*), purity (*amalatva*) and infinity (*ananta*). In the same text he equates these with the 'infinite knowledge and bliss' claimed by other texts to define Brahman essentially.[66] For Rāmānuja, Brahman's *svarūpa* consists of those qualities which define him as he is 'in himself':[67] perhaps the clearest translation is 'essential nature'.[68]

The term *svabhāva*, on the other hand, although similar in its literal meaning (which also suggests 'essential' or 'own' form or nature), is used by Rāmānuja more specifically to refer to Brahman's transcendent greatness in relation to his world. The 'noble qualities' attributed to him are those, for example, that attract devotees to the Lord and help them to realise him as their Self. These include lordship (*aiśvarya*), generosity (*audārya*) and compassion (*kāruṇya*).[69] They express the Lord's *vibhūti*: his Self-manifestation in the world.

It would appear that Rāmānuja deliberately distinguishes between these different yet related aspects of the Lord's nature. In chapter 18.55 of the *Gītābhāṣya* we have an example of this. The *Gītā* text is concerned with the devotee practising meditation in order to come to know the Lord – both 'who he is' and 'how great'. In Rāmānuja's words, both 'Who I am in *svarūpa* and, having regard to My *svabhāva*, how great I am in My *guṇa* (qualities) and *vibhūti* (realm or rule of glory)'.[70] Rāmānuja is developing the distinction present in the *Gītā* and reminding his followers that Brahman 'in himself' is distinguishable, if not separable, from what I translate as his 'manifest nature'.[71] The Lord's essential nature is the most important and his manifest nature – his qualities and rule or realm – are subsidiary.

This distinction between Brahman's *svarūpa* and *svabhāva* performs an important function of preserving and emphasising the transcendence of Brahman in relation to the world. It is, however, the nature of the Lord which determines the nature of the world: his essential form is manifest consistently in terms of noble and beautiful qualities embodied in 'worldly things'. Ultimately all belongs to Brahman and comprises his *vibhūti*. The world is part of his own Self-manifestation.

(iv) THE BODY'S PROPER OR ESSENTIAL FORM IS ACCESSORY TO THAT BEING

Having discussed Brahman's *svarūpa* in relation to other aspects of his nature, we should consider the *svarūpa* of the individual self (*ātman*), which, along with its macro counterpart, the world, stands in relation to Brahman as body to self. In Rāmānuja's relational worldview it is this that demonstrates his differentiated non-dualism most clearly: the individual self is different from Brahman (the Supreme Self), and yet, as we shall see, there is a fundamental identity within the difference.

Perhaps the most significant term Rāmānuja uses when speaking of the nature of the self or *ātman* is *śeṣa*.[72] What Rāmānuja means by the term we learn from his usage, which is frequently in the context of the function of the individual self (*jīvātman*) and the world as Brahman's body. They are (collectively) the accessory or 'servant' (*śeṣa*), he says, of the Lord, who is their 'master' (*śeṣin*). We can measure how important these relational terms are by the fact that he opens his *Vedārthasaṃgraha* by referring to them: 'Homage to the *śeṣin* to whom all conscious and non-conscious entities are *śeṣa*; Who reposes on *śeṣa*,[73] and Who is the treasury of immaculate and infinite beautiful qualities: Viṣṇu'.[74]

This opening passage clearly attributes all power, beauty and worth to Viṣṇu. All beings exist to serve him. This dependent relationship is explained in more detail in a subsequent paragraph:

> the *śeṣa* is in essence that which admits of application to, or which has its use for, another term inasmuch as it serves to support the transcending importance intrinsic to that other term that constitutes the *śeṣin*... [for example] it is the essence of born slaves that they have their use in so far

as they support the transcending importance of particular persons. In the same manner, all entities – comprising [conscious] and [non-conscious] beings, eternal and non-eternal – have essentially only their use inasmuch as they support the transcendence of the Lord. Thus everyone and everything is *śeṣa* to the Lord and the Lord is *śeṣin* to all.[75]

We learn here that the *śeṣa* serves to 'support the transcending importance' of the *śeṣin*. So all beings 'support the transcendence of the Lord'. This develops Rāmānuja's theme of the world existing through and for the Supreme Person. We saw in the preceding section how the world, as the body of Brahman, furthers his purpose. And through his concept of inner Ruler (*antaryāmin*), Rāmānuja presents this Brahman–world relationship as one not only of dependence by inherence. The terms *śeṣa-śeṣin* suggest more than this: they serve to present the relational nature of Rāmānuja's understanding of Person. The different 'modes' of Brahman complement and fulfil one another through serving their own true purposes.

Rāmānuja explains this in his *Śrībhāṣya* by discussing how the slave, for example, serves not only his master but also his own interest in feeding his master.[76] So although the relation is asymmetrical (the dependence and inherence are not mutual), functionally, each aspect of Brahman as Person has a different role to fulfil through the inter-relationship. The individual, for example, is both manifesting the Lord's greatness[77] and realising his or her own self through serving the Supreme Person as Master. Likewise, the Lord is showering concern and grace upon his devotees through his Self-manifestation.

We have already seen (p. 74 above) that it is through recognising the dependence of all things upon the Lord and through learning to see the world as his divine realm (*vibhūti*) that the individual secures the means to attain release from the false *ahaṃkāra* or 'independent' ego.[78] Identifying one's own self as *śeṣa* is an initial stage in the path of *bhakti*, and leads to an increasing love and worship of the Lord. Rāmānuja explains that it is, in fact, a person's 'sole essence (*rasa*) and delight (*rati*)' to be the *śeṣa* of the Lord.[79]

This brings us to Rāmānuja's understanding of the *ātman*'s *svarūpa* or essential nature. For him it fundamentally comprises uncontracted knowledge or consciousness, and is characterised by being *śeṣa*:

Then, when the *svarūpa* of one's *ātman*, whose nature (*svabhāva*) is to be a *śeṣa* of [Brahman] and whose form (*ākāra*) is unlimited knowledge, has been revealed and this *svarūpa* is not contaminated by the *kleśas*,[80] acts etc., one will not mourn over any being but [Brahman], nor desire any being but [Brahman], but be equal and indifferent towards all beings; not caring for anything, one will acquire *bhakti* towards [Brahman] – supreme *bhakti* which is the experiencing of the most dearly beloved One.[81]

This passage shows us particularly clearly the soteriological significance Rāmānuja gives to the term *śeṣa*: it is through realising one's own essential nature as *śeṣa* that one becomes a practitioner of *bhakti-yoga*, the way of uniting with the Lord through loving devotion. It is this which is both the goal and the means to attain that goal: loving the Lord devotedly. In his *Śrībhāṣya* Rāmānuja develops the metaphor of the servant and the master, explaining that the Lord blesses the person who performs good actions with piety, riches and release, whereas the one who does not respond to the Lord's rule experiences the opposite.[82]

This approach emphasises the dependence of the individual upon the Lord, and the enormous difference between the two. And yet, as Rāmānuja also makes clear, the true nature (*svarūpa*) of the individual's self (*ātman*) is *identical* with that of Brahman, being of unlimited knowledge or consciousness. The individual (*jīvātman*) is not *per se* the same as Brahman because, of course, his or her consciousness is circumscribed. But essentially his or her nature is 'of' Brahman: it is divine.

Rāmānuja's use of the terms *śeṣa-śeṣin* reiterates his understanding of the intrinsic relationship at the heart of life: all beings are both different from the Lord who brings them into existence, and supports and controls them from within; and they constitute who he is, in the sense that in his Self-manifestion in different 'names and forms', all these are essentially part of him. In other words, there is identity as well as difference in the Brahman–world relation.

We have already noted that the devotee's desired goal is, for Rāmānuja, a vision of the Lord's form and of the world as his *vibhūti*. This vision involves the realisation of the Lord's inherence in all things as their Self. It involves a recognition or perception of the essential identity of all the various things of the world:

One who has reached the highest stage of *yoga* approaches My nature, as is declared in the text, 'Stainless he attains supreme equality (*sāmānyam*)' (Isa Up. 6). Seeing that all *ātmā*-nature in its pure state beyond good or evil is equal to Me, he will see that I am in all *ātmās* and all *ātmās* are in Me, and in virtue of this equality, if he knows the nature of one *ātmā* he knows the nature of all *ātmās*. I do not veil Myself from the man who knows his own *ātmā* in its proper nature, for My nature is the same as his. Indeed, I consider him as My own Self (*ātmā*), as equal to Myself, and I always reveal Myself to him.[83]

It could be argued that to practise devotion to the Lord while claiming that the self (*ātman*) of each being is identical with Brahman (i.e. is divine) is contradictory. This is not, however, a correct understanding of Rāmānuja. As his use of the terms *śeṣa-śeṣin* indicates, he maintains at all times the dependent nature of the relationship between the self and Brahman. It is within the context of this dependency that he claims Self-realisation can take place. Correspondingly, the 'purposes' of Brahman and the world, though different, are ultimately the same. In other words, the individual self obviously has the goal of Self-realisation, but that is inextricably bound up with realising his or her dependence upon the Lord. Ironically, the Lord is 'attained' only by the devotee becoming truly him or herself.

(v) BRAHMAN AS SELF; THE WORLD AS BODY

Let us look a little more closely at Rāmānuja's understanding of Brahman as the Supreme Self (*paramātman*), since this radically affects his view of the world.

Rāmānuja asserts throughout his writings that Brahman is free from evil. This is, for him, a necessary corollary to his greatness and unsurpassability. But when we look at an example of his references to Brahman's greatness, we find that Rāmānuja includes all beings in this: they are seen to 'stand for' or, ultimately, represent the Supreme Person:

The word 'brahman' denotes the highest Person, who is essentially free from all imperfections and possesses numberless classes of auspicious qualities of unsurpassable excellence. The term 'brahman' is applied to any things which possess the quality of greatness; but primarily denotes that which possesses greatness of essential nature as well as of qualities, in unlimited fullness, and such is only the Lord of all.[84]

This definition speaks of greatness as a quality or attribute which is possessed by the Supreme Person in his 'essential nature' (*svarūpa*) and in 'unlimited fullness'. There is, as we have seen, an ontological continuity between Brahman and his world, because the former is ontologically determinative of the whole of reality. It is to Rāmānuja's credit that he tries to hold this claim together with that of Brahman's freedom from evil. He continually argues for

Brahman's transcendence as well as his 'involvement' with the world.

Rāmānuja maintains both claims simultaneously by means of the theory of co-ordinate predication (*sāmānādhikaraṇya*) (see p. 68 above). This enables him to argue for Brahman's inherence in the world without his assumption of the limitations of matter (*prakṛti*). To recapitulate his argument: Rāmānuja says that all terms denote Brahman ultimately, just as all beings 'stand for' the Lord, who, for the sake of his own sport,[85] constitutes the world with only a portion (*aṃśa*) of himself:

> all these entities are ultimately ensouled by Brahman. Hence [it] follows that all words which have definite denotative value owing to the combination of the radical element without suffix, e.g. god, man...etc., actually denote the entire composite entity: the body, the individual soul represented by it, and finally the Inner Ruler of that soul, the Supreme Person in whom that entity terminates. All words denote this entire *compositum* by merely denoting the material mass which has a certain generic structure that is commonly known as being denoted by a certain word.[86]

So Brahman's 'greatness' and perfection are represented, partially, in the world about us. The imperfections we experience are not those of Brahman, but rather the inevitable karmic constraints inherent in the elements of matter out of which life evolves. Nevertheless, all things ultimately express the divine, and Rāmānuja treads a fine line here to avoid both dualism and non-dualism. His answer is unique in the history of Indian philosophy: he maintains that only a qualified or 'differentiated non-dualism' (*viśiṣṭādvaita*) is an accurate representation of the way things are. The world is divine, but is also differentiated in certain respects from Brahman, who alone remains wholly 'great' and completely perfect.

Another feature of Brahman is that he is all-knowing. It is this 'knowingness' which defines his essential nature (*svarūpa*).[87] It also characterises his role as Self.[88] This becomes more comprehensible when we realise that Rāmānuja continually equates knowledge (or 'knowingness') with consciousness (*anubhūti*). In *Śrībhāṣya*, for example, he states that the Self is the knower (*kṣetrajña*),[89] and that the Self is I-consciousness.[90] He continues:

> What is established by the consciousness of the 'I' is the I itself... hence (it makes no sense) to say that the knowing subject, which is established by the state of consciousness, 'I know', is the not-I... Nor can it be said that this

'I', the knowing subject, is dependent on its light for something else. It rather is self-luminous; for to be self-luminous means to have consciousness for one's essential nature... The case is analogous to that of the flame of a lamp or candle... the lamp being of luminous nature shines itself and illumines with its light other things also.[91]

Rāmānuja is arguing here for the self-validating existence of Brahman as consciousness. He uses the metaphor of light to illustrate the self-disclosive nature of Brahman, who is 'self-luminous' and 'illumines with [his] light other things also'. This qualifies his relationship with the world. All things possess consciousness to varying degrees and hence are 'illumined' by Brahman. The light of their consciousness is attributable to him.

Rāmānuja propounds a teaching or doctrine of the body–self relation (*śarīra-śarīrī-bhāva*) to provide a theological structure which integrates both the difference and identity between Brahman and the world. This represents his unique interpretation of *Vedānta*, and provides an integration of differing spiritual approaches to the goal of knowledge of Brahman (*Brahmajñāna*).[92] Although this teaching is unique, nevertheless, Rāmānuja drew heavily upon traditional understandings of Brahman and the world. In particular he used the notion of the world comprising part of the divine Person (*puruṣa*) as expounded in the Vedas; and also the Upaniṣadic tradition of the self (*ātman*) being in some fundamental way identical to Brahman.

He goes further, and argues that 'all *Vedānta* texts' declare that 'the entire world... stands to the highest Self in the relation of a body'.[93] He quotes some of his sources:[94] these include the *Antaryāmī-brāhmaṇa* (p. 39 above), where it is said that both 'non-conscious things' and 'intelligent selves' constitute the 'body of the highest Self'; also the *Subāla Upaniṣad* ('he who dwells within the earth' and 'he is the inner Self of all'); and *smṛti* sources such as the *Viṣṇu-purāṇa*, which state that 'the whole world is thy body', 'all this is the body of Hari'. These sources show, says Rāmānuja, that the universe is the body of the Supreme Person.

The metaphors of the world as 'body' and of Brahman as 'self' were, as I have shown, not new. Rāmānuja, however, put them in direct relation one to the other as a means of qualifying each. He was critical of existing definitions of body (*śarīra*), for example, precisely because they did not allow for Brahman's transcendence of karmic actions, and of the limitations of matter.[95] He wanted a definition of 'body' which accommodated both the earth and all beings associated with matter *and* the Lord's divine form (*divya rūpa*) and descent (*avatāra*) forms (the latter two being independent of the karmic law of cause and effect). He was determined to define 'body' in such a way that the entire universe and Brahman were included in it, while remaining distinct from one another.

Thus Rāmānuja found the definition of 'body' that he wanted, and which we have used as the framework for this chapter. A body, he says, is a substance which a conscious being controls and supports for its own purpose, standing in a subordinate relation to that being. And in this sense, he continues, 'all conscious and non-conscious beings together constitute the body of the Supreme Person', since they fulfil these requirements exactly.[96] This definition enables him to integrate a divine–world unity (through the inherence of Brahman as Self) with Brahman's transcendence (through the world's ontological dependence upon him).

If we look at the ontological dimension of this definition, we find that in several of his most important texts about the body–self relation, Rāmānuja stresses above all that the body is defined by the self: in other words, the primary category in terms of ontological reality is the self. To put this in the context of Rāmānuja's view of the divine–world relation, we need to remember that he draws upon the style of earlier Vedic and Vedāntic *ṛṣis* and writers in assuming a homology between the individual self and the world.

Rāmānuja uses the body–self concept to relate these two homologous categories one to the other by their mutual centredness on Brahman as Self. They are 'micro' and 'macro' forms of Brahman's body, equivalent to one another in their total dependence upon Brahman. Furthermore, all 'micro' forms are subsumed under the 'macro' form, since the world comprises all conscious and non-conscious beings.

To turn to the epistemological implications of his definition, the important point is that Rāmānuja maintains the primacy of self-realisation. In other words, through consistently presenting Brahman as the Supreme Self of all beings, he remains firmly within the Vedāntic tradition of equating knowledge of Brahman with knowledge of self (*ātman*). In his *Gītābhāṣya*, for example, he interprets 10.20 thus: 'The meaning is that the entire aggregate of beings in all states are united with Me, who constitute their Self,'[97]

As we noted earlier (pp. 66–7 above), coming to know or realise Brahman is experienced as a transformed vision: to know him is to see him in all things (pp. 72–3 above). The world is then seen as the Lord's divine realm or rule (*vibhūti*). In theological terms, the world is the manifestation of the Lord's 'will to rule', which actualises his purpose of Self-manifestation.[98] This 'will to rule' is limitless: all auspicious objects exhibiting lordly power (*aiśvarya*), splendour (*tejas*) and beauty (*kāntimat*) come from a fraction of the Lord's ruling power.[99] So the Lord's will to rule is a unitive presence pervading and controlling the world. And it is through this same will that the devotee is helped to attain his or her goal. An example of this is the Lord's assumption of specific human or divine forms appropriate to the devotee's needs.[100]

It is the Lord's will which also enables the devotee finally to know and see him, to realise his true nature, his greatness and the universal dimensions of his body. Rāmānuja explains that when this happens, Brahman is seen as the 'Lord of all beings', and his splendour and glory are seen to manifest his body, the universe.[101] So it is that Rāmānuja presents the object of knowledge of Brahman (*Brahmajñāna*) as the Supreme Person, the personal ruler of a glorious realm. He it is whose divine form is realised by the individual self and is seen to indwell the world, his body, as its transcendent Self.

Thus the body–self doctrine provides a theological structure to hold together a vision in which the divine and the world are fully integrated, one with the other. It also provides a model for spiritual practice leading to knowledge of Brahman (*Brahmajñāna*) through coming to know the true nature of one's self and the world. In Part II we shall explore the ways in which Rāmānuja develops his body–self teachings to serve these spiritual and theological purposes.

PART II

CHAPTER 5

Functions of the divine body in Rāmānuja and Teilhard de Chardin

In this chapter I shall begin to compare the functions of the body of Brahman in Rāmānuja's works with those of the body of Christ in the writings of Teilhard de Chardin. At first glance it may appear extraordinary to place the thinking of a twentieth-century Frenchman next to that of a twelfth-century Indian. They came from totally different cultures, and the theological contexts in which they lived and wrote could hardly be less similar. Yet they shared a theological task: to expand and recreate the theological worldviews of their time. This task emerged from their spiritual commitment, and it seems remarkable that they both used a particular notion to underpin their respective visions: the body of the divine.

I suggest that the level at which we can best compare the respective 'divine bodies' is to consider, first of all, the functions of the term in each writer's work. I shall take for consideration two hypotheses: firstly, that the function of the divine body in each writer is metaphorical; and secondly, that it becomes a conceptual model for the way each theologian believes things to be. In this chapter I shall begin to look at these hypotheses.

What does it mean to speak of the divine body as a metaphor? By metaphor I mean a figure of speech which refers to something in terms of something else, thereby creating a new mode of perception. Janet Martin Soskice, in her book *Metaphor and Religious Language*, defines metaphor as 'a form of language use with a unity of subject-matter and which yet draws upon two (or more) sets of associations'.[1] In this context, the divine body is a metaphor with two sets of associations drawn from understandings of the terms 'divine' and 'body'. In Part I I sought to explore the different sets of associations drawn from the worlds of Rāmānuja and Teilhard de Chardin respectively, and to show how each thinker forged his metaphor of the divine body in his own unique way. Now I intend to bring the two presentations of the same basic metaphor together, with their various associations, to see whether they resonate with one another at all.

Metaphors are powerful tools of communication, and religious language abounds with them. This is partly because some things simply cannot be said in a literal way. Metaphors are non-literal ways of presenting things, and none the less 'true' for being non-literal. The truth of metaphors can only be assessed by their relative appropriateness as interpretative perspectives on reality. And metaphorical expressions, such as 'She's a gem!' or 'God is Light', evoke responses in the hearer or reader which confirm or deny their appropriateness: the 'truth' or meaning of the expressions is realised through appropriating a new way of seeing.

Talk of the 'divine body' is similarly powerful as a form of communication. It has a disclosive and evocative character in the writings of both Teilhard de Chardin and Rāmānuja. They use it to communicate their visions of the world, their ways of seeing. It becomes for them a method of spiritual teaching, which is the ultimate purpose of each (see the Introduction, pp. 3–4 above). But they teach in radically different religious traditions, so can we really compare the body of Christ in Teilhard with the body of Brahman in Rāmānuja?

Let us address this by returning to the question of how the divine body functions in each writer's work. When we look again at Teilhard and Rāmānuja, it is as if a pattern emerges: the divine body has a particular role to play in the theological framework of each writer, and that role is associated with what may be termed a 'root-metaphor'. This is a metaphor which has become dominant within its contextual usage to the extent that other interpretative perspectives of reality have become subordinate to it.[2] Most worldviews, consciously held or otherwise, have certain root-metaphors which act as keys to the total perspective. Comprehending such a root-metaphor can lead to an understanding of the worldview as a whole.[3] So in explicating the function of the divine body as root-metaphor in the theologies of Rāmānuja and Teilhard de Chardin, we are comparing the divine body in each at the level of theological symbolism. The structure of the divine body in Rāmānuja reflects his theological worldview, and this may or may not be similar to the structure of the divine body in Teilhard.

THE DIVINE BODY AS ROOT-METAPHOR

Key to divine–world unity

Let us look first of all at how the divine body in Rāmānuja serves as a root-metaphor. We saw how he defined Brahman in terms of the Highest Person (*puruṣottama*) and the Supreme Self (*paramātman*) ensouling the universe. For Rāmānuja, knowing Brahman (*Brahma-jñāna*) is equated with being granted a vision of his transcendent form, and this arises through devotion (*bhakti*) and the practice of devotional meditation (*upāsana*). In such a vision, or meditative insight, the Lord's form is seen to be of great beauty, incorporating all the elements that together comprise the world, which then appears as his 'body'. This vision of the Lord seen in terms of the world (or of the world seen in terms of the Lord) Rāmānuja takes as his key for interpreting the Vedāntic tradition: for him the Lord is the world's inner Self.

As he develops this in his major works, he builds up a composite picture of the nature of reality around this central theme, referring to the Lord and the world as inter-related aspects of one whole, guided and directed by the divine Person. Other metaphors are built up around this core metaphor to present a multi-faceted picture of a sacred cosmos. For example, Brahman is referred to as the inner Ruler (*antaryāmin*), the world as his divine realm or rule (*vibhūti*); he is the 'master' (*śeṣin*) of individual selves who are each his 'servant' (*śeṣa*); he is the possessor of modes (*prakārin*) to whom each person belongs as one of his modes (*prakāra*); as part (*aṃśa*) of him, the world does not exhaust the Highest Person who incorporates and transcends all as the whole (*aṃśin*). Finally, one of the most important supporting metaphors: Brahman is the Knower (*kṣetrajña*), having all things as his field (*kṣetra*). All these paired terms contribute to the disclosure of Rāmānuja's Brahman-centred world and the elucidation of his differentiated non-dualistic theology.

Teilhard, on the other hand, defines reality in terms of spirit or psychic energy. For him, spirit is the inner structure of matter, and Christ, as the essential Form and fulfilment of spirit, is the elemental structure of the world. Teilhard speaks of 'seeing' rather than 'knowing' divine reality and, like Rāmānuja, refers to the goal of humankind in terms of divine vision. For him, Christ is a perceptible, pervasive and indwelling presence, illumining the world from within. This 'seeing' transforms the world into a divine milieu. For Teilhard, it is the key to comprehending and entering the Kingdom or rule of God. The world appears as the 'body' of Christ, evolving towards completion. When discussing his phenomenology of the world, and especially of man, he refers again and again to this metaphor of a 'Christified' world, and he speaks of Christ being the 'flesh' of our flesh and Soul of our souls; all things, he says, are centred on him as a sphere is centred on a point. The metaphor of the divine body refers to the central theological notion of the incarnation: the universe is divine flesh, the embodiment of a consciousness that is evolving towards completion as Christ.

It is clear that for both Teilhard and Rāmānuja, the body of the divine points to and discloses a divine–world unity. In Rāmānuja's case he was advocating an alternative Vedāntic interpretation to Śaṃkara's *advaita* (non-dualism), synthesising different *śruti* texts and providing a framework which would incorporate the world in an understanding of Brahman. As we shall see later, the divine body becomes a model through which Rāmānuja can fulfil these purposes. And as a metaphor, it maintains the transcendent oneness of Brahman and the unity of the world's different elements. For Teilhard, as we have seen, the unity of the world and God was his paramount concern. He believed that only an understanding of Christ which took into account contemporary scientific worldviews was appropriate and meaningful; he sought to provide a Christology which incorporated current evolutionary theory, and in so doing argued for the unifying spiritual nature of matter. For him it was the metaphor of Christ's 'body' which enabled him to press his case: to be universal, Christ must, by definition, have a 'cosmic nature'; and the world must manifest his Form.

To look in more detail at how the divine body discloses a divine–world unity, it is useful to consider how Rāmānuja interprets the *Gītā* text on Arjuna's vision of the Lord. He does this in a way which presents Viṣṇu as 'the eternal *puruṣa*', who is present to the world through being its very support and protector:

Oh Lord! I see in your body all the gods, as well as all the groups of various kinds of living beings... O Lord of the universe, with the universe for your form, that is, O Ruler of the universe, having as your body the universe, because you are infinite, I do not see your end, nor your middle, nor yet your beginning. I see you who are a mass of light, resplendent everywhere, difficult to look at anywhere, effulgent like the brightness of the blazing fire and the sun, you [who are] indefinable and immeasurable, wearing a crown, carrying a mace and holding a discus... My conviction is that you are the eternal *puruṣa*... [You] have been cognised through direct perception by me now as of this nature.[4]

Rāmānuja interprets the *Gītā* material very specifically: 'Having the universe for Your form', he says (11.16), means 'having the universe as Your body'. The meaning of '[You are] the supreme abode of this universe', he goes on to say (11.18), is that 'You constitute the supreme support of this universe.' Being 'inexhaustible' means 'not liable to decline', unchangeable, he adds, in terms of form. Such language about the divine serves the theological purpose of affirming the world's reality in relation to Brahman as Person. *Puruṣa*, for example, is depicted in terms of the world (the universe is his 'body'; he is the 'support' of the universe). Rāmānuja vouchsafes the authenticity of this position by claiming the authoritative nature of direct perception.[5] The meaning of 'My conviction is that You are the Eternal *puruṣa*', he writes, is that 'You... have been cognised through direct perception by me now as of this nature.' In other words, the divine Person can be perceived or known directly.

We can see from this that the body of the Lord acts as a key to Rāmānuja's teaching about divine–world unity. The way he uses the metaphor is to disclose spiritual truth which is self-validating through inner knowledge and perception. It is the case that here Rāmānuja uses the divine body to structure his teaching about the transcendence of the Lord and his inseparability from the universe.

When we look at Teilhard's writings, we find that he also uses the divine body metaphor to disclose the divine–world unity:

The Diaphany of the divine at the heart of a glowing universe, as I have experienced it through contact with the Earth – the divine radiating from the depths of blazing matter: this it is that I shall try to disclose and communicate...[6]

You are the centre at which all things meet and which stretches out over all things so as to draw them back into itself: I love you for the extensions of your body and soul to the farthest corners of creation through grace, through life, and through matter...[7]

What I discern in your breast is simply a furnace of fire... all around it the contours of your body melt away and become enlarged beyond measure, till the only features I can distinguish in you are those of the face of a world which has burst into flame.[8]

We need to remind ourselves that in speaking of the world as the body of Christ, Teilhard, like Rāmānuja, was developing existing tradition. One of the things he brings to that tradition is a remarkable vividness of poetic expression which communicates authentic experience. His sentences abound in images of fire ('glowing universe', 'radiating', 'blazing matter', 'a furnace of fire', 'a world which has burst into flame') and passionate love ('I love you for...', 'what I discern in your breast...'). He communicates his vision through multiple metaphors associated with the body of Christ: in the 'fire' of love, the 'contours' of Christ's 'body' 'melt away' until all that is seen is 'the face' of the world. The 'fire', we learn, originates in Christ's heart – a heart which is found to extend throughout the world which 'has burst into flame'.

These two extracts clearly show that for Rāmānuja and Teilhard, the divine body is a root-metaphor of divine–world unity. Both writers use it as an interpretative tool to present the world in terms of a divine Person. In the given passages, where the experience described is intense, the imagery is very anthropomorphic ('wearing a crown', 'with many arms, stomachs, mouths and eyes', 'what I discern in your breast' and 'the contours of your body').[9] Yet this anthropomorphism is counteracted by a strong element of universalism, which transforms the term 'body' as it, in turn, influences the terms used to denote the world. It is not a human or Super-human 'personality' that is disclosed within the world, but a transcendent Presence – 'a mass of light', 'a furnace of fire'.

Key to divine Personhood

Let us consider the possibility that Teilhard and Rāmānuja share an interpretation of the world in terms of divine Personhood. Is it perhaps the case that the divine body refers, in both writers, to a unitary vision of the world in which all things are seen to manifest a transcendent Person 'filling all things' and 'resplendent everywhere'?

Rāmānuja uses the term *vibhūti* ('divine realm' or 'rule') to refer to the world in terms of the Highest Person (see p. 72 above). The devotee's goal is a vision of the Lord's transcendent form, and of the world as his divine realm. This vision, we are told, includes a perception of the unity of all things in Brahman, who inheres within as Supreme Self (*paramātman*) and inner Ruler (*antaryāmin*) yet transcends all through his greatness. It is the fullness (*bhuman*) of the

Lord which the meditating devotee experiences and which is found to be all-pervasive; she or he can no longer see anything apart from him (see p. 73 above).

Teilhard also has a specific term he uses to refer to the world seen in terms of Christ: *le milieu divin*. This denotes, for him, the 'sphere' in which matter is divinised, in which Christ, as the common 'Centre', unites all things in the formation of his 'body'. For Teilhard, this is the 'Kingdom' or 'rule' of God. The faculty to perceive the divine milieu he calls the 'pleromic sense', implying thereby Christ's 'fullness'. This is the crown (corona) of Christ, perceived as the inner radiance of all things, which gives life its 'consistence' and eschatological meaning (see pp. 59–60 above). For Teilhard, the ultimate goal for the Christian is to perceive, indwell and extend *le milieu divin*.

One of the most interesting points about these two perspectives is that they both present the Personhood of the divine in terms of a transformed perception of the world. The Lord (and it should be understood that both writers refer to the divine Person as 'Lord') 'fills' everything and is perceived to unite all things by indwelling them. He gives the world its inner reality. The descriptions overlap in one other main respect, and that concerns the descriptive language used about the experience of the divine Person: the world is seen as the very realm or milieu of the divine. These terms suggest that the world is the 'place' for the divine presence, the place of divine rule and power. It is interesting that the meaning of 'body' is extended by these terms to include divine transcendence. In other words, the world becomes the Self-manifestation of the Lord.

Key to self-knowledge

I think it is important to consider the functions of the divine body metaphor in terms of the writers' own purposes. As we noted earlier (p. 88 above), both writers' main purpose was spiritual: to teach others to know Brahman/see the divine milieu. And so the divine body becomes, in the writings of both Rāmānuja and Teilhard, a powerful epistemological tool evoking a response in the reader and pointing to the means of attaining release or salvation. It discloses a vision, different in each case, of the divine and the world as inextricably united. The world is shown to belong to the divine, and the Lord to possess a universal form.

Rāmānuja, for example, explains the relationship between

individual selves and Brahman in terms of the Knower (*kṣetrajña*) and his 'field' (*kṣetra*). This, he says, is the relationship of a knowing or conscious self to its body, or circumscribed 'field' of experience. The soteriological import of this is that the Lord is the very Self of each of us, who 'knows' us as a knower his 'field'. Clearly the spiritual task for each individual is to come to know the Lord as the Supreme Self of his or her being, and of the entire universe. In this sense it is true that the one who knows the Highest Person knows all, because all things are, through him, the means of attaining the Lord.

Teilhard speaks very differently of the relationship between the individual soul and Christ. He refers to individuals as 'conscious centres' and to Christ as their common Centre. In order to perceive and indwell the divine milieu (the 'Kingdom' of God), each person needs to place Christ in his or her heart as the primary directive influence, over and above the individual ego. To do this requires self-knowledge, and the effects are far-reaching. In the context of Teilhard's understanding of the human body as a microcosm of the whole world (see pp. 61–2 above), this practice results in the extension of Christ's influence and the completing of his body, the world.

The cultural and theological lenses through which Rāmānuja and Teilhard view the world determine the differences in their respective understanding of the spiritual process. In spite of radical differences, however, both thinkers share a theological insight: they insist that self-knowledge is the means of attaining that vision. To know Brahman/God, you need to know your true self or soul, which is a microcosm of the totality that is identified with the divine Person. The desired vision of the Lord is linked with realising our true nature in relation to the Lord: the individual sees him or herself as different from him yet ultimately sharing a common nature.

The self-knowledge which Teilhard and Rāmānuja advocate involves, as we have seen, a transformed perception of the world. Given that both thinkers describe the self or soul in terms of consciousness, we could refer to their teachings as ways of transforming consciousness. And the body of the Lord becomes a vehicle for practices designed for this purpose. As we shall see in a subsequent chapter, the divine body becomes a focus for different spiritual practices, all of which serve to awaken insight and love in the heart of the practitioner, and thereby to clarify his or her own awareness of the way things truly are.

Both Rāmānuja and Teilhard teach that the means to attain self-knowledge is, basically, devotional love. The individual seeking to 'attain' or unite with the Lord is encouraged to regard him with devotion (*bhakti*), to worship him, and cultivate an awareness of his all-pervading presence. Rāmānuja actually goes so far as to claim that *bhakti* is identical with knowledge (*vedana*) and devotional meditation (*upāsana*) (see p. 65 above). In other words, meditation on the Highest Person is a way of knowing him, a way to attain release from the individual, restricted ego. Teilhard does not make quite such a radical claim, but does stress the significance of human consciousness for the transformation of material energies into love or, as he calls it, 'radial' energy (see pp. 53; 58 above), which characterises Christ-consciousness. This transformation, he explains, involves devotion to the Lord of the universe, the universal Christ. We are reminded that it was while meditating on the Sacred Heart of Jesus that Teilhard had a vision of Christ's 'cosmic' body.[10]

This is important in relation to the spiritual purposes of Rāmānuja and Teilhard respectively. Coming to know and see the divine not only involves coming to know and see one's own true nature, but also transforming that nature through practising love and devotion. Teilhard believes that human love embodies Christ-consciousness; Rāmānuja that *bhakti* constitutes divine knowledge or consciousness. For both of them, it is through worshipping the divine in the world that his presence is realised.

There is now some clarification over the nature of a comparison between the body of Christ in Teilhard and the body of Brahman in Rāmānuja. When we explore how the divine body 'works' for each writer, it appears that the divine body acts as a root-metaphor to express fundamental presuppositions which both Rāmānuja and Teilhard share. Firstly, that the divine and the world are in some sense one whole. Secondly, that the divine is manifested in the world as Person. And thirdly, since human life participates in this process of divine manifestation, our task is to recognise this so that we can consciously integrate ourselves with the Lord's realm or milieu. Comparing the metaphorical functions of the divine body also reveals certain psychological parallels. For example, both writers, speaking authentically within their respective traditions, understand the divine and our world in terms of consciousness.

THE DIVINE BODY AS THEOLOGICAL MODEL

Turning now to the second of my two hypotheses concerning the functions of the divine body in both writers, we need to look at how the divine body metaphor, when articulated in conceptual terms, relates to each thinker's theological worldview. First of all, let us recapitulate our earlier findings: we saw in chapters 3 and 4 how Rāmānuja and Teilhard both expressed their understanding of the world and the divine through their respective definitions of the body and its relation to a self or spirit. You could say that the body, or the body–self/spirit is, in this sense, an analogical model for their views on the nature of reality. Rāmānuja, for example, through maintaining that a body is that which is 'controlled' and 'supported' entirely by a 'conscious being' for its own purposes, and which is characterised by being the *śeṣa* (accessory) of that being, was able properly to argue that since the world fulfils those requirements, it is the body of the Supreme Self, Brahman. Similarly, Teilhard, who defined the body in terms of the universality of each individual thing and its 'centredness' in an 'animating spirit', spoke of Christ as a 'universal element' and 'Centre of centres', the world being the physical extension of his centredness and corresponding universality.

The divine body is, however, more than an illustrative example of the way things are. It also has structural and ontological significance within each thinker's worldview.[11] As the term 'body' is extended to apply to the world and all within it, it comes to represent the structural relationship between the body and its self or spirit, and the world and the divine. And at the same time it represents an identity within that relationship: in Rāmānuja, the *ātman*'s *svarūpa* is basically the same as that of Brahman, although in limited form. And in Teilhard, the believer participates in the Form and cosmic nature of Christ. The extent to which the divine body 'models' reality for both thinkers is apparent when we realise that they are, in fact, defining individuals and the cosmos in terms of the divine Person. For example, Rāmānuja attributes consciousness to Brahman, speaks of him as the world's 'conscious being' (p. 63 above), and then defines the *ātman*'s *svarūpa* in terms of consciousness (p. 77 above). The individual and the world are defined in terms of Brahman; they are an ontological extension of him. Teilhard's ideas develop in a similar pattern. Consciousness is, for him, the 'centro-complex' structure of matter. But Christ is the inner spirit or Centre par excellence to whom all things relate as sphere to centre. So to speak of the universe as his 'body' implies a physical continuity between Christ and the world. In Teilhard and Rāmānuja, therefore, the term 'body' models an inter-related structural relationship between the divine and the world.

It is clear that for Rāmānuja and Teilhard the 'divine body' analogy is constructed upon a concept of inter-relationships. The divine Person is the primary 'analogue' to whom all else relates. This becomes a model for the very structure of reality. Different entities relate to one another through their relation to the divine Person (understood as inner Ruler, Centre etc.), but they are also, in themselves, microcosms of the totality attributed to the divine. There is a homologous relation, then, between the divine Person and the individual self/soul, and between the individual and the world (pp. 61–2; 82; 94 above). It is acceptable, therefore, to describe Rāmānuja's body–self doctrine (*śarīra-śarīrī-bhāva*) as an analogy, providing we also allow for its important structuring function as model. We can speak of Teilhard's understanding of the body of Christ as analogous, providing we acknowledge that in fact his criteria for defining 'body' are ontological. We need to realise that in both cases it is as theological model that the divine body operates most powerfully in the conceptual systems of each thinker.

Perhaps we should clarify this further: both Teilhard and Rāmānuja use the notion of 'body' as an analogical model for their respective understanding of the nature of reality. The body's inseparability, yet difference from, a self or soul is presented as representative of the world's inseparability, yet difference from, the divine. The body/world is therefore defined by the self/divine. In each case it is a particular view of the divine Person which determines each writer's understanding of 'body' in the first place. The preconception is theological.[12]

UNDERSTANDING THE DIVINE BODY

It could be said that in referring to two functions of the divine body, I am indicating different levels on which it can be understood. This distinction could be developed to identify the metaphorical function as primarily epistemological, and the conceptual or analogical function as primarily ontological. The important thing to remember, however, in making this distinction, is that the two functions belong together in the writings of both Teilhard and Rāmānuja.

The epistemological function

Let us consider firstly the epistemological function of the divine body metaphor. Earlier (pp. 90–2 above) we examined in some detail passages from both writers which disclosed, through the divine body metaphor, the divine–world unity. Rāmānuja, for example, presents the Lord in all his transcendent beauty, with the world as his body. The reason for this symbolism, however, is to communicate the possibility of knowing the Lord. This object of reverence, awe and beauty is, he says, the desired goal of meditation. To know him means meditating on him (*dhyāna*) and worshipping him (*upāsana*), because divine knowledge has the form of direct vision,[13] received through loving devotion (*bhakti*). 'Continuous sweet remembrance' is thus the way to attain the Lord, the means to final release, and Rāmānuja's descriptive picture of the Lord in all his beauty and glory symbolises this attainment.

For Teilhard the symbolism of the divine body is most apparent in those of his writings which deal primarily with the spiritual life. His 'La Messe sur le monde' is one obvious example. Here, the Eucharist symbolises the entire world in the process of divinisation through Christ ('Christification'). Teilhard's descriptions of a world that has 'the lineaments of a body and face – in Christ'[14] reveal his one 'basic vision of the union between [Christ] and the universe'.[15] Teilhard associates this vision with all joy, achievement, purpose and love of life. It is the goal of human life and death,[16] and so the divine body encapsulates for him the mystery of faith, which he locates in the 'heart' of matter.

The ontological function

The ontological function of the divine body becomes apparent as each writer articulates a structural relationship between the body–self/soul and the world–Person. I referred to this relationship as homologous in the sense that there is a parallelism between the two sets of relations. In other words, it is a relation between different sets of relations, yet the structure of both is identical. In this context we can speak of a micro–macro correspondence.

An example of this is to be found in Rāmānuja's *Śrībhāṣya*, when he explains in great detail how the co-ordination[17] of you (*tvam*) and that (*tat*) (in the *sadvidyā* text, see p. 68 above) expresses both 'oneness' (identity) and difference between the two terms. His model for this is the body–self relation. He speaks of the Supreme Self 'ensouling' the universe, his body:

All these texts declare that the world inclusive of intelligent souls is the body of the highest Self, and the latter the Self of everything. Hence those words also that denote intelligent souls designate the highest Self as having intelligent souls for his body and constituting the Self of them; in the same way as words denoting [non-conscious] masses of matter, such as the bodies of gods etc.... designate the individual souls to which those bodies belong. For the body stands towards the embodied soul in the relation of a mode (*prakāra*); and as words denoting a mode accomplish their full function only in denoting the thing to which the mode belongs, we must admit an analogous comprehensiveness of meaning for those words which denote a body.[18]

As we can see from this, Rāmānuja's precision with language enables him to express the full significance of his analogy. Since the Supreme Self is the self of everything, having all things as his body, words denoting 'intelligent souls', for example, refer ultimately to him in the same (i.e. parallel) way that words denoting the bodies of individuals, gods etc. refer ultimately to those individual selves. The reason for this, explains Rāmānuja, is ontological: the body 'stands towards the embodied self in the relation of a mode (*prakāra*)'. In this sense, the body is ontologically dependent upon the self for its very existence. And just as words denoting modes are only fully comprehended through referring to that to which the mode belongs, so 'analogously' (Rāmānuja), words denoting a body are only fully comprehensible in terms of a self.

This passage brings out several things quite clearly. Firstly, Rāmānuja's prior understanding of 'body': it is a 'mode' of something or someone. And as mode it is completely dependent upon its 'possessor'. This is the ontological assumption behind the analogy which derives from a theological understanding of the nature of reality (p. 97 above). Secondly, the parallelism is clearly indicated to be between the Supreme Self and its body, the individual self, and the individual self and body, non-conscious matter. What is interesting, however, is that the Supreme Self and its relation to individuals is referred to first. This is the primary 'analogue', not the human body–self relation (p. 97 above).

In Teilhard we find a radically different concept of the divine body:

By the Universal Christ I mean Christ the organic centre of the entire universe...[19]

In virtue of even the natural properties of the Universal Centre, the mystical Body of Christ is haloed by a *cosmic body*, that is to say by *all things* in as much as they are drawn by Christ to converge upon him and so reach their fulfilment in him, in the *Pleroma*.[20]

And this Cosmic Body, to be found in all things, and always in process of individualization (spiritualization) is eminently the *mystical Milieu*; whoever can enter into that milieu is conscious of having made his way to the very heart of everything...[21]

If we had to give a more exact name to the mystical Milieu we would say that it is a Flesh – for it has all the properties the flesh has of palpable domination and limitless embrace.[22]

Teilhard's way of expressing the structural relationship at the heart of his analogy is also different. He uses the metaphor of a sphere and its centre, and refers to the body as an aura, or corona, which 'haloes' an 'animating spirit' as a sphere surrounds its centre. It is a universal and 'universalising' central 'element' which links all things to one another. And it is perceived as a mileu, manifesting the properties of the unifying Centre, Christ. Just as in Rāmānuja the world as 'mode' is dependent upon Brahman, its 'possessor', so the world as milieu is dependent upon Christ, its Centre.

Here, Teilhard's prior understanding of body is implicit: the body is that portion of the cosmos that is formed through the life of a particular soul. It is, he says, the totality of the universe possessed by a person partially (p. 61 above). Christ is, analogously, the entire cosmos being formed through Christ–Omega, its spirit and Centre. The ontological implication of this is that Christ is the 'animating spirit' or Centre of all persons and all things. And Christ's 'body' indwells all forms of life because each particle of the whole is co-extensive with all others. In reality, therefore, Christ is co-extensive with the entire cosmos (p. 56 above).[23]

Teilhard's concept of the body of Christ is obviously different from Rāmānuja's concept of the body of Brahman. The functions, however, of the respective divine body concepts exhibit similarities. Basically, they both model a relational worldview. In addition, they both presuppose an understanding of the divine in terms of Person. There is, in each case, a homology between the world as the divine

Person's body and an individual's body, and all things are assumed, by both writers, to exhibit a shared identity in a divine source (self or centre). Thus the divine body becomes an inclusive model of the nature of reality in each case. In theological terms, the world is the divine Person.

THE DIVINE BODY: COMPARATIVE FINDINGS

While beginning to sense underlying patterns or theological themes running through and between the writings of Rāmānuja and Teilhard de Chardin, let us remind ourselves that on the surface, their works are radically different. Rāmānuja is concerned with interpreting the received tradition of *Vedānta*, and with systematising different aspects of that tradition. His main subject, as he states at the beginning of his *Śrībhāṣya*, is *Brahmajijñāsā*, or the desire to know Brahman, the Highest Person. Teilhard de Chardin, on the other hand, is concerned with reconciling received Catholic doctrine with contemporary research in the fields of science. He attempts to formulate a Christian philosophy of evolution. Rāmānuja's concept of the body of the Highest Person serves primarily, therefore, to model a theory of divine Self-realisation, whereas Teilhard's concept of the body of Christ models a theory of the evolution of consciousness.

This said – and we need to bear it in mind throughout – it is important to realise that theology comes in many different shapes and forms, and while at one level, a writer is giving specific teachings within an apparently 'closed' system of spiritual practice and doctrine, nevertheless at another level the same teachings can be received in a more universal way, as manifestations of the spiritual or theological import of metaphors and symbols. It is on the latter level that I have chosen to focus this enquiry, and it is interesting to note that through exploring the writers' uses of the divine body concept, I have found some fundamental similarities of spiritual outlook and theological understanding.

One of the most striking similarities between the body of Christ as understood by Teilhard and the body of Brahman represented in Rāmānuja is their interpretation in terms of consciousness. For both writers, consciousness is the fundamental 'property' or 'attribute' of the Supreme Person/Super-Person.[24] The world is thus a divine 'body of consciousness'.[25]

Another parallel is the shared interpretation of divine knowledge in terms of attaining or realising the divine as Lord. In both Rāmānuja and Teilhard, this understanding is expressed in terms of 'seeing' him. The vision or awareness involved is, in both cases, a vision of unity through, or in, difference. 'Seeing' the Lord involves 'seeing' the world as an inseparable part of him and seeing all things as manifestations of him.

Rāmānuja and Teilhard are both involved in transmitting experience and received teaching concerning the attainment of this knowledge or vision of the Lord. For both it is seen to involve a change of perception, which accompanies a transformation of consciousness (pp. 93–4 above). The theological context for this transformation is, for Rāmānuja, the spiritual teachings of the *sadvidyā*: 'you are that'. For Teilhard it is the mystical Christian teaching epitomised by Colossians 1:17b: 'In him all things hold together.' Both sets of teachings, and their respective contexts, present different frameworks for knowing and seeing the divine. But the concept of the divine body helps to form, in both cases, an experience of the world which reflects unity with and difference from the divine Person.

Perhaps one of the most interesting points for comparison is between the visual descriptions of the Lord 'seen' through this transformed vision. In spite of very great differences, the imagery is remarkably similar. The Lord is, for both, a Person of considerable beauty, who is perceived to indwell every aspect of the world as its inner Ruler (*antaryāmin*) or Centre. He is also greater than the entire universe, the different forms of life being 'limbs' or 'parts' of his body.

Related to this description is the reference by both Rāmānuja and Teilhard to the divine body in terms of a divine realm (*vibhūti/milieu*) (pp. 53; 72–3 above). Clearly this is connected with the universal dimensions of the divine, and with the human perception of its all-pervasiveness. This important metaphor illustrates the inseparability of the divine from the world, and the inseparability of the object from its perceiving subject. For both Teilhard and Rāmānuja, the divine is known or 'seen' through personal experience of the Lord in the world. This divine 'knowing' involves 'seeing' the Lord in relation to all things. Rāmānuja speaks, for example, of Kṛṣṇa's vision of the Lord's form, which involves seeing all elements of the universe as comprising his body; together they form his *vibhūti* (realm or rule). And Teilhard refers to Christ as binding all things together through their inner consistence in him. 'Seeing' him involves perceiving a milieu radiating Christ's presence.

This vision of the divine realm or rule (the body of the Lord) is associated, in both Rāmānuja and Teilhard, with a transformation on the part of the individual, explicitly connected with the heart and the power of love. In Teilhard we have already noted the passionate language in passages referring to 'seeing' Christ in the Eucharist (see, for example, p. 55 above). We also know that some of his meditations arose in connection with devotion to the Sacred Heart of Jesus. Indeed, throughout his writings there is an underlying attitude of devotion and 'burning' love. His teachings in *Le Milieu divin* on purity and chastity focus specifically on love of Christ. In his vision, it is the power of this love which moves mankind 'forward' and 'upward' towards Christ–Omega, the goal of creation. Teilhard describes human love as transformed radial energy. Loving the Lord becomes a way of transforming oneself into his body, and participating in his 'work' of divinising the world. It is Christ's love which burns in the world as its inner light (p. 91 above), transforming everything into his consciousness of God (Christ-consciousness).

Rāmānuja explicitly equates *bhakti* or loving devotion with knowledge (*vedana*) and with the form of meditation (*upāsana*) which facilitates a vision of the Lord (p. 65 above). We saw how Rāmānuja sought to evoke this *bhakti* in his readers by describing the beauty of the Lord's transcendent form (p. 65). It is the desire for Brahman in the devotee, together with dedicated devotion, which enables him or her to receive the Lord's gift of grace (the 'divine eye' of Kṛṣṇa's vision). This desire and devotion Rāmānuja identifies with the individual's nature as *śeṣa* (p. 78): the individual self joyfully and willingly 'serves' the Lord as 'master'. Through learning to recognise his or her own true nature, the individual comes to a realisation of the Lord. Such a realisation transforms the individual self-consciousness.

It is significant that not only is consciousness understood by Teilhard and Rāmānuja to be a divine 'property' or 'attribute' which is manifest in the world, but also that coming to know the Lord involves a change of heart which signifies a change in consciousness and hence, in perception. It appears to be the case that knowing the divine is believed by both writers to be connected with seeing from the heart. In psychological terms, we could speak of the individual experiencing a transformation of his or her consciousness.

Theologically this is understood by Rāmānuja and Teilhard to be a question of realising the Self (Brahman) and attaining union with Christ (Christ-consciousness).

This desired transformation is understood in terms of reflexive consciousness. We have seen how in Teilhard's schema, consciousness becomes increasingly complex in 'higher' forms of life because it is increasingly deeply centred. In humankind this consciousness becomes 'eu-centred', and takes the form of self-consciousness (not to be confused with egocentricity). This is brought about, Teilhard says, by a reversal or involution of consciousness upon itself, through which a new intensity and form of consciousness evolves. It is human self-consciousness which plays a significant role in the world's completion. A 'Super-Centre' or 'Super-Person' evolves from the many centres of reflective consciousness, and in this (or him) the world is completed.

Rāmānuja's perspective is, of course, very different. In his commentaries on the *Bhagavad-gītā* and the *Brahma-sūtras* we find the traditional Vedāntic theme of the individual's need to find and realise his or her 'true' nature or self. Rāmānuja explains that human self-awareness needs to identify itself in relation to Brahman, the Supreme Self. The form of this ultimate 'Self-consciousness' (as Rāmānuja describes it) is referred to by metaphors of light, for example. The individual comes to perceive this form by realising that his or her own nature is a limited form of the divine nature, and that she or he stands in an intimate relation to the Highest Person.

Whether the consciousness in question is understood in terms of one individual (Rāmānuja) or humankind generally (Teilhard), it is believed to manifest the form of 'moving' inwards, towards its own central point of reference, in order for it to become whole. The theological terminologies are different in both writers, but the pattern towards centration remains the same.

The findings of this brief comparison between the divine body as understood by Rāmānuja and Teilhard de Chardin respectively can be summarised in the following way: for both, the divine body is inextricably linked to their understanding of consciousness. In fact, as we shall see in the succeeding chapters, it becomes a model 'of' and 'for' consciousness in each thinker's worldview. Consciousness is, for each, the true nature or form of the world and the attribute or property of a divine Person (the Highest Person/Christ). In this context we can refer to the world as a 'body of consciousness'.

The spiritual goal (for both) of knowing or seeing the Lord involves the recognition that all things participate in his body. Both thinkers refer to this in terms of 'seeing' his presence pervading all things as their inner reality. They describe a vision of divine Self-manifestation, using metaphors which link ordinary human experience with images of light, power and self-transformation. 'Seeing' the Lord is, for them, to see everyday reality in the light of his consciousness. It involves partaking of divine consciousness.

CONCLUSION

In this chapter we have begun to look at the metaphorical and conceptual functions of the divine body in Teilhard de Chardin and Rāmānuja. In both writers it has been shown to serve as a root-metaphor, revealing a divine–world unity by disclosing the world's relation to the divine as Person. This is the theological heart of both writers' worldview. It is significant, in this context, that Rāmānuja and Teilhard both refer to the world as the Lord's realm or rule (*vibhūti*/milieu). These metaphors of the divine body reveal the world manifesting the power and transcendence of the Lord. The divine body metaphor thus discloses a vision of the world as divine. Teilhard and Rāmānuja indicate, through their usage of the divine body metaphor, that self-knowledge (considered by both to involve knowledge of the divine) takes the form of a transformation of awareness or consciousness. This is both cultivated by,[26] and reflected in, a transformed perception.

As we have seen, the divine body is developed to become a key concept in the framework of each thinker's theology. The divine body serves as an analogical model for the true nature of reality. The structural relationship between the divine as Self/spirit and the world is presented as homologous to the relationship between the individual person and his or her body. In both Teilhard and Rāmānuja, however, the primary, defining relationship is the former. In other words, comprehension of the nature of the divine as Person determines an understanding of the nature of the human being and of the cosmos. In addition, there is considered to be an ontological continuity between the two sets of relations in the sense that the individual is viewed as a microcosm of the divine–world totality. Thus there is both a structural correspondence between the divine and the human and also an identity[27] of form or nature.

In the light of the comparative theological findings at the end of this chapter, we can conclude that this structural correspondence and identity of form or nature between the individual and the divine Person is understood by each thinker in terms of consciousness. To know the divine as Lord is to 'see' his form in the world, and this represents a partaking of divine consciousness. Attaining such knowledge also involves a realisation of the nature of the relationship between oneself and the divine. This, for both Rāmānuja and Teilhard, is one of devoted dependence.

Thus the divine body provides a model in the writings of Teilhard de Chardin and Rāmānuja for the identity and the difference between the form or nature of the world's consciousness and that of the divine Person to whom the world belongs. In the next two chapters I shall consider in more detail how the divine body works as theological model for each thinker. In particular I shall address the question of how the divine body serves as a model *of* consciousness (understood as the basic form of reality) and as a model *for* the transformation of consciousness involved in the realisation and knowledge of the Lord.

CHAPTER 6

The divine body as model of the integration of consciousness

In this chapter I intend to consider in more detail the second function of the divine body in Teilhard de Chardin and Rāmānuja (see p. 87 above), namely, the divine body as a theological concept. In particular I shall explore how the divine body metaphor, when articulated conceptually, provides a key to understanding each thinker's theological worldview.

In this context it is appropriate to refer to the divine body as a 'model', in that it represents connections made between things in order to help us structure and interpret what we see. Like metaphors, models are intrinsic to our thought-processes: we look on things in terms of other things and act upon their perceived connections.[1] Models are thus maps of inner processes. Stephen Katz explains:

> The model provides a cosmological–metaphysical and inter-related mystical mapping of the order of things. It shows us how things are; where we are in the scheme of things; what is before and what after; what is expected of us; what is above and what below; and especially important in mystical traditions, how we get from where we are to where we want to go... It provides what we can call conceptual coherence; a quite particular understanding of the nature of the inter-relationship existing among entities in space and nature and beyond.[2]

The potential relationship between a model and metaphor is brought out by Janet Martin Soskice's definition of a model. She says it is 'an object or state of affairs viewed in terms of its resemblance, real or hypothetical, to some other object or state of affairs'.[3] A thing is not a model in itself, but becomes such when it functions in a certain way in relationship to other things.[4] She distinguishes two main types of models: those in which the subject of the model is also its source, as in a model aeroplane ('homeomorphic' models), and those where source and subject differ, as in a discussion of the properties of gases in terms of billiard balls ('paramorphic' models).

A model is made through its function, or functions, in relation to other things (occurrences, events). 'Paramorphic' models have a particular type of relation to other things in that they provide explanations through their structure, like the billiard ball model of the properties of gases. Of course, the explanations emerge from culturally determined perspectives. Thus a Christian may find heavenly fatherhood a useful model because she or he believes this to represent the way things are.[5] A Buddhist may not find this a helpful model, and may prefer, say, a model of the wheel, which represents more accurately his or her view of life.

In this sense a model represents a particular way of looking at things. It serves as a map of a worldview. As a map it interprets things in terms of certain features or relationships. It has the potential to create meaning.[6] Thus the model of heavenly fatherhood interprets God's dealings with human beings in terms of a father's relationship with his children. In this case a hypothetical structural correspondence between the two sets of relations leads to a particular theological understanding.

Models indicate the structure of things, their constituent inter-relationships. Whether in a 'homeomorphic' or 'paramorphic' way, they are intrinsically informative: they are either models 'of' something (a structure) or models 'for' understanding and creating meaning[7] – or both.

The potential link between metaphors and models lies in the fact that they both present something in terms of something else. And of course a metaphor can become a model. Paul Ricœur writes: '[A] theory of metaphor tends to merge with that of models to the extent that a metaphor may be seen as a model for changing our way of looking at things, of perceiving the world.'[8]

In Rāmānuja and Teilhard de Chardin the divine body metaphor serves to model, in each case, a relational view of reality. In the last chapter we saw how the divine body models, for both writers, the identity and difference between the form and nature of the world's consciousness and that of the divine Person (p. 96 above). The divine body becomes, therefore, a model of consciousness. What we find when we read Rāmānuja and Teilhard, therefore, is that the divine body is a theological model[9] for the differentiated and unitive structure of consciousness.

BACKGROUND TO THE DIVINE BODY AS MODEL IN TEILHARD DE CHARDIN AND RĀMĀNUJA

Before looking at how the divine body works as a model in the writings of both thinkers, let us consider how others have understood this important theological function.

Eric Lott, in his book *Vedāntic Approaches to God*, provides a useful introduction to the modelling function of Rāmānuja's body–self teaching. He refers to the Vedāntic model of the self, which he sees as its most significant point of reference for determining the nature of reality, as the context for Rāmānuja's exposition of the self's relational nature.[10] He develops this point in his article 'Iconic Vision and Cosmic Viewpoint in Rāmānuja's Vedānta', by arguing that Rāmānuja's body–self doctrine is far more than a 'mere cosmological metaphor'. Rather he sees it as a 'fundamental model' for understanding reality and how we apprehend reality. It is a key, he says, for unlocking the mystery of our existence: 'As psycho-physical beings we are eternally in an inseparable relationship with the supreme Self; we are his body.'[11]

Clearly Lott interprets metaphor according to common parlance, in which it is seen to be a dispensable mode of speech. In this sense, of course, the divine body has no status or value as metaphor or model in the way I have indicated. However, it should be noted that he does speak of the 'fundamental' character of the divine body as model, which suggests that he attributes to it great significance for Rāmānuja's theology. He goes on to refer to the function of the model in terms of representing for Rāmānuja the 'organic' and 'inseparable' relationship between individuals and the Supreme Self. Clearly, then, Lott understands Rāmānuja to be using the body–self doctrine to represent a direct correspondence between the notions of body–self and world–divine.

Julius Lipner perceives the body–self model in Rāmānuja to be more complex. He presents his viewpoint concisely in his article 'The World as God's "Body": in pursuit of Dialogue with Rāmānuja'.[12] He states that the model is to be understood in terms of the macrocosmic and microcosmic applications of the constituent relationships of Rāmānuja's body–self doctrine. He claims that these represent to Rāmānuja 'the interplay between the One and the many'.[13]

Signifying the 'ensouling self' of this body–self model as 'self_m'

and its body as 'body$_m$', Lipner gives a detailed exposition of Rāmānuja's use of the model in terms of three constituent sub-models, including the support–thing-supported relationship (*ādhāra-ādheya*), the controller–thing-controlled relationship (*niyantṛ-niyāmya*) and the principal–accessory relationship (*śeṣin/śeṣa*). He analyses Rāmānuja's use of this model (in its constituent three parts) by positing a 'system of polarities' which is applied to each sub-model both microcosmically[14] and macrocosmically.[15] This illustrates, for him, Rāmānuja's theological method, as it 'pivots' around the divine body concept.

Lipner interprets Rāmānuja's method as 'polarity theology', taking the body–self model to represent various inter-related 'sub-models', each of which has micro and macro components. However, he refers to Rāmānuja's literal, as opposed to metaphorical, usage of the term 'divine body',[16] so we can only assume that like Lott, he is anxious to preserve the theological import of the term by affirming its non-figurative meaning.

It is interesting that few have referred to Teilhard de Chardin's body of Christ as a theological model. Robert Hale, however, in his book *Christ and the Universe: Teilhard de Chardin and the Cosmos*, begins by discussing the use of models in theology, and in particular, the 'body' model.[17] He gives a very general definition of models to begin with: 'One has recourse to a more manageable reality to illumine some aspect of a less manageable one.' The model articulates mystery, he goes on to explain, and in order that it can be easily understood, simplicity, familiarity and a 'down-to-earth' quality are required of it.[18] Like Lipner and Lott, Hale rejects a link between the model and metaphor and, like Lipner, he uses the argument that the body model contains a realism that the metaphor lacks: 'Teilhard understands his category "cosmic Body of Christ" to be much more than mere metaphor. He always interprets the phrase in a thoroughly realistic manner... One must, then, be chary of speaking of "the metaphor" of the Body of Christ.'[19]

The idea that a model 'stands' for a reality that is ungraspable ('unmanageable'), although popular, seems inappropriate: if a reality is ungraspable, how can a model for it be selected? Hale interprets the divine body in Teilhard de Chardin as signifying aspects of reality which many would take to be mysterious. He does not discuss its value or whether the divine body model, in 'articulating' such mystery, makes it more accessible and comprehensible.

Lott, Lipner and Hale all demonstrate the modelling function of the divine body by the way they use it as an interpretative key to the theologies of Rāmānuja and Teilhard. Lott, for example, sees Rāmānuja's whole theological enterprise in terms of his relational understanding of the self; Lipner views his theological method in terms of the polarities represented in Rāmānuja's body–self doctrine. Clearly the concept of the body–self still serves as a model for Rāmānuja scholars. For Hale, Teilhard articulates something of God's mystery through his model of the body of Christ.

All three writers disclaim any metaphorical value for the examples of the body of the divine in Rāmānuja and Teilhard respectively. Lipner maintains that the term has 'literal' rather than metaphorical significance; Lott argues that it is a 'fundamental model' for understanding reality. For Hale, it is much more than 'mere metaphor'. It appears that they all wish to underline the realism of the body–self/soul model. And clearly Rāmānuja believes there to be a 'homeomorphic' equivalence between the body–self relation in individual and cosmic forms of manifestation.

Perhaps the realism they all seek to emphasise stems from the analogical nature of the model.[20] The 'divine body' is a model of the world, for example, in the sense that the divine is to the world what a self is to its body. Just as people live out their lives 'bodily', so the divine lives 'bodily' in the world.[21] We could even say that the 'structure' of the divine is analogous to the 'structure' of the human body. In all these examples, analogy is a kind of 'connective' language extending the usage of the given terms.[22] For example, Rāmānuja extends the term 'body–self' to refer to Brahman's relationship with the world. Teilhard extends the term 'milieu' to refer to the sphere of divine creativity which is the world.

Of course, not all analogies are linguistic. For example, there is an analogy between ritual sacrifice and the Eucharist. Here the symbolism of the Eucharist involves a tacit analogy of action, which contributes to its power to structure reality. It is in such a symbolic way that the divine body analogy comes into its own. Its subject matter renders it capable of affecting the way people see things, and it becomes an analogical model of the way the world 'is'.

It is precisely in relation to this symbolic power that we can see why metaphors make good models. Metaphors feed upon symbols, and express them. Indeed it is their symbolic roots which give metaphors the power of evocation: they call up associations and experiences which arouse the reader's own creative imagination. A model which has not first been a metaphor has not the same epistemological potential. It does not have the same power to disclose a way of seeing things. The divine body model is, for Rāmānuja and Teilhard, a theologically indispensable metaphor. It encapsulates the spiritual insights each thinker wishes to communicate concerning the inter-relatedness of all things and, furthermore, in defining the nature of this inter-relatedness it provides a structural model of reality which can be appropriated as a mode of viewing, and hence experiencing, the world.

THE STRUCTURE OF THE DIVINE BODY MODEL IN TEILHARD DE CHARDIN AND RĀMĀNUJA

The key to the power and realism of both thinkers' use of the divine body model is to be found in the fact that it serves as an analogical structure of consciousness. And consciousness is, for Teilhard and Rāmānuja, the fundamental characteristic of all that exists.

Micro-Macro homology

Teilhard claims, for example, that consciousness is a function of being centred and a property, therefore, of every living thing from a molecule to a complex organism. He maintains that there are levels of consciousness representing different degrees of spiritualisation, the highest of which is human self-consciousness. Integrating these levels is one Centre which draws all forms of matter towards an ever-increasing intensity of centredness: Christ. Each individual, through his or her 'centredness', participates in the consciousness of Christ, the Centre of centres. As such she or he represents Christ's universality.

It is the relationship between the individual as microcosm and his or her function in the world's 'pleromisation' which is of interest here. Hale comments that, 'For Teilhard, the traditional image of man the microcosm takes on a new and dynamic character: in the human body is focused and in-folded the entirety of the cosmos.'[23] He is speaking of the individual person as the *locus* of the world's convergence or in-folding. To understand this we need to remind ourselves of Teilhard's view of the human body (see pp. 61–2 above): it is an incomplete nucleus, an 'organisational centre' of a life which extends to the very boundaries of the universe. The human body is the context, therefore, for the world's completion and self-integration. Each individual contributes, through the integration of the elements of his or her life (p. 62), to the realisation of the whole. Not only does each person represent the life of the world, but she or he also enables that life to come to its own self-fulfilment.

From this brief summary it is clear that for Teilhard, the human being represents an important level of consciousness (the noosphere) in the divinisation of the world. From his perspective on the human body's true extension (the boundaries of the universe), there is an isomorphism between that and Christ's body. Or, to put it another way, consciousness has a universal form. Correspondingly, consciousness has, in Teilhard's eyes, a universal Centre which is Christ. All references, therefore, to consciousness refer ultimately to the one reality the divine body represents, both microcosmically and macrocosmically.

Turning to Rāmānuja, it is important to remember that he drew upon the Upaniṣadic tradition to refer to a homology between the self (*ātman*) and Brahman (p. 39 above).[24] Rāmānuja refers to both these levels of reality interchangeably. Both, however, are centred on Brahman as inner Ruler (*antaryāmin*) and Supreme Self (*paramātman*). In Chapter 4 I connected this with Rāmānuja's references to different analogical directions and spaces which in fact have one referent.[25] For example, all things are said to be both 'indwelt' by the Lord and 'encompassed' by him. The 'inner' and 'outer', like the 'minute' and the 'huge', are somehow equivalent; they refer to the same reality.

It is interesting to note that when Julius Lipner analyses Rāmānuja's theological method he retains a separation between these two aspects of the divine body:

> [Rāmānuja's] method consists in the identifying and then the holding together of a system of polarities. In other words it is this 'system of polarities' which finds expression in the body–self model comprising as it does its three sub-models or component relationships which themselves have, as we have seen, a two-tiered application: in microcosm to the finite *ātman* and its body$_m$, and in macrocosm to Brahman and his body. It is through the interplay and the inter-relationships of the various polarities of this complex two-tiered structure that the range and depth of Rāmānuja's theology are expressed.[26]

This is a very perceptive analysis of how Rāmānuja's body–self model works. Lipner goes on to explain that the 'polarities' in Rāmānuja's thought are indicated by 'centripetal' and 'centrifugal' modes of theological discourse which operate within the micro and macro expressions of the body–self relationship. Thus in the controller–controlled (*niyantṛ/niyāmya*) relationship, the Lord's absolute control over the world is preserved (a 'centripetal' mode of discourse) as well as the moral and physical freedom of individuals (a 'centrifugal' mode of discourse), through the notion of divine grace.

Lipner's exposition of Rāmānuja's theological method reveals the inner dynamic of Rāmānuja's worldview. Yet side by side with what he calls 'polarity' discourse, which preserves the theology of difference even in the 'holding together' of the divine and human realities, there is also a discourse of union. This expresses a perception of the world in which all things are seen as one reality, whether on a micro or macro level. Thus the essential nature (*svarūpa*) of both the Highest Person and the individual self (*ātman*) comprises knowledge or pure consciousness, and the goal for the devotee is to see all in the light of the divine totality (see pp. 66; 78 above). The divine body thus represents both the differences between the individual's consciousness and that of the divine Person, and the identity of form or structure revealed through a transformed perception (p. 105).

Unitive discourse and integrated consciousness

Rāmānuja and Teilhard both demonstrate unitive discourse, understood in this sense. It is expressed through their representations of the divine in terms of 'body'. These representations disclose the true nature of reality in terms of consciousness. They both perceive consciousness to be inseparable from forms[27] of self-manifestation. In this context it is appropriate to speak of the divine body as a model of the relational structure of consciousness.

Let us consider this in more detail. Teilhard de Chardin refers to the 'form' of Christ in terms of his universal function (pp. 50–1 above). Describing how he 'sees' Christ as present in the world, he speaks of a 'universal physical reality'[28] which surrounds all things in the way that auras surround individuals. This is Christ's crown or corona. It is an extension of Christ himself and the milieu in which all things are transformed into his likeness and drawn towards him, their Centre. Thus Christ's 'form' is his all-embracing consciousness, con-centrating itself in the process of divinising the cosmos.

Teilhard also tries to define the Christ–world relationship. He speaks of Christ as the formal cause[29] of the cosmos, determining its structure from within, and causing matter to 'take on' form in him. As its cause, he is the world's Soul.[30] All things stand in relation to him as matter does to form.[31] It is thus as physical cause that Christ becomes universal 'Element', 'informing' matter from within. As the world's 'form' or Soul, Christ is also its body or the natural extension of that form. He is the inner consciousness that evolves its own complexity, and the transcendent goal or fulfilment of that consciousness (Christ–Omega). To adapt Teilhard's terminology, Christ is both the world-sphere and its Centre (p. 49 above).

Teilhard is claiming here that the very structure of reality comprises spirit-in-relation-to-matter or centre-complexity. As the model of this integration, Christ is himself 'animating spirit' and 'flesh'.[32] Through evolving new forms of life, not only is the cosmos attaining completion but also Christ, since the progressive integration of the elements of our world effect the actualisation of divine consciousness.

Rāmānuja speaks of the self's proper form (*svarūpa*) comprising consciousness or uncontracted knowledge (p. 77 above). Brahman himself is referred to as the Supreme Self (*paramātman*), whose defining attributes are described generally as 'infinite knowledge and bliss'. His essential form (*svarūpa*) is self-luminous[33] (i.e. self-generating) consciousness which 'illumines' all things. In this context the individual's true nature is to be the Lord's accessory or 'servant' (*śeṣa*) in that she or he is in a relationship of complete dependence upon the Lord for consciousness and life. At the same time Rāmānuja is quick to point out that ultimately, the form of Brahman and the self (*ātman*) is the same; so there is identity within the difference.

One example in Rāmānuja of the transcendence of the Lord's form is to be found in his *Gītābhāṣya*, where Arjuna actually perceives the divine form (*divya rūpa*)[34] of the Lord: all things are seen to be pervaded by him, and they appear to be part of him (pp. 92–3 above). Suddenly the whole world is seen as the realm or rule (*vibhūti*) of the Lord. Nothing can be seen apart from him.

Rāmānuja argues for the validity of direct perception in his more philosophical texts, such as the *Vedārthasaṃgraha*. Here he shows, through his skilful use of grammatical constructions, that meanings of different terms can be inter-related. For example, *sāmānādhikaraṇya* constructions demonstrate that several terms can have the same ultimate denotation, one term being the predicate of another (p. 68). In this way he shows how the individual self signifies a modified form of Brahman. Thus all things are modifications of Brahman and exhibit his *svarūpa* and *svabhāva* (pp. 74–6).

Clearly, then, Rāmānuja presents us with a model of Brahman and the world in terms of differentiated non-dual consciousness. The world is built into his definition of Brahman, who is disclosed as the Supreme Self of all. And knowing Brahman means seeing the world as his body, his realm. Thus the body–self model presents Rāmānuja's understanding of reality as one integrated whole. He understands reality in terms of an inter-related structure of consciousness dependent upon a Self. The 'proper' form of the Self, the ultimate form, is unlimited consciousness, which manifests itself in the world as all conscious and non-conscious beings. Thus for Rāmānuja, all things express the divine 'body of consciousness' (p. 101).

Similarities of perspective

When we compare the 'form' of Christ and Brahman in Teilhard de Chardin and Rāmānuja respectively, one feature immediately presents itself: the divine is understood by both thinkers to comprise unlimited or de-limited consciousness.[35] Another similarity is that the world is included in the understanding each has of the divine. By that I mean that the essential nature of the self is ontologically identical to that of Brahman. And Christ is viewed as the universal Element animating the whole of matter. Epistemologically, the vision of the Lord (exemplified in Rāmānuja's description of Arjuna's vision, and Teilhard's vision of Christ in the heart of matter) represents an integrated level of consciousness in which the divine is actualised. So human experience is seen to belong to and be part of divine consciousness.

Teilhard and Rāmānuja communicate this through their various presentations of the divine body model. Of course they express this integration[36] of consciousness in their own respective terminology, but the function is the same. The divine body models a cosmological integration of the divine and the world; a psychological integration of human and divine consciousness.

Structurally, the divine is the central 'point' through which the individual self and for Teilhard, the world, is integrated. For Rāmānuja Brahman is the Self, the Knower of all conscious and non-conscious beings, realised through meditation upon and knowledge of the self. For Teilhard, Christ is the Omega Point drawing the cosmos (comprising different levels of consciousness: the geosphere, biosphere and noosphere) inwards through thresholds or boundaries of consciousness to fold in upon itself and hence sur-create new and 'pleromised' being. Rāmānuja refers to knowledge of Brahman as Self-realisation, and he teaches the individual's path to this goal. Teilhard speaks of the whole of matter[37] being 'Christified' and teaches that the individual can seek his or her goal as part of a cosmic process of redemption. In both cases the polarities of divine, world and self are integrated through a transformative experience in which all is seen as a divine realm/milieu, the 'body' of the Lord.

The respective philosophical formulations of the divine body model reflect this structure. Rāmānuja's clearest presentation is, perhaps, in a passage preceding his discussion of co-ordinate predication (*sāmānādhikaraṇya*) in the *Vedārthasaṃgraha*, where he says:

All these entities are ultimately ensouled by Brahman. Hence [it] follows that all words which have definite denotative value owing to the combination of the radical element without suffix, e.g. god, man...etc., actually denote the entire composite entity; the body, the individual [self] represented by it, and finally the Inner Ruler of that [self], the Supreme Person in whom that entity terminates. All words denote this entire *compositum* by merely denoting the material mass which has a certain generic structure that is commonly known as being denoted by a certain word.[38]

Teilhard's most succinct formulation is a syllogism he uses in *Le Milieu divin*:

At the heart of our universe, each soul exists for God in our Lord,
But all reality, even material reality, around each one of us, exists for our souls.
Hence all sensible reality, around each one of us, exists, through our souls, for God in Our Lord.[39]

These two passages argue for the *a priori* existence of the divine as the inner point or source of all life. Rāmānuja concludes that all words stand ultimately for the entire structure comprising the gross and subtle layers of energy or consciousness which together make a being. Teilhard argues that the whole of matter exists because of and in relation to God in Christ, and this relationship is concretised in each individual soul which represents God-in-the-world. Human life seems to be of major significance in the path towards the realisation of the divine. In us the cosmic and personal processes converge.

The ways in which Rāmānuja and Teilhard describe this are, naturally, very different. But they are both claiming that each object in the world ultimately derives its significance or *raison d'être* from a personal Centre or inner Self to whom it owes its existence. In fact, there is a progressive intensification of consciousness according to the proximity or otherwise to the divine centre. The microcosm (individual) and the macrocosm (world) are conceived as a series of inter-related layers or sheaths of consciousness.[40] Teilhard develops this in his analysis of the evolution of consciousness, explicitly referring to physical reality in terms of concentric spheres around Christ, the Centre of centres.[41] Rāmānuja expresses this through his use of the metaphor of knower and 'field' (i.e. of knowledge). Of course Teilhard's model is within the context of time, and his perspective evolutionary. Rāmānuja, however, is not concerned with linear time. His teachings remain at the level of symbolic time, within the broad context of a cyclic process of birth, growth and decay.

THE SYMBOLISM OF THE DIVINE BODY MODEL

The structure of consciousness revealed in Rāmānuja's and Teilhard de Chardin's divine body model is a symbolic structure,[42] in which the divine is disclosed to be the innermost self or heart of the universe and each thing within it. Teilhard actually acknowledges this by referring to 'our symbol of the "polycentric sphere"',[43] and to Christ as 'cosmic Centre'.[44]

It is the symbolic function of the divine body model which gives it the power to communicate truths about the way things are (see p. 111 above). This is because symbols represent and suggest things to us in a language which speaks to the depths of our experience. We can not only 'hear' what is being communicated by symbols, but we have the ability to respond by recreating and resonating with that which is 'heard', thereby consciously aligning ourselves more fully with what is 'given' in our experience of the world.[45]

In other words, the divine body not only teaches about the nature of the divine, the nature of the way things are in the world, but also reveals something of this nature to our own consciousness. This is the most powerful form of theological language because it is potentially transformative. It does not separate the ideas it seeks to express from their symbolic roots. Renewal of spiritual life remains a possibility through such discourse.

Identifying the symbolic structure

In the case of the divine body, we can see the application of this structure to individual growth: there is a movement implicit in the model, from the outer spheres or layers of consciousness inwards, towards the common centre of integration. In Rāmānuja this is presented as an orientation towards the individual's true self (*ātman*), within which Brahman, the Supreme Self, is to be realised. This is the goal of the individual's spiritual quest. In Teilhard, the individual, in seeking to fulfil his or her commitment to the world, develops love which enables her or him increasingly to see from the energetic 'heart' of Christ. This movement of consciousness in the divine body model symbolises a fundamental pattern of energy manifesting as form in the world. The structure of the model reflects this movement. There is a divine centre of consciousness with a surrounding 'sphere' or 'field', which depends upon that centre for its existence.

As a symbolic structure, the divine body is not unique. In fact it exhibits features of mandalas, which have been identified by C. G. Jung as 'universal' symbols arising from a collective unconscious. It may be interesting at this point to consider the structure of the mandala and its possible relationship with human consciousness, since this may have some bearing upon our understanding of the divine body symbol in Teilhard and Rāmānuja.

The original term *maṇḍala* is derived from the Sanskrit root *maṇḍ*, which has a variety of meanings,[46] mostly connected with circular, spherical or corporate entities, often used as diagrammatic forms for visualising and summoning a deity. A mandala can be two- or three-dimensional in form, and its circular[47] or spherical shape is constructed around a central axis or point, known as the *bindu*. This is the focus of the entire symbol, and represents the divine (whether deity or Buddha). Certain mandalas are abstract,[48] and in these the different aspects or levels of consciousness are represented solely by colours and syllables. Others are representational in form, incorporating reconstructions of divine figures in specific places. Whatever the form of the mandala, the structure always includes indications of the four cardinal points of the universe because the mandala is a cosmic, as well as an individual, symbol.

In Hindu and Buddhist traditions, mandalas serve as exterior aids to inner practices of transformation. When visualised, they represent the elements and energies which together constitute ourselves and our world. The practitioner recognises these elements and energies by the colours and shapes of the mandala, often matching them with specific sounds. She or he integrates them by progressing gradually from the outer rim of the mandala, through the four 'gates' to the inner 'realms' and finally to the centre – a process involving specific techniques in the transformation of consciousness. In his book *The Theory and Practice of the Mandala: with Special Reference to the Modern Psychology of the Subconscious*,[49] Giuseppe Tucci claims that the origins of the mandala lie in the psychological experience or intuitions of diversification and unification. It is essentially, he says, a 'geometric projection of the world reduced to an essential pattern', not just a cosmogram but also a psychocosmogram.[50] He is drawing here upon the findings of Jung in his psycho-analytical work with patients, and especially his research into dreams. Jung himself came to believe that mandalas signify 'nothing less than a psychic centre of the personality'[51] exhibiting a 'so to speak, metaphysical nature'.[52]

When we look at the divine body model in Teilhard de Chardin and Rāmānuja, the structure of divine Person as the Centre or Self (*bindu*) surrounded by spheres or layers of consciousness exhibits the same features as the structure of the mandala. It represents, for both thinkers, the individual and the cosmos. Teilhard explicitly refers to the different cardinal points of the universe,[53] whereas in Rāmānuja they remain implied.[54] In both, we have a model of cosmic and individual self-realisation, through the gradual integration (and in Teilhard, this is an evolution) of 'spheres' or realms of consciousness into a focal divine centre.

At an experiential level the divine body is referred to as a divine milieu or realm (*vibhūti*). This is described as a state of being in which all things are seen in terms of the divine Person. This represents for each thinker a level of consciousness in which 'ordinary' awareness is transformed in proportion to the realisation of the divine. From this perspective the individual experiences the beatific vision of the divine (Teilhard speaks of 'diaphany'). This is equated with knowledge of Brahman or Christ-consciousness.

The cosmic and psychocosmic homology in the divine body model (see pp. 112–13 above) corresponds to the structure of mandalas. Heinrich Zimmer maintains that when used in visualisation and ritual transformative practices, mandalas must be seen both as 'reflections of the divine essence in its production and destruction of the universe' and as emanations radiating from the meditator's psyche.[55] In the context of the latter, he explains that when used in yoga, the contents of the mandala represent stages of consciousness, ranging from the everyday state of ignorance (*avidyā*) through to Self-realisation.[56]

It is precisely this correlation between individual and divine consciousness which Teilhard and Rāmānuja seek to express. Rāmānuja, for example, speaks of the individual as knower (*kṣetrajña*) and his or her world of experience as field (*kṣetra*), but also refers to the divine Person as *kṣetrajña*, with the universe, composed of all individual *kṣetrajña*s, as *kṣetra*. Similarly, Teilhard refers to individuals as 'centres of consciousness', and to Christ as the 'Centre of centres'. As noted previously, the nature and structure of the individual is understood, by both, to derive from and express the divine Person. The divine body model represents, therefore, a theological understanding of the relational structure of consciousness. In the following chapter I shall look at this model in the context of the spiritual disciplines of Rāmānuja and Teilhard which aim to help individuals transform and integrate consciousness.

Centroversion: the pattern of movement within the structure

As we continue to consider the structural forms the divine body exhibits, it is important to note the inherent movement within the model. In the cosmic application of Teilhard de Chardin's model he posits a process of involution, whereby the energies of the earth converge upon their common centre, creating a new 'critical point' in the evolution and transformation of the world.[57] He puts this another way by saying that the 'Spirit of the Earth' finally 'disappears in depth' through totally centring upon itself.[58] In other words, spirit or consciousness collectively centres itself and folds back upon itself in a final act of unification. This, for Teilhard, is envisaged as the end or 'outcome' of the world. In Christian terms, he refers to this as the pleroma: the consummation and integration of the world in God through Christ.

Rāmānuja's understanding of cosmic integration, on the other hand, is not evolutionary in the western, historical sense of the term. But he speaks of a process whereby Brahman created the universe for his play or sport (*līlā*).[59] In the beginning, it is traditionally explained, Brahman resolved to become many, so the elements in subtle form were submerged in him to become non-conscious matter. The 'aggregates' of individual selves were also submerged in him, to become manifest through differentiation. From these subtle elements he created the gross elements, which the individual selves animated by entering. Then Brahman brought the whole world into being from those elements, animating the whole by conscious principles in various combinations. Finally Brahman entered all entities as their ultimate Self with all existence comprising, thereby, his body.[60] Both perspectives, therefore, reveal a progressive inward movement as the divine is manifest in the cosmos.

Teilhard's understanding of individual, psychological integration is expressed in terms of inner states or 'circles' of reality, through which a person progresses, to become imbued with the divine milieu. He equates this progress with the development of the 'mystical sense'.[61] Rāmānuja's understanding of the individual's cultivation of the path of loving devotion (*bhakti-yoga*) involves an accumulation of merit (which destroys negative karma) and the development of qualities such as mind-control, sense-control, purity and compassion. The individual increases his or her devotion and self-surrender to the Lord in meditation and worship, and finally attains a state of consciousness in which *bhakti* takes the form of continuously 'remembering' the presence of the Lord.

From these macro and micro applications of the model we can see an increasing focus on and movement towards the divine centre, from which all things initially come forth. The individual's path to liberation is mapped out by an inner progression to 'higher' states of consciousness in which the divine Person becomes increasingly realised and his presence more perceptible. As the individual (or the cosmos) becomes 'nearer' to the divine Person, the more integrated she or he (or the cosmos) is: transformation of consciousness means here integration into the divine.

This process could best be described as 'centroversion':[62] by this

I mean the integration of different components through centring. Concerning the individual, this term is especially helpful, since it suggests a conscious initiative to create unity and wholeness. As with all mandala symbols, Teilhard's and Rāmānuja's divine body model implies the identification, objectification and integration of the different elements of individual consciousness.

CONCLUSION

At the beginning of this chapter I spoke of models as maps of inner processes, of the way things are. The divine body serves, in both Teilhard de Chardin and Rāmānuja, as a paramorphic model providing a symbolic structure of a unified worldview. It is a model of the nature of life on earth; a map of consciousness.

The language used by each thinker reflects the uniqueness of his spiritual tradition. The structure, however, has fundamental aspects in common. In particular, the divine body discloses a relational dimension to consciousness: each person or thing exists in relation to the divine core of his or her being. This core is presented as the divine Person, the Self, the Centre. A person or a thing can both be identified with this transcendent core and be differentiated from it. Depending on the perspective, we are inherently at one with, and distinguishable from, the divine.

To speak of the divine body as a metaphor of consciousness raises questions about the realism of the model. To speak of the cosmos, or the individual, as part of the Lord in this way is not, we may argue, just a figure of speech. There is truth in it. But if by metaphor we mean an indispensable non-literal way of disclosing lived experience, the question of realism is answered. This is so especially if we accept the value of metaphors for structuring and giving meaning to our own lives. The models or maps we create may need to use such hieroglyphs to reveal the true nature of the terrain we seek to explore, because literal terms are inadequate.

In theological terms, the language of metaphors and symbols is close to the apophatic tradition. We cannot say the divine *is* x or y, but we can create symbolic pictures to evoke and communicate our 'sense' of it. This 'sense' of the divine can lead to the creative use of symbolic means of communication which draws upon the very depths of our existence to fashion forms for what is perhaps at that level alone fully known. Rāmānuja and Teilhard drew upon the depths and richness of their respective spiritual heritages to create a language which would transmit and disclose truth at this level of symbolic understanding. They used a metaphor of consciousness to communicate the inseparability and integration of the divine with the world: the body divine.

When we analyse the symbolic structures they formed for this purpose, the similarities are notable. They both refer to the divine in terms of limitless consciousness, which is manifest as layers or spheres radiating out from and moving inwards towards a central point of integration. The model is presented analogously as both self and body or centre and sphere. This represents the micro form of consciousness, such as the individual, for example, and the macro form, which comprises the cosmos itself. There is an isomorphism between individual and cosmic consciousness: the one extends to include the other. At one level the boundaries of the individual are those of the universe, and at another, the vastness of the cosmos is contained within an individual life-form. This understanding of reality in terms of the integration of consciousness is expressed symbolically in what I have identified as the mandala structure of the divine body model.

Learning to grasp the significance of this teaching involves, for both thinkers, total commitment to the spiritual path which leads, ultimately, to a transformed knowledge and perception: a transformed consciousness. From this perspective all things are seen to belong to the Lord, and to manifest his divine qualities. This vision represents an integration of the differing elements which make up physical and psychological existence, and in this sense the divine body presents holiness in terms of integrated consciousness. The following chapter will address the question of how the divine body also serves as a model for such holiness.

CHAPTER 7

The divine body as model for the transformation of consciousness

I have shown how Rāmānuja and Teilhard de Chardin, in presenting their visions of the world, have drawn upon rich symbolic understandings inherent in their respective traditions. Representations of the Lord whose body is the world date back to the earliest recorded literature associated with Vedic and early Christian traditions. Whether we accept theories of universal symbols or archetypes or not, clearly this notion is deeply imprinted in both eastern and western consciousness.

One reason why certain symbols reappear in different times and cultures is quite simply their 'workability'. If a religious symbol is prevalent, it works well for people. By this I mean that it has transformative power. Patrick Sherry claims that religious concepts often involve reference to spiritual transformation;[1] but it is symbols that can provide the means to attain that transformation. Even if we have a map of where we are, showing us where we want to go (in other words, a model), we still need the means to get there. Symbols provide such means of transport; they are vehicles for transformation.

Perhaps the symbol of the divine body is of key significance in the works of both Teilhard and Rāmānuja because for them it has been proved to work. In the last chapter I said that the divine body presents holiness in terms of integrated consciousness. In this chapter I would like to consider how it does this, and how the divine body actually works as a model for the transformation of consciousness leading to integration and wholeness.

To put this in the context of what has gone before, we need to remember that both Teilhard and Rāmānuja present their world-views in terms of consciousness. We have seen how they identify a divine Person as the Centre or Self of a 'body' of consciousness. They each speak of the goal of humankind in terms of attaining the Lord and sharing in divine consciousness. What concerns us now is the way in which both thinkers use the divine body symbol as a tool for attaining the divine Person and becoming part of him. Through certain religious practices associated with the form of the divine, the individual becomes Christ/Self-conscious. In this chapter we shall explore these practices and see how they lead to integration into the body of the Lord.

THE DIVINE VISION: THE SYMBOL OF THE LORD'S FORM

We saw earlier how 'attaining' or 'knowing' the Lord is depicted by both Teilhard and Rāmānuja in terms of seeing him. This is what the aspiring individual longs for: a vision of the Lord. But what does this desired vision comprise? A study of their writings suggests that the divine vision is conceived by both in terms of the Lord's unique or proper form (see pp. 114–15 above) as it pervades, encompasses and illumines the world, his body.

Consider Teilhard's use of language:

> Glorious Lord Christ: the divine influence secretly diffused and active in the depths of matter, and the dazzling centre where all the innumerable fibres of the multiple meet... you whose forehead is of the whiteness of snow, whose eyes are of fire, and whose feet are brighter than molten gold; you whose hands imprison the stars; you who are the first and the last, the living and the dead and the risen again; you who gather into your exuberant unity every beauty, every affinity, every energy, every mode of existence... All of us, inescapably, exist in you, the universal milieu in which and through which all things live and have their being... For me, my God, all joy and achievement, the very purpose of my being and all my love of life, all depend on this one basic vision of the union between yourself and the universe.[2]

This is an intense and poetic statement of Teilhard's vision of Christ as the universal milieu surrounding and incorporating all things. The light symbolism which is prevalent is reminiscent of earlier passages we have looked at (for example, on p. 91 above). The theme is of Christ's beauty and of the individual's awe and reverence before him. Teilhard's use of metaphors builds a structural image of Christ: he is the 'centre' of all, and within their 'depths', gathering everything into an 'exuberant unity'.

Teilhard uses anthropomorphic imagery to describe the Lord of the cosmos: his forehead is as white as snow, his eyes are of fire, his feet are brighter than molten gold and his hands imprison the stars. Non-anthropomorphic features portray eschatological aspects of his nature: he is the first and the last; the living, dead and risen again; the universal milieu in and through which all exists.

Now let us look at Rāmānuja's language when he is describing the vision of the Lord:

He who exists within the orb of the sun, whose splendour is like an impressive mountain of burning gold, whose brilliance is of a hundred thousand suns, whose eyes are pure and long like the petals of a lotus or a translucent stalk, rising out of deep waters, [and] opening out in the sun's rays, whose forehead has well matched eyebrows, whose nose [is shapely]... and who has a pair of graceful feet like full blown lotuses... he has attracted the eyes and thought of all by his manifold and wondrous beauties. The nectar of his beauty completely fills all animate and inanimate beings... The endless space between the [four] cardinal points is perfumed by the fragrance of his holiness. He shines in his supreme majesty as he envelops the three worlds. This supreme Person, seen within the sun, is the ultimate one who sports, [i.e. plays], through the creation, maintenance and dissolution of the whole world, who is antithetical to all evil, who is an ocean of all auspicious attributes and who stands above all other entities. He is the supreme Brahman, the highest Self, Nārāyaṇa...[3]

Then Arjuna... having seen the Lord, who constitutes the support of the highly wonderful universe in its entirety with but a part of his own body... became overcome by wonder:[4] O Lord! I see in your body all the gods, as well as all the groups of various kinds of living beings...
I see you everywhere – you who are of boundless form, with many arms, stomachs, mouths and eyes...
I see you who are a mass of light, resplendent everywhere, difficult to look at anywhere, effulgent like the brightness of the blazing fire and sun...
You, the supreme abode of this universe (that is, what constitutes the supreme support of this universe is you alone)... Of whatever nature, quality or dominion you are, you remain always with that same form... My conviction is that you are the eternal Person (*puruṣa*).[5]

The first extract in this passage gives a vivid description of Brahman as a Person of incomparable beauty and splendour. The two most prevalent themes are of light (compare p. 81 above) and lotus blossom. The splendour of the Supreme Person is like a mountain of gold; his brilliance is that of 'a hundred thousand suns'; he 'shines' in his majesty throughout the three worlds; and above all, he is seen 'within' the sun. The lotus metaphor develops the theme of the Lord's pervasive presence: not only are his eyes and feet like lotus flowers, but the 'nectar' of his 'loveliness' fills and overflows the whole of existence; and his fragrant holiness 'perfumes' the entire universe.

In the second passage (see pp. 90–1 above), which refers more specifically to the body of the divine Person, anthropomorphic imagery is combined with non-anthropomorphic language of transcendence. For example, Arjuna sees the Lord's body as having 'countless stomachs, faces and eyes', but this leads into a reference to seeing a mass of light which is 'resplendent everywhere'. What is of especial interest is the structure alluded to in this passage: the divine body is such that the universe comprises only one small part of it. The body is divided and differentiated into the various categories of conscious and non-conscious forms of existence, with Brahman at the head. And the various levels of existence are denoted by the different worlds. The divine body, therefore, comprises a cosmological structure in which the different hierarchies of existence are held together.

At first sight, the contrasts between the divine visions depicted by Rāmānuja and Teilhard are clearly apparent. Each picture has its own code or symbolic language. For example, Christ is, for Teilhard, the 'first and the last'; and for Rāmānuja, the Highest Person is seen 'within the sun'. In addition to these inherited symbolic themes, there are ideas and interpretations unique to each writer: Teilhard, for example, refers to spiritual energy as the 'heart of the world'; and Rāmānuja, for example, interprets the Person seen 'within the sun' to be none other than Brahman. It is hardly surprising also to note that the form of Rāmānuja's Highest Person differs structurally from that of Teilhard's Christ. The latter appears to be co-terminous with the universe, whereas the former contains the universe within it as but one small part of it.[6]

On closer examination, however, the divine Person in each passage is found to have certain features in common. To begin with, the Lord is seen, in both instances, to be characterised by brilliant, self-luminous light. He has 'brilliance' (R),[7] 'radiance' (T) and 'splendour' (R). He is a 'dazzling centre' (T), is seen 'within the sun' (R), he 'shines forth' (T), and 'shines in his supreme majesty' (R) through all things. Rāmānuja's sun image may be compared with Teilhard's fire symbolism, both being the source of light and heat.

We saw in Chapter 2 how the early *puruṣa* concept was associated with light, and with the sun in particular. Indeed, the connection was made between *puruṣa* (the divine Person) and Agni (the god of fire), and hence with sacrificial ritual (p. 33 above). So Rāmānuja is drawing upon a rich symbolism when he speaks of the Lord having the splendour of a 'hundred thousand suns'.[8] In addition, there are other references to fire which, in a sacrificial context, refer to purification and contemplative devotion.[9] No doubt Rāmānuja was aware of these.

In Chapter 5 we saw how Teilhard refers to the heart (literally 'the breast') of Christ as a 'furnace of fire', the source, it is inferred, of the world's primal energy and light.[10] When he speaks of 'a world which has burst into flame' (p. 92), he is referring to the world being 'consumed'. He means by this the consummation or divinisation of the world.[11] Teilhard sees this in terms of sacrifice, or more specifically, renunciation: 'All our work, finally, goes into making up the host on which the divine fire will descend.'[12] In his 'La Messe sur le monde', he presents the whole world as the host, which is continually being offered and transformed into the consecrated body of Christ.[13] This requires in man the development of 'a power to adore' or, as he puts it elsewhere, 'a capacity to renounce' oneself, to give oneself to the divine.[14] Teilhard believes that such renunciation made in love effects the transformation which leads eventually to the pleroma, when the fullness of Christ is in all, for all.[15]

The symbolism of light is associated, in both writers, with the vision of the Lord. The focus of the vision is, in both cases, a divine Person of light,[16] whose beauty[17] evokes awe and adoration. The images of fire and the sun are connected, in both writers' minds, with divine creativity, sacrifice, and the human response of devotion. There appears to be a fundamental link between all of these. They represent different aspects of the reality (or the 'consistence', as Teilhard would say) of the material universe. Teilhard and Rāmānuja, each in his own way, express the idea that the divine Person, who envelops the whole world (T)/three worlds (R), and who is the key to its comprehension, exists 'behind' the world of everyday existence and can be seen 'through' it at moments of significance. At such times the individual is granted release from the restricted vision of the ego, and everything is seen in terms of this divine Person. In their words, there is a 'Diaphany' of the divine (T) who is seen as a 'mass of light' (R). The world is then revealed in its completeness as a Person whose pervasive presence transfigures and unites all things, a divine realm or milieu, whose fundamental 'element' is light.[18]

In the context of the divine form (pp. 90–2 above), it is interesting to find that in Rāmānuja and Teilhard, the respective terms used are specifically associated with light and colour. The term *rūpa*, for example, includes 'outer colour' as one of its primary meanings. Rāmānuja develops the Upaniṣadic tradition of referring to the divine *svarūpa* ('proper form' or 'essential nature') in terms of self-luminosity and Self-consciousness (p. 115 above). Light symbolises, for him, pure consciousness. And when we look again at Teilhard's understanding of *forma Christi* (pp. 114–15), we find that he speaks of auras (encircling bands of colours/light) when referring to the 'universal physical reality' he identifies as Christ's 'crown' (corona). This 'crown' or universal 'Element', which is the divine Milieu, comprises 'circles' (p. 122) of increasing transparency to the divine radiance (p. 93).[19] Given Teilhard's equation of spirit with consciousness, this inner radiance symbolises for him divine consciousness. Both Rāmānuja and Teilhard, therefore, disclose the divine vision of the Lord through light symbolism. This, for both, is associated with divine consciousness. To see the Lord is to see from an enlightened perspective an illumined world which is revealed to be the body of the divine.

Such a vision implies a transformative process by which the viewer is enlightened. It represents the transformation of consciousness involved in coming to 'know' the Lord. Attaining the divine vision is synonymous in both cases with realising divine 'sight' or consciousness.[20] The limited ego or self-centred worldview is opened out into a universal, infinite perspective (pp. 52; 83), the focus of this new realm being the Lord, who is experienced as one's true 'Self' or 'Centre' of consciousness.

TRANSFORMATIONAL PRACTICES AND THE BODY OF THE LORD

If these descriptions of the divine vision represent a transformation of perception and consciousness, then how is this transformation worked out in the lives of individuals? What spiritual practices do Teilhard and Rāmānuja recommend as valuable, or necessary even, for spiritual advancement and personal fulfilment? In the rest of this chapter we shall look at the ways advocated by Teilhard and

Rāmānuja to attain the transformation of consciousness effected in the vision of the divine.

The religious practices advocated by Rāmānuja and Teilhard are, broadly speaking, devotional in character (p. 95 above). Love of, and devotion to, the Lord is believed, by both, to be a prerequisite for every believer or devotee. We could go further and classify these practices as ritualistic, in so far as they entail prescribed acts, physical and mental, pertaining to worship of the Lord. The attitude and awareness cultivated in this way is intended to be carried over into everyday life. It could be argued that Rāmānuja's spiritual discipline appears to have a more interior focus than that of Teilhard, and is, in fact, a form of meditation. It must, however, be pointed out that the cultic life of contemporary Vaiṣṇavism would have involved many practices of a more external character, which Rāmānuja would have taken for granted on the part of his listener or reader,[21] as indeed the Catholic contemplative tradition is equally taken for granted by Teilhard. Generally speaking, though, the different practices referred to by Teilhard and Rāmānuja have similar aims: to displace ego-centredness, through visualisation and worship of the divine, and to identify with the divine 'Centre' or 'Self'.[22]

Rāmānuja

In the case of Rāmānuja, loving devotion (*bhakti*) is divine knowledge and a form of meditation (*upāsana*).[23] His spiritual practice or *sādhana*[24] is a form of *bhakti-yoga*,[25] a discipline integrating devotion, knowledge and meditation in the context of worship of the Lord. Obviously this implies a relational perspective: the devotee's spiritual practice is in relation to the Lord, cultivating devotion towards him. Rāmānuja's definition of the self as 'accessory' (*śeṣa*)[26] should be viewed in this context. He writes: 'The *jñāni* [one practising the discipline of divine knowledge]... is one whose nature is to feel happiness and misery solely on account of union with or separation from Me. No being whatever is born with such a nature.'[27]

When we look more specifically at what Rāmānuja understands by *bhakti-yoga* we find several, inter-related aspects. These can be seen most clearly, perhaps, in a passage from his *Vedārthasaṃgraha*[28] where he describes the path through which the Supreme Person is attained. He speaks first of all of the individual's accumulation of merit, which destroys all impurities, and of the person seeking refuge at the feet of the Supreme Person. Such self-surrender, he explains, develops an 'inclination' towards him. The aspirant is then instructed in the Scriptures' knowledge of reality by holy teachers, and through 'steady effort' develops the 'qualities of the self', such as control of the mind and senses, purity, forgiveness, straightforwardness, discrimination, compassion and non-violence. He (traditionally this process refers to a man or boy, although theoretically it could refer to a woman or girl as well) is helped in this endeavour by regular ritual practices, appropriate to his caste and stage of life, and by rules of conduct which enable all actions to be viewed as worship of the Supreme Person. In fact the individual offers himself and all he has at the Lord's feet, and is encouraged to praise, remember, meditate upon and adore the Lord continually, as a form of total self-dedication. The Supreme Person, Rāmānuja continues, who is 'overflowing with compassion', showers his grace upon the aspirant, thus destroying all his 'inner darkness'. Thus *bhakti* develops in the individual towards the Supreme Person, 'which is valued for its own sake, which is uninterrupted, which is an absolute delight in itself and which is meditation that has taken the character of the most vivid and immediate vision'.[29] It is through such *bhakti*, he concludes, that the Supreme is attained.

It appears from this that some form of 'taking refuge' in the Lord initiates the aspirant into this practice of *bhakti-yoga*. Taking refuge, which may or may not be formalised, should lead, on the part of the individual concerned, to firstly, an 'inclination' toward the Lord; secondly, instruction in the Scriptures from 'holy teachers'; and thirdly, the development of 'qualities of the self [*ātman*]', affecting, lastly, his or her course of conduct. This conduct becomes governed by an overall desire to worship the Supreme Person, and includes the performance of prescribed ritual observances. These attitudes and practices generate *bhakti*, which is understood here as the condition or state of consciousness seeking and attaining union with the Lord. *Bhakti* is expressed through 'perpetual remembrance' of the Lord, enacted through acts of humility, adoration, praise and self-dedication, and above all, through meditation (*dhyāna*). These serve to increase *bhakti* in the devotee, causing the Supreme Person to respond out of his compassionate grace, enlightening the mind of the devotee (all his 'inner darkness' is destroyed) and granting him or her 'the most vivid and immediate vision', which characterises attainment of the Lord.

This passage illustrates how the disciplines of knowledge (*jñāna*) and action (karma) are both seen by Rāmānuja to stem from an act of self-dedication or taking refuge. They lead to the release (*mokṣa*) of self through the attainment of the Lord. In this way, knowledge and action are transformed through the inner attitude of the aspirant (*sādhaka*). *Bhakti* signifies, here, the entire process, from taking refuge to continuous remembrance of the Lord in meditation, and finally, attaining him. For Rāmānuja it refers to the means (*upāya*) and the end (*upeya*) of knowledge of Brahman (*Brahmajñāna*).

In Rāmānuja's *Gītābhāṣya* and *Śrībhāṣya* there is more detailed information about the nature of the practices involved.[30] To begin with we find that the development of the 'qualities of *ātman*', including control of the mind and senses, is referred to in the *Gītā*[31] as yoga or 'knowledge of the self'.[32]

In fact it is this 'knowledge of the self' which destroys past sins,[33] and this knowledge which transforms actions of self-centred desire for gain into acts of worship.[34] To attain it the *Gītābhāṣya* outlines several meditation practices,[35] one of which is to meditate on the equality[36] of all selves.[37] This helps the individual to break free from his or her self-identification with his or her impermanent body and establish him or herself in the 'vision of the enduring self'.[38] Such contemplation of the self, when practised continually, leads to the attainment of bliss.[39]

There are four specific aspects of this meditation[40] on the equality of all: firstly, the individual should see no difference between his or her own form and those of others, because all selves are perceived through the vision of one's own self; secondly, this equality is found to stem from a fundamental 'similarity of nature'[41] between the self and the Lord; thirdly, this realisation leads to worship of the Lord by giving up 'practices based on *prakṛti*' (i.e. all that is not centred on the Lord) and by continually visualising him, and finally, the devotee experiences constant 'oneness' with the Lord which renders material happiness or sadness the same in terms of experience. These four aspects incorporate the 'qualities of self [*ātman*]' referred to in the *Vedārthasaṃgraha* passage, and it can be seen how knowledge of one's self passes over into knowledge of the Lord. The relinquishment of ego-centredness leads, in this context, to the perception of the divine Person as one's true Self.

Rāmānuja gives quite specific indications as to how the Lord enlightens the mind of the practitioner of *bhakti*. In the *Gītā* he refers to this subject as 'most secret knowledge'. The Lord, who is 'established' in the 'mental state' of the devotee as the 'object of thought', destroys his or her darkness[42] by means of the 'shining light called knowledge', which manifests divine and auspicious qualities.[43] In more practical terms this means that through focusing on the Lord as the sole object of thought, that vision or sight is attained which is equated with knowledge, and which reveals the Lord's qualities. Kṛṣṇa explains this to Arjuna:

Be one whose mind is placed on Me. That is, have your mind fixed well on Me without any interruption like a stream of oil...

[Be] My devotee. The meaning is, 'Be one whose mind is placed on Me by meditating on Me as exceedingly dear'...

Be My worshipper. That is, become engaged in My worship, which is brought about by your experience of Me, which is dear and excellent beyond limits. Worship, indeed, means the cause of conduct of one who is completely subservient...[44]

Rāmānuja identifies this knowledge of, and devotion to, the Lord as *upāsana*, a form of meditation comprising visualising and 'remembering' the Lord continually (see p. 65 above). He explains:

What is enjoined in *Vedānta* texts... is knowledge (*vedana*) of the Lord: it can be expressed [more specifically] by the words, 'meditation' (*dhyāna*) and worship (*upāsana*): it is of the form of direct vision: it is continued remembrance: and it is inexpressibly dear. This [knowledge] is enjoined here (when the direct means to final release has to be taught) in 'Be one whose mind is placed on me'...
Being thus, you will straightaway attain Me... In regard to him whose love for Me is very great, My love for him also becomes very great. Therefore, unable to bear separation from him, I cause him to attain Me.[45]

This passage reveals that the injunction 'Be one whose mind is placed on me' refers to knowledge of the Lord attained in meditation and worship. *Upāsana*, which represents both of these, is a form of devotional meditation in which the divine is objectified (visualised)[46] and internalised. As in tantric practices, this involves a process of symbolic appropriation. By that I mean that a symbol of the divine is objectified and then meditated upon in such a way that transformation occurs through identification with the symbol.

Let us look a little more closely at what Rāmānuja is saying about *upāsana*. Above all, he is telling the devotee, through Kṛṣṇa's words to Arjuna, to focus on the Lord. We learn from the ensuing description that he is referring here to the Lord's transcendent or divine form. Arjuna is told to 'remember' this (form) continually ('have your mind fixed well on Me without any interruption like a stream of oil').[47] This suggests an imaginative reconstruction of the image through visualisation (cf. p. 34 above). It is, Rāmānuja explains, a form of 'seeing'. The devotee is projecting a symbolic representation of the Lord through visualisation. This is easier to understand when we find that in the *Śrībhāṣya* Rāmānuja refers to this as knowledge (*jñāna*). This is, he explains, 'A mental energy different in character from the mere cognition of the sense of texts... which is of the nature of remembrance (i.e. representative thought)'.[48] It is this visualisation which renders the Lord 'immediately present' to the devotee[49] in the form of 'direct vision'. In other words the image becomes a symbol of the Lord's presence. It is the consciously received[50] and objectified form of the Lord which provides the means of knowing him.

The devotee is encouraged to repeat this practice frequently, even continually, in order to perfect it.[51] The impression given is that it is self-generating. It is, in effect, the actual formation of the 'mental energy' that Rāmānuja calls *bhakti*. The experience arising from the continual practice of *upāsana* is referred to as joy,[52] and the object as 'inexpressibly dear'.[53] The subsequent 'vision' or perceived form of the Lord is characterised by a mass of light (p. 90 above). Given the significance, already noted, of light in this context, we could say that the experienced vision of the divine Person represents the integration of the devotee's consciousness with the divine. This is what Rāmānuja calls a 'direct intuition' of Brahman,[54] because the divine has to some extent been 'realised' in the devotee.[55]

Rāmānuja states that this realisation is ultimately due to the grace of the Lord, who reveals himself to those devotees whom he has chosen, on account of their love and devotion.[56] Clearly, divine grace is of paramount importance to Rāmānuja. Only when the devotee proves his or her love for the Lord is the divine vision granted. The initiative, even when the individual's efforts are great, is always taken by the Lord. Meditation using visualisation is not in itself the key to release (*mokṣa*), but rather the inner attitude of love and devotion which, when expressed through *upāsana*, can precipitate the divine response in the form of the gift of inner sight and knowledge of the Lord. I referred to the entire process as *bhakti-yoga* because the term *bhakti* embraces both the attitude of the devotee and the divine response, which are two aspects of a single movement.

Teilhard de Chardin

Turning to Teilhard de Chardin, we find a different path pointing towards what is seen as a state of union with God. Like Rāmānuja, he envisages a final state in which the individual transcends his earthly form of existence through a radical integration or at-onement with the Lord. But Teilhard conceives this fulfilment (pleroma)[57] as located in a future moment in the evolution of the human race.[58] He refers to this as the completion of Christ's body.[59] In other words, the body of Christ symbolises, for him, the final and complete integration of the world in God.[60] The individual is seen as a partial element of this total reality, each with his or her own contribution to make (pp. 52–4 above). Every person participates partially in Christ's fullness and helps to bring about his completion in the world. It is in this context that Teilhard speaks of Christ as a Super-Person. he is described as a being who is evolving with humankind; a corporate figure including yet transcending all individuals and drawing them to self-fulfilment in him.[61] It is his power of attraction which draws individuals beyond their ego-centricity and into a greater Centre of energy: the 'heart' (p. 92) of Christ. For Teilhard, personal fulfilment is found through entering this 'greater' life, which is the life of the universe lived and experienced as the body of Christ.

The question of how Teilhard envisages the individual's entrance into Christ's body, and the transformations necessary along the way, may be rephrased to address how he views human sanctity. This is for him a state of inner transparency to the universal life of Christ, involving tremendous purity and faith, and resulting in the manifestation of an energy of love and prayer which alone can centre all things in Christ. For him, the fundamental transformation[62] is the awareness and development of the shared spiritual resources of the earth:[63]

> To 'conform' to Christ is to share, through a partial identity, in the unique, fundamental act constituted by the Whole. There is, in reality, *only one* humility in the world, *one* loving-kindness, *one* sacrifice, *one* passion, *one* lying in the tomb, *one* resurrection – and it is Christ's. It is all one in him, multiple in us – begun and perfected by him, and yet completed by us.[64]

We need to place Teilhard's understanding of Christian devotion in this context of human life as a participation in the life of the universe (pp. 61–2 above). The unique relationship between the individual and the cosmos expressed in the body of Christ he refers to as 'mystical' (pp. 54–5; 58).[65] It is the 'mystical sense', he says, which gives a person an awareness of the 'total and final unity of the world, beyond its present sensibly apprehended multiplicity'.[66] And it is this perception or consciousness which causes all things to be seen as a 'mystical milieu'.[67] Thus, the path Teilhard advocates to attain the vision of the Lord, which signifies participation in his body, he calls the 'third'[68] or 'mystic' way[69], which involves 'all one's strength and all one's heart... coinciding with the Focus of universal unification, as yet diffuse but nevertheless already in existence', and '*loving*, co-extensively and co-organically with all the past, the present and the future... a Universe which is in process of centration upon itself'.[70]

Teilhard's 'mystic' way involves aligning oneself with Christ, the spiritual Centre of the universe, and thereby entering the 'sphere' or realm of his influence, power and love. When we look for more specific spiritual teachings, we find a wealth of material compressed into three main sources: 'Le Milieu mystique', which is a paper he wrote in 1917,[71] 'La Messe sur le monde', which was written in 1923,[72] and *Le Milieu divin* (1927).[73]

Drawing upon these texts, we can best summarise his teachings on sanctity by putting them in the context of his understanding of the Eucharist, since for him, this symbolises the entire transformative process by which the universe and the individual become part of Christ's body, or *le milieu divin*. What comes to light in this context is the inseparability of human 'salvation' from that of the cosmos. It must be remembered, however, that just as in the Mass each successive section of the liturgy, while overlapping with others, nevertheless represents one movement to consecrate the elements and the whole of life, so too the aspects of the path summarised below indicate a progressive, yet overlapping transformation of the inner life.[74]

By way of a preface, however, we need to point out that this unfolding of the 'mystic' path, corresponding to a development of the 'mystical sense', is primarily due, not to the individual's efforts, though these are of paramount importance to Teilhard, but to God. In *Le Milieu divin*, Teilhard refers to the gradual perception of the 'divine omnipresence' as a gift, 'like life itself, of which it is undoubtedly the supreme experimental perfection'. Thus the initiative always comes from God, and any development with regard to a person's mystical faculties is a new gift, to be responded to appropriately.[75]

The beginning of the individual's path towards unity with God lies simply in recognition of the 'mystical sense'. It is experienced, says Teilhard, as the perception of an 'aureole' (p. 60), a 'universal milieu', which discloses the 'unique essence of the universe' in all things.[76] This awareness causes a longing, a 'thrilling', a feeling of being 'inundated',[77] and it evokes a response of love: 'the Presence that spreads through all things is the only source that gives me light and the only air that I can ever breathe'.[78] Given that the Christian mystic becomes increasingly aware of the divine presence, it is not surprising that at the opening of his 'La Messe sur le monde', Teilhard takes for his offering all those aspects of the world in which the divine presence is hard to perceive: the labours and sufferings of the world. It is on these that he, as priest, will 'call down the Fire'.[79]

Teilhard makes it quite clear that the individual's initial response to a sense of the divine presence must be one of prayer for the 'fundamental gift': *Domine, fac ut videam*. 'Lord', he writes, 'we know and feel that you are everywhere around us; but it seems that there is a veil before our eyes. Let the light of your countenance shine upon us in its universality.'[80]

He explains that this 'intense and continual' prayer contributes towards a conscious 'sharpening' of the 'mystical sense'. The inner realities of things become clearer, and imperceptibly, the 'structure' of 'a sublime love' of God begins to take shape within the person concerned.[81]

When Teilhard speaks of the 'structure' of 'a sublime love', he is referring to the recentring of a person around Christ. If Christ comprises the inner structure of all matter (p. 51 above), then for him to be fully realised, love – the energetic and spiritual component of this structure – needs to become conscious. The individual seeking to follow his personal 'sense' of the divine is, in fact, giving birth to a new consciousness: Christ-consciousness. For this to be born, Teilhard teaches that purity is absolutely necessary.[82] By purity he means transparency, a total openness to the divine; a focusing upon the emerging Christ perceived within the world. In *Le Milieu divin* he writes: 'The purity of being is measured by the degree of the attraction that draws [individuals] towards the divine Centre, or, what comes to the same thing, by their proximity to the Centre.'[83]

Only such concentration and clear awareness can allow the unity diffused throughout the world[84] to become conscious. For Teilhard, purity acts as the eye with which the individual begins to see Christ's universal presence, the 'consistent' form of things. He explains: 'This means that the incorruptible principle of the universe is now and for ever found, and that it extends everywhere: *the world is filled*, and filled with the Absolute. To see this is to be made free.'[85]

In a very real sense, the person who is pure participates, through his or her transparency, in the transformative power of Christ. Through 'seeing' his universal presence, the individual is making that presence conscious and accessible to others. 'Seeing' can be understood here as the reflection and realisation of the divine.[86] It becomes a form of consecration in that it is a function of Christ's divinisation of the world.[87]

Openness to the divine, which is experienced by the person who is pure, leads, says Teilhard, to the desire to surrender oneself completely to God. He calls this the 'phase of communion'.[88] In *Le Milieu divin* we are shown two aspects of communion with the divine, active and passive,[89] which can be viewed as complementary facets of living by faith.[90] Basically, Teilhard says that the world can become for us the body of Christ *if* we believe so. Faith is the conscious assent to the divine Centre, influencing all features of our life and world by allowing them to be 'charged' with the divine. To surrender to God is to share in his continuing creativity[91] by affirming the divine presence in every situation and especially, perhaps, in experiences of diminishment. This does not lead to the annihilation of self, but rather to an identification with the divine:[92] 'the more perfect an instrument he becomes, the more does [the individual] *become one* with the creative Act'.[93] So this 'phase of communion' is a conscious immersing of oneself in the divine by believing, and hence making, Christ's presence universally available.

In time, the mystic who has travelled thus far is able to perceive the divine in all things and at all times.[94] His faith has 'made' the world the body of Christ, the divine milieu:

> If I firmly believe that everything around me is the body and blood of the Word, then for me (and in one sense for me alone) is brought about that marvellous 'diaphany' which causes the luminous warmth of a single life to be objectively discernible in, and to shine forth from, the depths of every event, every element.[95]

Teilhard maintains that in addition to faith the mystic needs to develop what he refers to as 'fidelity', in order to maintain his or her orientation towards the divine continuously. 'Faith consecrates the world. Fidelity communicates with it',[96] he explains. In a way, it is a person's continual rededication of self in daily living that frees him or her to relate honestly to the world. What he understands by fidelity I would call a form of 'centring' in the Lord through the confluence of inner and outer circumstances. 'Through fidelity', he clarifies, 'we situate ourselves and maintain ourselves in the hands of God so exactly as to become one with them in their action.'[97] This means that the individual becomes a channel for the divine. She or he is moulded by the milieu and power which was the initial attraction. In 'Le Milieu mystique', Teilhard describes how the mystic ceases to be only him or herself: 'Body and soul, he has become a fragment of the divine. Henceforth, as though through a sacred door opening on to the universe, God passes through him and spreads his radiance.'[98]

To the extent that the mystic is 'faithful', she or he also has charity, because in losing egocentricity, the person is acquiring a common form and Centre in the love of Christ. In fact the whole process of evolution becomes one of Christification, because of the transformation of individual centres of consciousness and their respective worlds or 'spheres'. And in this common remoulding, Teilhard envisages a mutual acceptance and integration taking place. He defines charity as the 'greater or lesser cohesion of souls engendered by their communal convergence *in Christo Jesu*'.[99] 'The individual divine *milieux*', he explains, 'in proportion as they establish themselves, tend to fuse one with another.' This leads to a 'boundless increase in ardour' and love for all things, as demonstrated in the lives of saints. It is this love, he says, which carries in itself the germ of eternal life. Hence, the only subject ultimately capable of mystical transfiguration is the whole of humankind, forming one body and soul 'in charity'.[100]

That individuals experience an 'increase of ardour' is due, as we see from the passage above, to a fusion of energy, and especially of love, which Teilhard identifies as the supreme power of spirit. It is natural, then, for a person to exhibit more devotion the further she or he travels along the path. Correspondingly, the world increasingly assumes the 'form' and 'features' of a Person worthy of adoration:

> We have seen the mystical milieu develop and assume a form at once divine and human... What name can we give to this mysterious Entity, who is in some small way our own handiwork, with whom, eminently, we can enter into communion, and who is some part of ourselves, yet who masters us, has

need of us in order to exist, and at the same time dominates us with the full force of his Absolute being?...
I can feel it: he has a name and a face, but he alone can reveal his face and pronounce his name: Jesus![101]

This is the point at which the mystic attains a transformed vision, which signifies establishment on the path of holiness.

Teilhard understands a saint to be a mystic who is deeply rooted in the cosmos. She or he demonstrates, through an inner openness and joyful acceptance of life, the love of a Universal Christ. She or he also manifests more than a personal ego. Through purity, faith and fidelity, a new Centre of Consciousness shines through the individual soul. The individual's progression along the path becomes a form of self-offering in which the person, together with all those elements that comprise his or her life, becomes the matter that is slowly transformed into the consecrated body of Christ. So personal purity and faith represent properties of a world that is evolving a divine Person. The development of a 'mystical sense' of the divine Presence, which leads through prayer to the evolving of a 'structure' of love within the individual, is an intense process of self-transformation. It requires total honesty and transparency through which the universe's energies are encouraged to flow. This leads to an actual perception of the divine 'consistency' of things, which influences every thought and action, enabling these to become acts of self-surrender to, and communion with, God. When practised continually this leads ultimately to the recognition of Christ's form in the world.

Such self-offering is symbolised for Teilhard in the Eucharist, which is also the single most specific act in which the Christian aligns him or herself with this process. In the Eucharist,[102] the individual seeks to attain and realise the very 'mind' or consciousness of Christ.[103]

Similarities in the transformation of consciousness

The spiritual practices advocated by Rāmānuja and Teilhard de Chardin, however differently they are conceived and described, clearly lead in both cases to an integration of the individual with divine consciousness. The results of such practices are referred to in terms of 'seeing' the Highest Person/Christ in the world. This is described symbolically as seeing the 'body' of the Lord.

The point of convergence in both the divine vision descriptions and the spiritual practices considered above lies in the experience of personal transformation. There are recognisable features common to descriptions of Rāmānuja's *sādhana* and Teilhard's spirituality. In both cases, the initiative to embark on the spiritual quest is understood to come from the divine (pp. 135; 137 above). The Lord 'reveals' himself to those he has chosen. Nevertheless, it is the devotion and dedicated effort of the individual which enables him or her to become increasingly aware of the divine presence. In particular, we find that Teilhard and Rāmānuja emphasise that continuity of effort and a cultivation of love are the most important factors. The Lord should be focused on continually, either through meditation (p. 134) or prayer (p. 138). To both thinkers, what follows is an ex-centration of self: the individual's focal point of awareness gradually changes as the divine object is internalised through symbolic appropriation (pp. 134; 137).

In the respective religious traditions of Teilhard and Rāmānuja, the divine form serves as a tool for the process of internalising and appropriating the divine. This is not to say that the divine form is simply a human invention. As we have seen, the divine form arises in conjunction with the transformed perception of the initiate or devotee. It belongs to that new 'divine' consciousness. We could say, therefore, that the divine form is perceived and realised through subjective experience. It is, however, 'received' by those seriously committed to their respective paths. Using Rāmānuja's term (from the *Gītā*), I call this a 'secret' teaching. It is a teaching to be understood and realised by those initiated into the inner life. The ritualised forms of this experience are meditation in Rāmānuja's tradition, and the sacraments (especially the Eucharist) in the Catholic tradition. The divine is objectified in a symbol, such as an icon of his transcendent form, or as the consecrated offering for the Mass, and then appropriated in a ritual of self-transformation.

Through the practices of meditation, prayer and the sacraments, the individual integrates the disparate elements of his or her life (and hence, in Teilhard's view, the elements of the world). During the act of meditating and participating in the sacraments, the 'true' nature of reality is revealed to the subject. This nature is experienced as a 'seeing' and a 'knowing'.[104] It unites and liberates through the very act of perceiving the world and the divine as one.[105]

The divine body symbolises this change of perception and consciousness. It is visualised as the Lord's transcendent form in *upāsana*, and in the Eucharist the elements are envisaged as being changed into Christ's body and blood. The relationship here between visualisation and faith is interesting: in meditation, including visualisation practices, faith plays an important part. And in the Eucharist, where faith is of fundamental importance, the believer responds to the bread and wine as to Christ's body and blood, and visualisation can play a part in this response. Teilhard, of course, visualised the whole cosmos being transformed by one continuing Eucharistic consecration (see Appendix II).

It is extremely interesting to find that these very different religious traditions include practices which, although different in outward appearances and conceptual formulations, nevertheless have the same fundamental function of enabling the individual consciousness to realise its true, divine 'form' (see pp. 114–16 above). The practices are undertaken in relation to the divine Person, and it is this perspective of the divine as Person which leads to certain similarities of purpose and language in Rāmānuja and Teilhard.

In both cases the divine is viewed as the Lord, and it is he who is focused upon and visualised. The individual approaches the divine as devotee, as 'servant'. The nature of this relationship facilitates the cultivation of devotional love, for example, in the heart of the individual. Devotion can then lessen ego-centredness and render the heart more open and less circumscribed by habitual patterns of emotional response. This enables the person concerned to experience the divine presence within his or her world. All things are gradually perceived in relation to him. This leads to the development of love in the devotee, who begins to see all things, including his or her own life, in terms of the Lord, who is the true Self or Centre of consciousness.

A gradual identification of the individual with the divine develops, especially through the ritual practices of *upāsana* and the Eucharist. The devotee practises surrender to the Lord (the relinquishment of the ego) (p. 132), and builds a new 'structure' or pattern of love in daily life (p. 138). The divine presence is felt to be everywhere, and the individual begins to perceive a correlation between the divine as Self or Centre and the 'mass of light' or 'divine milieu' seen to pervade all things. By self-offering, therefore, the individual receives a new 'form' of consciousness, and realises his or her participation in the 'body' of the cosmos which belongs to the Lord who is its 'heart'.

Experiencing this integration of consciousness and identifying with it releases the individual from his or her normally restricted mode of vision. It frees the person concerned to participate, through a transformed awareness, in a broader vision (literally 'seeing'). Being centred and integrated in the divine (as Self/Soul), she or he perceives all things in the 'light' of that consciousness. The divine, present everywhere, is 'seen' through the 'divine eye' or the 'mind of Christ'. All things are then experienced as equal facets of one divine reality (pp. 133; 139).

THE DIVINE BODY AS SOTERIOLOGICAL MODEL

It is clear from the material explored in the latter part of this chapter that the spiritual practices which play such an important part in the theological teachings of both thinkers are, in spite of radical and obvious conceptual differences, concerned with the same soteriological question of the transformation of consciousness. In this context the divine body becomes both a means and an end. It is a symbolic model of that transformation, and a symbol for that transformation.[106] The techniques appear different, but they both represent devotional means for self-transformation.

At the beginning of the chapter we looked at Teilhard's and Rāmānuja's respective depictions of the divine form; the 'visions' of the Lord as envisioned by both thinkers. It became apparent that their descriptions of the divine form are constructed from a symbolic code of language, incorporating both unique and common elements. Fundamental similarities include allusions to light (p. 129) to a divine Person of unsurpassable beauty who evokes a response of awe and adoration, and to experiences of unity and completeness. All things are described as being seen in the light of the presence of the Lord and as being experienced as his glorious *vibhūti* or milieu.

When this is put in the context of an analysis of the theological content of the terms *svarūpa* and *forma Christi*, it becomes clear that both Teilhard and Rāmānuja equate radiant light with divine (Self-) Consciousness (p. 130). Visions of the divine form refer, then, to a realisation of divine consciousness. Perceiving the Lord is synonymous, for both Rāmānuja and Teilhard, with knowledge of the divine. To 'see' the Lord is to 'attain' him or be united with him.

If, as I suggest, metaphorical and symbolic language can actually initiate a changed state of perception and consciousness, then these descriptions of the divine form are indeed 'secret' teachings which, when combined with spiritual practice, can potentially be instrumental in leading to a transformed vision of the world. They are potent symbols which have been proven to be useful in their respective spiritual traditions when practised in the context of a continuing spiritual discipline. Daily practice thus provides the context for the creation of the divine body model in theological teaching.

Given that traditional and cultural factors almost certainly influence the nature of a mystic's experience (as well as his or her recording of that experience),[107] it would be extremely difficult to account for the similarities between the visions of Teilhard and Rāmānuja, were it not for the shared spiritual concern of integrating the individual and the world with the divine. Both writers identify *bhakti* or love of the Lord as being of particular significance in this process. And for them this represents not simply an attitude on the part of the devotee or believer, but also a participation in the form or consciousness of the Lord (see pp. 133; 141 above).

Thus the inherent form of the world is experienced as being the Lord's own true form or nature. In other words the theological presupposition of both writers is that the world is inherently divine, and that the very 'Person' of the Lord is manifest as our world. 'Attaining the Lord', 'realising his blissful nature' and 'surrendering to the power of love' within each person and the world refer to an experience of living in a world that is fundamentally sacred. The similarity of language used to describe the divine vision suggests a phenomenological likeness of experience in that the divine body discloses a vision of fulfilment both at the level of the individual, and of the world. It also reveals ways to attain that fulfilment.

It is perhaps in the experience of self-transformation that the language of the divine vision and the divine body originates. And it is here, within the context of spiritual practice, that another explanation for the similarities between the divine body in Teilhard and Rāmānuja may be found.[108] Both forms of the practices aim at integration of human consciousness. And it may be that the various ways to attain such a state of consciousness have certain elements in common. Perhaps they all exhibit a similar pattern, or perhaps consciousness itself in its various forms has a common fundamental structure.[109]

CHAPTER 8

The body divine: paradigm of a conscious cosmos

I have shown in the previous chapters how the divine body symbol functions in the writings of Teilhard de Chardin and Rāmānuja. It serves, for both, as a metaphor to disclose an apprehension of reality in terms of the divine Person (Christ/the Highest Person). It also becomes an analogical model of an integrated worldview. In other words, the term 'body' is extended in its usage to apply to all aspects of reality which together constitute a mode or part of the divine. And since the divine is understood, in both cases, in terms of consciousness, the whole of the material world is presented as being alive and conscious.

The term 'divine body' acts as a root-metaphor for both writers to disclose this non-dualistic vision. The world is perceived as part of a divine totality. Rāmānuja and Teilhard both describe how it is to 'see' the world in the 'light' of the Lord's presence. Clearly, for them this sacred knowledge is experienced as a transformed perception. The symbolic language they employ communicates something of this transformed state of being.

As a model representing a theological 'map', the divine body reveals a way of viewing things in terms of relationships: it refers to the inter-related unity of the divine and the cosmos at every conceivable level. Teilhard, for example, speaks of Christ as the Centre of the cosmos, to which all things are physically related. Rāmānuja refers to Brahman as the Self of all selves, to whom all relate as to their source and inner Ruler.

One feature common to both models is the correspondence between the individual and the universal, the psychological and the cosmological. The divine body functions for both writers on micro and macro levels simultaneously. Another way of looking at this is to say that the whole is instantiated in the part; the divine is represented partially in the individual. So spiritual growth can be seen to include personal and cosmic responsibility and awakening.

This relationship between the whole and the part provides the theological basis for the spiritual paths of transformation advocated by Rāmānuja and Teilhard respectively. These involve practices of *bhakti* or devotional love which focus on integrating with the divine. Brahman or God is related to as Person, and the supreme goal is referred to by both writers as union with, or attainment of, the Lord.

This attainment is spoken of in terms of perceiving the Lord. Descriptions are given of a divine vision in which the divine Person is referred to by metaphors of light, beauty and transcendence. In both cases the divine is experienced as a pervasive presence and a manifestation of light, which illumines the entire vision of the individual concerned. Rāmānuja refers to the world being seen as the divine realm (*vibhūti*), and to Teilhard, the world becomes the divine milieu. This perception denotes for them an en-lightened consciousness.

This vision encapsulates a pattern of cosmic wholeness. All the layers of life are integrated. The integration is represented symbolically through allusions to the beauty and transcendence of a divine Person. Rāmānuja speaks of the perfections, unsurpassability and all-pervasiveness of the Lord and of the illimitability of his transcendent form. He is depicted as being both infinite and containable within the space of a human heart. Likewise Teilhard describes the infinite prolongations of the divinely created cosmos, which is the body of Christ, who is both a universal Element and also the Omega Point and telos of the whole creation.

Today, this unified vision need not be regarded as the view of a 'mystic' minority. Contemporary scientists and psychologists have been coming together with practitioners of spiritual disciplines for over a decade to explore the bases of their worldviews.[1] In fact, the physicist David Bohm speaks of reality in terms not dissimilar to those used by Teilhard and Rāmānuja. Viewing the cosmos as 'one unbroken whole', he refers to the unmanifest matrix of the cosmos as the 'enfolded' or 'implicate' order which manifests itself in gradations of gross to subtle forms of matter, which he calls the 'explicate' order. The whole undivided reality he describes as a 'holomovement'.[2] Perceiving this unity has been likened to having 'lensless vision'[3] in which the 'lens' of our limited (explicate) and independent consciousness falls away to allow de-limited (implicate) consciousness to be fully present. Thus scientists are using metaphors to speak of the world in terms of unified vision and consciousness.

Bohm calls his unified understanding of the cosmos a form of monism. There is no divine Person in his worldview – or at least, he does not discuss this. Rāmānuja and Teilhard de Chardin, on the other hand, interpret the cosmic unity as Person, and the manifestation of divine consciousness. Bohm uses a metaphor of attribution when referring to the divine totality. He speaks of 'field consciousness', by analogy with field physics. His perspective throws light on Rāmānuja's references to Brahman as Knower (*kṣetrajña*) and the world as his 'field' (*kṣetra*). For Bohm the knower and known are not two realities, but are apprehensible as one 'holomovement' in which knowing and being known are part of one process. Such a unified 'field' of consciousness is, Renée Weber explains, 'neither neutral nor value-free' but 'an orderly and compassionate energy articulating itself in a new domain where physics, psychology, ethics and religion merge'.[4]

Rāmānuja's disclosure of Brahman as the Supreme Self in an inseparable relation with the world can be interpreted in dualistic terms. And perhaps for a certain stage in spiritual growth this is appropriate, or indeed as a model for an inner integrative process at any time: the devotee practises *bhakti* with the Lord as his or her divine focus. However, Rāmānuja's theme throughout all his writings is of reality as non-dual although differentiated (*viśiṣṭādvaita*). The spiritual goal, described in terms of the divine vision, is portrayed as an experience of total integration, when the individual perceives and knows all things through their identity in the Lord. For Teilhard the goal is similarly integrative: perceiving or knowing Christ is to see his 'radiance' pervading the entire world.

INTERPRETING THE DIVINE BODY IN TERMS OF CONSCIOUSNESS

Micro-macro homology

One structural similarity in the divine body of Teilhard and Rāmānuja concerns their claims for identity between the individual self or soul and the divine Person. I explored this (in Chapter 5) in the context of the essential form or nature of the individual and the Lord. The self is to its body what the divine Person is to the world, and these two sets of relations are not just parallel but a continuity of relationship. As Teilhard puts it, 'My matter is not a part of the universe that I possess totally, but the totality of the universe that I possess partially' (p. 61 above). In his terms, the human person partially represents the cosmos. She or he represents the cosmic body of Christ.

Renée Weber, when discussing David Bohm's 'holocosmic metaphors', points out that for him, as for esoteric religions and philosophical worldviews, there is seen to be a crucial relationship between the part and the whole, between 'particle' and 'wave', 'explicate' and 'implicate' – and, we might add, the individual 'self' and the 'cosmic Self/Spirit'. 'Instead of stressing their divergences', she explains, 'as in the case of exoteric religion and philosophy, the esoteric systems and Buddhism, in particular, assert [their] identity.'[5] She discusses this concept in the context of the Buddhist notions of *saṃsāra* and *nirvāna*, and adds: 'Inaccessible to Western science until the discovery of the hologram, Buddhist logic, holographic logic, and quantum logic defy common sense by stating that the whole is in the part.'[6]

Obviously such a position radically affects our understanding of the world about us. We are challenged to acknowledge that the whole, which in religious terms is understood in terms of the divine, can express itself partially in any object or living being, rather like light being reflected through a prism. Such a view requires that even in the most mundane of our activities we act in accordance with greater awareness. For Mother Teresa to talk of 'seeing' Christ in dying beggars is no longer so incomprehensible. In each encounter we make, we are affecting the cosmos, and in Christian terms this can be interpreted as helping to heal, or deepening the wounds in the body of Christ. The traditional Indian form of greeting, which is to place the palms of the hands together, to bow to the person and greet him or her, is understood in terms of giving reverence to the divine within that individual. This is, in itself, an 'enwholing' act,[7] acknowledging and creating wholeness.

To appropriate this view is to instigate changes in attitude and understanding.[8] The ways in which we conduct our relationships, for example, mirror and influence the ways in which we are relating to nature as a whole. It is not only that our 'inner' actions affect the 'outer' ones; rather the two are related as part of one continuum of movement and resonance. The maxim 'do to others what you would have done to yourself' appears startlingly applicable in this context, since there is seen to be an inherent relationship between others and ourselves.

In theological terms, the salvation or release of each individual is understood to be directly connected to the redemption or completion of the cosmos as a whole. Individual spiritual growth is placed, of necessity, within this broader framework. One implication is that each person is seen to be partially responsible, through the way she or he lives, for the 'well-being' of the earth. Rāmānuja does not speak in terms of social responsibility, but he is suggesting that knowing Brahman involves seeing the world's unity in terms of his body. A person who knows Brahman cannot, therefore, harm a living thing. Teilhard de Chardin does, however, speak explicitly about the duty of the individual to participate in the process of divinising the cosmos and hence, of completing Christ in God. For both of them, the world's inter-relatedness is perceived and understood in terms of the integrity and transcendence of the body of the Lord.

The Divine Body as theistic paradigm

In the context of the continuing consciousness debate, the divine body visions of Rāmānuja and Teilhard de Chardin may serve as examples of a useful paradigm for a conscious cosmos. And this is a paradigm with a respected lineage in the history of religion. It offers a way of seeing the world which relates all the elements and inhabitants of our world to one another. Each particular individual or thing is viewed in connection with others and in the context of the whole. Furthermore consciousness, which is usually attributed only to certain forms of life, is recognised as an inherent structure of every cell, every atom. From this perspective the entire world appears as a multi-faceted expression of consciousness.

For Rāmānuja and Teilhard de Chardin, the divine body is a symbol which can help transform existing ways of knowing and seeing things. Through practising love and devotion to the Lord, however he is conceived, through visualising him around and within us, and through attaining deeper insight and understanding of the sacramental nature of reality, it is possible, they claim, to begin to perceive the world differently and to allow its inherent 'form' to shine forth.

Such practices of integration with the divine I referred to as centroversion. The Lord is attained through 'centring' in the divine, and the experience is spoken of in terms of perceiving the Lord. The state of integration with the Lord is alluded to in similar symbolic language by both Teilhard and Rāmānuja. This language communicates the perception of a divine universality in which all things are seen to be equal and 'illumined'. In this sense we can speak of a transformed perception.[9]

The divine body symbolises, therefore, the way of self-transformation. It serves as a cosmological and psychological map of consciousness to guide the individual committed to realising his or her Centre or true Self. In fact the practices advocated by Rāmānuja and Teilhard respectively, while different in form, reveal strong similarities of emphasis: the main feature of both is the cultivation of *bhakti* or love of the Lord.

What is of particular significance for this enquiry is that neither Teilhard nor Rāmānuja speaks of *bhakti*/love as simply the means to attain the Lord: it also represents the goal. In other words, the experience of *bhakti*/love belongs to and characterises union with the divine. This is an interesting claim. It is *bhakti*/love which leads to and precipitates the divine vision, yet this also signifies the experience of divine consciousness. As we discovered, the initiative for movement towards the divine is believed to come from the Lord, and yet the experienced impulse or energy of *bhakti*/love is also found to be divine. So divine consciousness is manifest and experienced as love within the human heart. It is this which is the force actualising the integration of consciousness.

A comparison of the practices taught by Teilhard and Rāmānuja reveals fundamental similarities in spite of obvious differences. In particular, it indicates a shared concern with displacing the ego by increased consciousness of the divine presence. This is developed in both systems by a continuous focusing on the divine as Person, in prayer and meditation. The individual quite literally surrenders him or herself to the Lord and in so doing accepts the divine as the new Self or Centre of consciousness. To the extent that the individual is integrated in the new Centre, to that extent is she or he 'realised'/'divinised'. And to that extent does she or he experience the bliss or joy that such integration manifests, and the 'equality of vision' expressed by terms such as the 'divine realm' or 'milieu' of the Lord.

In Rāmānuja and Teilhard, it is through a daily, continuous practice of the presence of the Lord that the human heart and mind are transformed, so that the individual's very perception alters. His or her awareness is clarified and purified, allowing for the development of a 'mystical' sense (Teilhard) of the way things are, a sense which functions as a refined form of seeing. Teilhard's description of the path of the mystic is of one who passes into an ever-increasing penetration by the divine presence. Rāmānuja teaches that the true nature of the self is de-limited knowledge or consciousness. But it is important to point out that neither Teilhard nor Rāmānuja accepts that complete release or salvation occurs before death. Only after death (or through death?) is full integration with the divine possible.[10]

WORLDMAKING

To speak of the divine body as a theistic paradigm[11] of a conscious cosmos is to raise fundamental issues regarding the interpretation of traditional doctrines and beliefs. In the time of the Early Church the 'hermeneut' was one who interpreted the message of the gospel for those who spoke another language. Perhaps today there is a need for hermeneuts to focus more specifically on the relationships between the languages of existing religious traditions and those of contemporary physics, for example, and transpersonal psychology.[12]

One area which would profit, perhaps, from such exploration, is contemporary Christology. What does it mean to speak of the 'woundedness'[13] and 'resurrection' of Christ's body in the context of a conscious cosmos? And what are the ecological implications of learning to 'see' Christ's aliveness expressed in the natural world about us? In the Postscript to her book *God's World, God's Body*, Grace Jantzen claims[14] that the model of the universe as God's body helps us to do justice to nature and to recognise the importance of conservation and ecology. But how do Christians translate this into their devotional and liturgical life, and how does it influence their life-styles?

One major implication of the divine body model concerns the relationship between different religious traditions. If the cosmos is an inter-related whole, then we are unquestionably linked to those of very different worldviews and spiritual practices from our own, and equally indeed to those who are atheistic in outlook. Is it possible, in this context, to look at any one religious tradition as being in sole possession of 'the truth', or indeed for a 'family' of traditions to be sole interpreters of human experience? The divine body could provide a valuable theistic paradigm to contribute towards continuing research into the nature of consciousness. This in itself may prove to be a useful area for inter-religious sharing and discussion which could broaden out into a common enquiry with scientists and those of non-religious worldviews.

In the context of inter-religious sharing, Bede Griffiths, in his book *A New Vision of Reality*, makes the point that nowhere until now has the Church evolved a theology which is based on 'the experience and the wisdom' of Asia and Africa.[15] This is not to deny the work of contemporary Christian theologians but rather to suggest that even they, in their initiation into Christian life, are steeped in a worldview based on Greek or European thought. If this is to change, then it is the symbolic bases of eastern religious traditions which need to be encountered and appropriated. And this, if done with integrity, could lead to the evolution of new forms of Christianity altogether. Maurice Wiles once suggested that there may come a time when distinctively Buddhistic or Islamic forms of Christian theology, for example, may emerge: in other words, forms in which insights central to those traditions – 'and only fully accessible and expressed within these faiths' – will have moulded Christian belief. This would, he thought, illuminate and deepen aspects of belief, imperfectly realised in existing forms of Christian theology.[16] If such a mutual process of revisioning and enriching religious life is undertaken with commitment, the outcome could be of major significance, not just for Christianity, but for many people worldwide who are seeking to integrate the truths they are learning from different religious sources.

If a position of 'integrational wholeness' is appropriated, whether in the context of a religious or non-religious worldview, a methodology based on an understanding of the relationship between the whole and the part, the cosmos and the individual, needs to be created. If the disciplines of contemporary psychology and ethics are taking on board emerging theories of the nature of consciousness,[17] what about disciplines involved in the study of theology and religion? Could it be that here too, a new methodology will emerge in which the whole is addressed as the key to the local and particular?

The question arises, 'How authentic is it to study something from a perspective of wholeness if such a perspective is not fully appropriated as one's own?' This relates to Weber's question as to how humankind can express and embody this vision in its daily life.[18] The appropriate response to both of these questions is, perhaps, that the answer lies in the doing. Only through acting as if there is an inherent unifying pattern to our world can we create tools for studying and living within it. By the very process of living and working from an integrational perspective we are contributing to the 'enwholing' of the cosmos.

Worldmaking as we know it always starts from worlds already on hand: the making is really a re-making. (Nelson Goodman)

APPENDIX I

Composition and publication dates of papers by Teilhard de Chardin cited in this work

Title	Composition date	Publication date
'L'Atomisme de l'esprit: un essai pour comprendre la structure de l'étoffe de l'univers'	1941	1963
'La Centrologie'	1944	1963
'Le Christ dans la matière'	1916	1961
'Le Christique'	1955	1976
'Le Cœur de la matière'	1950	1976
'Comment je vois'	1948	1973
'L'Elément universel'	1919	1956
'L'Energie humaine'	1937	1962
'En quoi consiste le corps humain?'	[1919]	1965
'L'Esprit de la terre'	1931	1962
'Esquisse d'un univers personnel'	1936	1962
'L'Etoffe de l'univers'	1953	1963
'La Foi qui opère'	1918	1956
'Forma Christi'	1918	1956
'Introduction à la Vie chrétienne	1944	1965
'Ma position intellectuelle'	1948	1955
'La Messe sur le monde'	1923	1961
'Le Milieu divin'	1926–7	1957
'Le Milieu mystique'	1917	1956
'Mon univers'	1918	1956
'Mon univers'	1924	1965
'Note sur l'élément universel du monde'	1918	1956
'Panthéisme et christianisme'	1923	1969
'Le Phénomène spirituel'	1937	1962
'Le Prêtre'	1918	1956
'La Puissance spirituelle de la matière'	1919	1961
'Quelques remarques "pour y voir clair" sur l'essence du sentiment mystique'	1951	1976
'Super-humanité, super-Christ, super-charité'	1943	1965
'L'Union créatrice'	1917	1956
'La Vie cosmique'	1916	1965

APPENDIX II

Teilhard de Chardin on the Mass

For Teilhard, the Mass is a deeply symbolic ritual in which the individual offers him or herself, through the sacramental elements, to become part of the consecrated body of Christ. He believes that she or he participates through this act in the very life and spirit (which, of course, he refers to in terms of consciousness) of the Lord. His cosmic understanding of the process of the Mass is most clearly set forth in his 'La Messe sur le monde', but he refers to it at intervals throughout his writings. One passage in 'Mon univers' clearly explains how he views the relationship between the consecration of the host and the consecration of the world:

> There is but one Host, ever growing greater in the hands of a long succession of priests – the Host of bread, I mean, [which] is continually being encircled more closely by another, infinitely larger, Host, which is nothing less than the universe itself – the universe gradually being absorbed by the universal element. Thus when the phrase 'Hoc est Corpus Meum' is pronounced, 'hoc' means 'primario' the bread; but 'secundario', in a second phase occurring in nature, the matter of the sacrament of the world, throughout which there spreads, so to complete itself, the superhuman presence of the universal Christ. (*SC*, p. 65 (*Oeuvres* 9, pp. 93–4))

The structure of the Mass can be viewed in the context of the mandala[1] structure of the divine body. The host represents, in this instance, the *bindu* or central point of the mandala. The individual is understood to appropriate the mind or consciousness of Christ through moving towards and identifying with the body of Christ in the form of the host. In Teilhard's view this means integrating with the 'heart' of the world.

[1] See Eric Thacker, 'Teilhard in Ordos: a Mandala Mass', *CR* 299 (Christmas 1977), 15–19.

Glossary of Indian terms

ācārya, spiritual guide or teacher (especially one who invests the student with the sacrificial thread, and instructs him in the *Vedas* and religious practices)

acit, without consciousness or knowledge

ādhāra, support

ādheya, supported

advaita, non-dualism; the school of *Vedānta* started by Śaṃkara

āgama, traditional collection of sacred doctrines and precepts, in particular a *tantra* or work concerning religious practices related to Śiva and Śakti

aṃśa, part; share

aṃśin, whole; having a share

antaryāmin, inner Ruler; Brahman as the inner controller or guide of all things and selves

ātman (derived from *an*, 'to breathe'; *at*, 'to move'; *va*, 'to blow'), the self

bhakti, loving devotion

bhakti-yoga, the discipline or path of *bhakti* leading to release (for Rāmānuja this incorporates *karman* (works) and *jñāna* (spiritual knowledge))

bhūman, fullness; abundance

brahman, term for the divine which Rāmānuja understands to be personal (*nirguṇa brahman*, 'unmanifest brahman', *saguṇa brahman*, 'manifest brahman')

brahmajñāna, knowledge of Brahman

brāhmaṇas, explanations of sacred knowledge, especially for the use of brahmins; a class of works comprising part of Vedic knowledge

cit, to be conscious; appear: shine

darśana, seeing, audience: view, philosophical system
dharma (literally 'that which is established'), law; prescribed duty; right
divya rūpa, divine form; celestial figure

guṇa, a quality associated with one of the five elements; a characteristic of living things; quality of the divine

jīvātman, the living or personal self

kṣetra, field; the body considered as the field of the indwelling self
kṣetrajña, the knower, the conscious principle of the body

mokṣa, release, liberation, setting free

niyāmya, controlled
niyantṛ, controller

paramātman, Supreme Self
prakāra, mode
prakārin, mode-possessor
prakṛti, original or primary substance
puruṣa, person; the primaeval man as source of the universe; the personal, animating principle in living beings
puruṣottama, the Highest Person, the Supreme Person

ṛṣi, seer, sage; one of the inspired persons to whom the Vedic hymns were revealed
rūpa, outward form, figure, shape or colour

ṣaḍguṇas, the six qualities of the Lord (knowledge, strength, sovereignty, valour, power and splendour)
sādhana, spiritual means of attaining a goal
sāmānādhikaraṇya, theory of co-ordinate predication
sāṃkhya, one of the great divisions of Hindu philosophy (ascribed to the sage Kapila), so called either from 'discriminating' or 'reckoning up'
śarīra-śarīrī-bhāva, body–embodied-self doctrine
sat, being
satkāryavāda, the theory that the effect is existent in the cause
śeṣa, servant; owned; accessory
śeṣin, master; owner; principal
śiva, name of the Supreme for those who worship him (*śaivites*); name of the destroying and recreating deity, sometimes called 'the auspicious One', and linked with Brahmā and Viṣṇu

smṛti (literally 'that which is remembered'), a non-Vedic traditional religious work

śruti (literally 'that which is heard'), the revealed texts of the *Vedas*

svabhāva, inherent nature; manifest nature

svarūpa, essential form; proper form

upāsana, worship through loving meditation; devotional meditation

upāya, means

upeya, goal

vedānta (literally 'the end of the *Vedas*') name of one of the main divisions of Hindu philosophy, being concerned either with teaching the complete *Vedas* or explaining the *Upaniṣads* which come at the end of the *Vedas*

vedas, sacred knowledge; name of celebrated works which constitute the revealed (*śruti*) basis of a pre-Hindu religious tradition in India

vibhūti, divine realm; manifestation of divine glory and rule

viśiṣṭādvaita, differentiated or qualified non-dualism; the school of *Vedānta* started by Rāmānuja

viṣṇu, name of the Supreme for those who worship him (*vaiṣṇavites*); name of one of the principal deities and known as 'the preserver', alongside Śiva and Brahmā

Notes

INTRODUCTION

1 I am indebted to Ninian Smart's approach to the study of religion. An introduction to this is to be found in his *Worldviews: Crosscultural Explorations of Human Beliefs* (New York: Charles Scribner's Sons, 1983).

2 For Rāmānuja and Christianity, see A. J. Appasamy, 'Christological Reconstruction and Rāmānuja's Philosophy', *International Review of Missions* 41 (1952), 170–6; and C. Duraisingh, 'Towards an Indian–Christian Theology: Rāmānuja's Significance', Ph.D. dissertation, Harvard University, 1979.

3 The reader is referred to Ursula King's excellent summary of Teilhard's own comparison of his and Rāmānuja's positions. See Ursula King, *Towards a New Mysticism: Teilhard de Chardin and Eastern Religions* (London: Collins, 1980), pp. 243–5. It is interesting to learn from Teilhard's notes that he was aware of Rāmānuja's concern to present the world as 'real' (in contradistinction to Śaṃkara), and that he did this by regarding it as within God. He remarks that this is a more 'static' view than his own, and without 'centre-complexity' (p. 244).

4 Patrick Sherry, in his book *Religion: Truth and Language Games* (London: Macmillan Press, 1977), speaks of religious doctrine as a kind of 'grammar' needing to be 'located' in its historical evolution, within the theological system, for example, in which it has developed, and 'related' to the religious way of life which gave it birth.

5 Experiences 'arise within an already existing tradition and receive their fundamental shape and interpretation from that tradition ... [Descriptions of them] are not absolutely fixed and unalterable in meaning, but they do bring with them a rich texture of meaning from the past,' Maurice Wiles, *The Remaking of Christian Doctrine* (London: SCM Press, 1974), p. 84.

6 I am deliberately referring to the worldviews of Teilhard de Chardin and Rāmānuja as 'theological', because both have faith in *theos*. In the West, theology is usually understood in Christian terms, but religious reflection is done everywhere, and often within the context of belief in the divine (whatever name is given for that); hence theology is 'done' all over the globe by people of different religious traditions. Rāmānuja,

for example, refers to Brahman consistently as 'the Highest Person', and his entire philosophical enterprise is devoted to 'knowing Brahman'.

7 Kurt Goldammer says, 'We attempt to expound the symbol through its own methodology.' 'Is there a Method of Symbol Research?', in *Science of Religion: Studies in Methodology*, ed. L. Honko (The Hague: Mouton, 1979), p. 503.

8 For his theological aims see *CE*, p. 176 (*Oeuvres* 10, p. 206).

9 To avoid problems of reference, the terms 'God' and 'Brahman' are used throughout to stand for the Christian and Hindu conceptualisations of the divine.

10 Rāmānuja, *Vedārthasaṅgraha*, trans. S. S. Raghavachar (Mysore: Śrī Ramakrishna Ashrama, 1978), p. 2.

11 'Le Prêtre' (1918), in *WTW*, p. 219 (*Oeuvres* 12, p. 328).

12 'A la base de mon attitude' (1948), in *HM*, pp. 147–8 (*Oeuvres* 13, pp. 181–2).

13 e.g. Introduction, *MD*, p. 46 (*Oeuvres* 4, p. 17).

14 'Le Prêtre'. The translation is my own (*Oeuvres* 12, p. 329).

15 The term 'milieu' will remain untranslated throughout since it has become part of English usage. From the Latin *medius* ('medium') and French *lieu* ('place'), it has the associations of middle, medium and surroundings. *Compact Edition of the Oxford Dictionary* (Oxford: Oxford University Press, 1979 edn), 1, p. 1974.

16 See *Rule of Metaphor: Multi-Disciplinary Studies of the Creation of Meaning in Language*, trans. R. Czerny (Toronto and Buffalo: University of Toronto Press, 1977), and *Hermeneutics and the Human Sciences*, ed. and trans. J. B. Thompson (Cambridge: Cambridge University Press, 1981).

17 M. Eliade, *The Two and the One* (London: Harvill Press; New York: Harper & Row, 1965), p. 14.

18 Ninian Smart, 'The Scientific Study of Religion in its Plurality', in *Contemporary Approaches to the Study of Religion* 1, ed. Frank Whaling, Religion and Reason 27 (Berlin: Mouton, 1984), pp. 369–70.

19 Ninian Smart adapts the American Indian proverb, 'Never judge a man till you have walked a mile in his moccasins' to 'Never describe a man until you have walked a mile in his moccasins', for the student of Religious Studies. *Contemporary Approaches to the Study of Religion* 1, p. 369.

20 Ibid., p. 378.

21 Eliade, when discussing the methodology of working with symbols, refers to a stage of 'reconstituting' the symbolic significance of religious facts. It is not a question of reducing the material to a common denominator, but a process of integration, he explains. The comparison and contrasting of two expressions of a symbol are not to 'reduce them to a single, pre-existent expression, but in order to discover the process by which a structure is capable of enriching its meanings'. *The Two and the One*, p. 201.

22 Goldammer, 'Is there a Method of Symbol Research?', p. 498.

23 Ibid.

24 e.g. Ernst Cassirer, *The Philosophy of Symbolic Forms* (New Haven: Yale University Press, 1953–7), I–III and *Language and Myth* (New York: Dover, 1953); Suzanne Langer, *Philosophy in a New Key: a Study in the Symbolism of Reason, Rite and Art* (Cambridge, Mass.: Harvard University Press, 1960).

25 Sherry, *Religion: Truth and Language Games*, p. 112.

1 THE BACKGROUND TO THE DIVINE BODY IN TEILHARD DE CHARDIN

1 By this I mean his perception and knowledge of the body of Christ. It would appear from certain writings that these were derived in part from visions or meditative states. See 'La Messe sur le monde', in *HU*, pp. 39–55 (*Hymne de l'univers* (Paris: Editions du Seuil, 1961), pp. 17–37). For Teilhard as visionary, see Georges Crespy, 'L'Intention théologique de Teilhard de Chardin', in *Le Christ cosmique de Teilhard de Chardin*, ed. Attila Szekeres (Paris: Editions du Seuil, 1969), pp. 305–6.

2 It has been suggested that Teilhard derived his appreciation of St Paul from Ferdinand Prat's *The Theology of St. Paul*: C. E. Raven, *Teilhard de Chardin: Scientist and Seer* (London: Collins, 1962), p. 46, quoted in J. A. Lyons, *The Cosmic Christ in Origen and Teilhard de Chardin: a Comparative Study* (Oxford: Oxford University Press, 1982), p. 43.

3 Lyons, *The Cosmic Christ in Origen and Teilhard de Chardin*, p. 149.

4 'Chute, rédemption et géocentrie', in *CE*, p. 44 (*Oeuvres* 10, p. 57).

5 Ibid.

6 Lyons has demonstrated that Teilhard was probably well aware of contemporary references to cosmic aspects of the incarnation by German and English theologians, and of J. R. Illingworth's evolutionary views (*The Cosmic Christ in Origen and Teilhard de Chardin*, pp. 25–7; 43–4). He was not alone in valuing this verse, since Maurice Blondel, Pierre Rousselot and Edouard Le Roy found it significant as well (ibid., pp. 161–7; 151–3; 176–7).

7 Colossians 1:16–20 (RSV).

8 See 'L'Union créatrice', in *WTW*, pp. 151–76 (*Oeuvres* 12, pp. 193–224).

9 Ibid., p. 174 (p. 222).

10 In 'Le Dieu de l'evolution' (1953), Teilhard writes: 'In a universe in which we can no longer seriously entertain the idea that thought is an exclusively terrestrial phenomenon, Christ must no longer be *constitutionally* restricted in his operation to a mere "redemption" of our planet... Christ, as still presented to the world by classical theology, is both too confined (localized) astronomically, and evolutively too extrinsic, to be able to "cephalize" the universe as we now see it.' *CE*, pp. 241–2 (*Oeuvres* 10, p. 290). Cf. *SC*, pp. 221–3 (*Oeuvres* 9, pp. 291–3).

11 Notes taken during C. F. D. Moule's lectures on Pauline Christology at the Divinity School, University of Cambridge (1972–3). See his *Origin*

of Christology (Cambridge: Cambridge University Press, 1977), pp. 69–89.

12 Colossians 2:9 (cf. Ephesians 1:23, 3:16–19).

13 We shall see in Chapter 4 how Teilhard uses the term 'form' (*morphē*) to denote Christ's role in the world, which is perhaps a more concrete term than 'image'.

14 J. A. T. Robinson translates *eis tēn eleutherian* as 'into' the freedom. *The Body: a Study in Pauline Theology* (London: SCM Press, 1952), p. 83.

15 Romans 8:19–23 (the translation is my own).

16 Cf. Philippians 3.21: '[He] will change our body of humiliation, conforming [*summorphon*] it to his body of glory.' (The translation is my own.)

17 John 14–15.

18 *Katalabesthai* can also be translated as 'perceive'.

19 Ephesians 3:14–19 (RSV).

20 *SC*, pp. 55–6 (*Oeuvres* 9, pp. 83–4).

21 Maurice Blondel referred to this 'realism' in a letter to Auguste Valensin (1919): 'It is a real joy for me to find that [Teilhard de Chardin] has a sense of total realism, of reintegration, and of the sanctification of the universe as it undergoes divinization *per gradus debitos*. This sense of realism is rare among Catholics, and is rarely sustained with the motivation and justification he brings to bear.' *Pierre Teilhard de Chardin, Maurice Blondel: Correspondence* (New York: Herder & Herder, 1967), p. 38; (*Blondel et Teilhard de Chardin: Correspondance* (Paris: Beauchesne, 1965), p. 35).

22 Three months before his death, Teilhard wrote in a letter to a friend, 'We now need a new Nicaea to define the cosmic aspect of the Incarnation.' Letter to Bruno Solages, *Lettres intimes de Teilhard de Chardin à Auguste Valensin, Bruno Solages et Henri de Lubac 1910–1955*, introduction and notes by Henri de Lubac (Paris: Aubier Montaigne, 1972), p. 459.

23 Robert Hale, in his book *Christ and the Universe: Teilhard de Chardin and the Cosmos* (Chicago: Franciscan Herald Press, 1972), refers to Origen's vision of the universe as an organism '"informed", as it were, by God himself' (p. 43).

24 Origen, *On First Principles*, II.1.3, quoted in Robert Hale, *Christ and the Universe*, pp. 43–4.

25 Lyons, *The Cosmic Christ in Origen and Teilhard de Chardin*, pp. 105–45.

26 *Schol. in Apoc.* 7, quoted ibid., pp. 130–1.

27 *The Cosmic Christ in Origen and Teilhard de Chardin*, p. 212.

28 Ibid. For a detailed comparison between Teilhard de Chardin and Origen, see especially pp. 85–7; 211–19.

29 See Emile Mersch, *The Whole Christ: the Historical Development of the Doctrine of the Mystical Body in Scripture and Tradition*, trans. J. R. Kelly (London: Dennis Dobson, 1938), pp. 227–47.

30 By deification Irenaeus does not mean that man becomes God, but rather that he is 'quickened by God's energies'.

31 Irenaeus, *Demonstration*, 4.38, quoted (by ed.) in 'Réflexions sur la probabilité scientifique et les conséquences religieuses d'un ultra-humain', in *AE*, p. 279 (*Oeuvres* 7, p. 290).
32 *Journal of Ecumenical Studies* 13 (Philadelphia, 1976), 86.
33 Irenaeus, 'Against Heresies', in *The Anti-Nicene Fathers* I, ed. Alexander Roberts and James Donaldson (Grand Rapids: W. B. Eerdmans, 1985), 2.14.2, 376, quoted in Dai Sil Kim, 'Irenaeus of Lyons and Teilhard de Chardin: a Comparative Study of "Recapitulation" and "Omega"', *Journal of Ecumenical Studies* 13 (Philadelphia, 1976), 70.
34 Athanasius, *Contra Arianos*, II.48; 60, quoted in Roderick Strange, *Newman and the Gospel of Christ*, Oxford Theological Monographs (Oxford: Oxford University Press, 1981), p. 136.
35 Ibid., ii.70 (*Newman and the Gospel of Christ*, p. 123).
36 Trans. J. C. O'Mahony (London: Sheed & Ward, 1935).
37 Thomas Aquinas, *Summa theologiae* 1a.xii.12. See *St. Thomas Aquinas: Philosophical Texts*, ed. and trans. Thomas Gilby (London: Oxford University Press, 1951), p. 87.
38 Published in 1908.
39 Introduction to *The Intellectualism of St. Thomas*, pp. 1–14.
40 Cf. Aquinas' theory that knowing something means being 'in-formed': to know what a horse is, for example, is to have the form of a horse in one's mind. Teilhard's description of Christ's presence to human consciousness as personal source, centre and goal, enabling individuals to come to know God (i.e. 'see' the divine milieu), is not dissimilar.
41 *Journal*, vol. 1 (Librairie Arthème Fayard, 1975), 17 July 1916, p. 90.
42 Ibid., 4 February 1916 (p. 28); 23 February 1916 (p. 41).
43 Ibid., p. 41.
44 Letter to Victor Fontoynont, 15 March 1916, quoted in Henri de Lubac, *The Religion of Teilhard de Chardin* (London: Collins, 1967), p. 243.
45 Ibid. For another reference to the *Apologia* see letter to Marguerite Teillard-Chambon, 2 February 1916, in *MM*, p. 93 (*Génèse d'une pensée: Lettres (1914–1919)* (Paris: Bernard Grasset, 1961), p. 118). See also pp. 167; 215 (pp. 114, 145).
46 *The Mystery of Newman*, trans. H. C. Corrance, with Introduction by Rev. George Tyrrell (London: Williams & Norgate, 1907).
47 This movement stemmed in theological circles from Augustinian thought. It appeared in seventeenth-century French spirituality, and later in nineteenth-century English thinkers such as Coleridge and Newman. See Gabriel Daly, *Transcendence and Immanence: a Study in Catholic Modernism and Integralism* (Oxford: Clarendon Press, 1980), p. 24. Teilhard's contact with seventeenth-century French thought would have been indirectly through Henri Bremond's studies of seventeenth-century spirituality and through Germain Foch's *La Vie intérieure* (6th edn, Paris and Lyons: Librairie Catholique Emmanuel Vitte, 1919). See *LLZ*, p. 56 (Teilhard de Chardin, *Lettres à Léontine Zanta* (Paris: Desclée de Brouwer, 1965), p. 61). In Foch, the *fait intérieure* tradition

is expressed in language of *la divinisation* of the individual, which is interesting in the light of Teilhard's use of the term. In the Foreword to *La Vie intérieure*, he speaks of St Paul as the best teacher on 'ce grand mystère de la divinisation du chrétien par la grâce'.

48 *Transcendence and Immanence*, p. 61.

49 J. A. Lyons claims that Teilhard's concept of doctrinal synthesis 'undoubtedly depends on Newman's *Essay on the Development of Christian Doctrine*'. *The Cosmic Christ in Origen and Teilhard de Chardin*, p. 81.

50 Pp. 125–6.

51 *Parochial and Plain Sermons* 8, p. 253, quoted in Strange, *Newman and the Gospel of Christ*, p. 126.

52 Letter to Samuel Wilberforce, 29 January 1835, quoted in Strange, *Newman and the Gospel of Christ*, p. 140.

53 See above, p. 14.

54 Although we know that his friend Auguste Valensin had a good knowledge of German theology.

55 See below, pp. 22–4.

56 'Despite their objections to Protestant liberalism [the Modernists'] viewpoint was in large measure determined by the criticism and religious philosophy of the Protestant *avant garde* of their day.' Bernard Reardon, 'Roman Catholic Modernism', in Ninian Smart, John Clayton, Stephen Katz and Patrick Sherry (eds.), *Nineteenth Century Religious Thought in the West* (Cambridge: Cambridge University Press, 1985), p. 171.

57 Alfred Fawkes refers to Rothe as 'one of the greatest of German theologians': *Studies in Modernism* (London: Smith, 1913), p. 274. E. Schott describes him as perhaps the most original among theologians of mediation: 'Richard Rothe', in *Die Religion in Geschichte Gegenwart* III (3rd edn, Tübingen: J. C. B. Mohr, 1961), p. 1197.

58 Richard Rothe, *Dogmatik* II (Heidelberg, 1870), p. 120. (The translation is my own.)

59 See Claude Welch, *God and Incarnation in Mid-Nineteenth Century German Theology* (Oxford: Oxford University Press, 1965), p. 242. Also Anne Hunt, 'Rothe's Christology: a Study of "Sermons for the Christian Year"', unpublished BA dissertation, University of Cambridge, 1975.

60 Richard Rothe, *Sermons for the Christian Year*, trans. W. Clarke (Edinburgh, 1877), p. 3.

61 In addition to Auguste Valensin, he might have come across the idea through Blondel (who would be familiar with it) or P. T. Forsyth, in whose *Person and Place of Jesus Christ* (London: Hodder & Stoughton, 1909) he openly acknowledges a debt to Rothe (p. viii).

62 See Teilhard de Chardin, 'Christology and Evolution', in *CE*, p. 87 (*Oeuvres* 10, p. 106).

63 The name was given by critics at the turn of the century to a general movement within the Roman Catholic Church. See *Au Cœur de la Crise moderniste: le dossier inédit d'une controverse: lettres de Maurice Blondel, H.*

Bremond, Fr. von Hügel, Alfred Loisy, Fernand Mourret, J. Wehrlé..., ed. René Marlé, SJ (Paris: Aubier, Editions Montaigne, 1960).

64 In his autobiographical introduction to *A Variety of Catholic Modernists*, Alex Vidler refers to a conversation he had with Maude Petre in 1941 in which she said that Modernism was still at work in the Church though not under that name, and instanced the writings of Teilhard de Chardin: *The Sarum Lectures in the University of Oxford for the year 1968–1969* (Cambridge: Cambridge University Press, 1970), p. 11.

65 Teilhard de Chardin corresponded with Maurice Blondel, who, although avowedly uninvolved in the movement, nevertheless expressed, in his theory of 'action', an understanding of Christian doctrine in terms of the totality of human experience (including its inner dimension). He was, as we shall see, influenced by Blondel's 'panchristisme', and may have been introduced to Blondel's ideas as early as 1900 through Auguste Valensin (Lyons, *The Cosmic Christ in Origen and Teilhard de Chardin*, p. 159). Teilhard de Chardin also came to know Edouard Le Roy, a follower of Henri Bergson and religious pragmatist, whose *Dogme et critique* was put on the Index in 1907. Their exchange of ideas led to Le Roy's confession that he was no longer sure which ideas were his own and which were derived from Teilhard (Vidler, *A Variety of Catholic Modernists*, p. 93).

66 *Nineteenth Century Religious Thought in the West*, ed. Smart *et al.*, p. 141.

67 Italian representatives are excluded here.

68 Reardon, 'Roman Catholic Modernism', in Smart *et al.* (eds), *Nineteenth Century Religious Thought*, p. 152.

69 Ibid., p. 163.

70 *Through Scylla and Charybdis: Or, the Old Theology and the New* (London, 1907), p. 305, quoted by Gabriel Daly, OSA, in *Transcendence and Immanence*, p. 159.

71 Tyrrell, pp. 374f., quoted in Daly, p. 151.

72 *Encyclical Letter 'Pascendi Gregis' of Our Most Holy Lord Pius X by Divine Providence Pope on the Doctrines of the Modernists* (London, 1907).

73 Ostensibly due to a paper given at Enghien on 'Three Possible Representations of "Original Sin"'.

74 At the beginning of her book *Bergson et Teilhard de Chardin*, Madeleine Barthélemy-Madaule quotes Teilhard's own words: 'What you tell me about Bergson has moved me deeply. I am praying for this amazingly gifted man whom I revere as a kind of saint.' Lettre de Teilhard, 3 April 1930 (Paris: Editions du Seuil, 1963).

75 *HM*, p. 25 (*Oeuvres* 13, p. 33).

76 Henri Bergson, *Creative Evolution*, trans. A. Mitchell (London: Macmillan, 1911), p. 285.

77 Ibid., pp. 29; 192; 275.

78 I.e. from 1902 to 1905; 1908 to 1909; 1913 to 1914.

79 J. A. Lyons states that in what they say about the body of Christ, Rousselot and Teilhard 'adopt virtually identical positions' (*The Cosmic Christ in Origen and Teilhard de Chardin*, p. 154).

80 G. A. McCool, *Catholic Theology in the Nineteenth Century: the Quest for a Unitary Method* (New York: Seabury Press, 1977), p. 250. The 'intuitive mind' is in contradistinction to the *ratio* or 'discursive intellect'.

81 Pierre Rousselot, Preface to *Pour l'histoire du problème de l'amour au Moyen Age* (Münster: Druck und Verlag der Aschendorffschen Buchhandlung, 1908), p. 1. The translation is my own. For further study of Rousselot's thought, see his controversial paper 'Les Yeux de la foi', in *Recherches de science religieuse* 1 (1910), pp. 241–59; 444–75. Also *Christus: manuel d'histoire des religions*, ed. J. Huby (Paris: Beauchesne, 1912), to which Rousselot contributed.

82 Appendix 1 in de Lubac, *The Religion of Teilhard de Chardin*, pp. 244–5.

83 For a study of Blondel's German influences see J. J. McNeill SJ, *The Blondelian Synthesis: a Study of the Influence of German Philosophical Sources on the Formation of Blondel's Method and Thought* (Leiden: E. J. Brill, 1966).

84 J. M. Somerville, 'Blondel, Maurice', in *New Catholic Encyclopedia* II (1967), p. 617. See also his book, *Total Commitment: Blondel's 'L'Action'* (Washington: Corpus Books, 1968).

85 This was his doctoral thesis, presented in 1893, which later became the basis for part of his trilogy (published in two volumes between 1934 and 1937) entitled *La Pensée*, *L'Etre* and *L'Action*. To this two subsequent volumes were added in 1944 and 1946: *La Philosophie* and *L'Esprit chrétien*. For the rewritten form of his thesis, see *L'Action*, 2 vols. (Paris: Presses Universitaires de France, 1936–7; reprinted 1949–63); and *Action: Essay on a Criticism of Life and a Science of Practice* (Notre Dame, Ind.: University of Notre Dame Press, 1984). See also '*The Letter on Apologetics*' and '*History and Dogma*', trans. A. Dru and I. Trethowan (London: Harvill Press, 1964).

86 *L'Action*, pp. 467–70; trans. J. C. Guinness in J. Lacroix, *Maurice Blondel: an Introduction to the Man and his Philosophy* (London and New York: Sheed & Ward, 1968), pp. 114ff. Blondel believed it is the dialectic of will and action which constitutes the fundamental character of life as we know it: both will as that which determines what shall be done, *la volonté voulante*, and will expressing an underlying intention seeking fulfilment, *la volonté voulue*. The realisation of the latter comes, he argues, through choosing to share in what may be termed the 'divine' will. See *La Philosophie et l'esprit chrétien* 1, 30–1; trans. Guinness in Lacroix, *Maurice Blondel*, pp. 142ff.

87 In a letter of 1712, responding to the question of how the Catholic doctrine of transubstantiation could be stated in terms of his philosophy, Leibniz explained that the monads comprising the bread need not be envisaged as being removed through transubstantiation: the *vinculum substantiale* of the Body of Christ is applied to those monads formerly united by the substantial bond of the bread, and the phenomena of bread and wine remain. F. Copleston, *A History of Philosophy* IV (London: Burns & Oates, 1965), p. 315.

88 Maurice Blondel, *Une énigme historique: le 'vinculum substantiale' d'après Leibnitz et l'ébauche d'un réalisme supérieur* (Paris: Beauchesne, 1930), pp.

105–6, quoted by Lyons, *The Cosmic Christ in Origen and Teilhard de Chardin*, pp. 162–3.

89 See *MD*, pp. 123–6 (*Oeuvres* 4, pp. 138–40). Cf. 'La Messe sur le monde', in *HU*, pp. 19–38 (*Hymne de l'univers*, pp. 17–37). In this I disagree with J. A. Lyons' argument that Blondel's starting-point is 'a consideration of sacramental metaphysics' and Teilhard's 'a sense of cosmic unity' (*The Cosmic Christ in Origen and Teilhard de Chardin*, p. 163). Teilhard's main concern throughout is sacramental.

90 *MD*, p. 122 (*Oeuvres* 4, pp. 135–6). For Christ's power of attraction see 'Forma Christi', in *WTW*, pp. 254–6 (*Oeuvres* 12, pp. 370–2).

91 See Lyons, *The Cosmic Christ in Origen and Teilhard de Chardin*, p. 41 n. 172.

92 *Correspondence*, pp. 26–7 (*Blondel et Teilhard de Chardin*, pp. 23–5).

93 *Correspondence*, p. 25 (*Blondel et Teilhard de Chardin*, p. 23).

94 I.e. treatment of God's transcendence in terms of the physical universe.

95 We know more, perhaps, of what Maurice Blondel thought of some of Teilhard de Chardin's ideas than vice versa, from their published *Correspondence*.

96 See 'Mon univers' (1924), in *SC*, pp. 58–9 (*Oeuvres* 9, p. 87).

97 I.e. a doctrine which refers all phenomena of the universe to physical or material forces.

98 *Correspondence*, p. 25 (*Blondel et Teilhard de Chardin*, p. 24).

99 'Mon univers', in *SC*, p. 59 (*Oeuvres* 9, p. 87). See also 'Panthéisme et Christianisme', in *CE*, pp. 56–75 (*Oeuvres* 10, pp. 73–91).

100 'Mon univers', in *SC*, p. 74 (*Oeuvres* 9, pp. 102–3).

101 'Mon univers', in *SC*, p. 74 (*Oeuvres* 9, pp. 102–3).

2 THE BACKGROUND TO THE DIVINE BODY IN RĀMĀNUJA

1 Śrīvaiṣṇavites worship Viṣṇu and his consort, Śrī.

2 As opposed to *smṛti* ('that which is remembered'), which derives its authority from the *śruti* it supports.

3 Swami Ramakrishnananda, *Life of Śrī Rāmānuja* (Madras: Śrī Ramakrishna Math, 1977), p. 257. Bodhayana is believed to be the author of a commentary, no longer extant, on the *Brahma-sūtras* among other *vṛttis* (commentaries). Tanka wrote the *vākya* (speech or argument) referred to by Rāmānuja in his *Vedārthasaṃgraha* (*VS*) and *Śrībhāṣya* (*SB*), as well as an earlier commentary on the *Brahma-sūtras*. The other references are to the author of *Dramidabhāṣya*, and to three followers (Gudadeva, Kapardi and Bharuci) of the *Cārvāka* or Materialist school. See Rāmānuja, *VS*, trans. Raghavachar (henceforth *VS*(R)), para. 130, p. 102; *VS*, ed. and trans. J. A. B. van Buitenen, Deccan College Monograph (Poona: Deccan College Postgraduate and Research Institute, 1956) (henceforth *VS*(VB)), para. 93, p. 251.

4 Kōil Oḷugu (Śrīrangam temple record).

5 Namely, his *Śrībhāṣya* and *Gītābhāṣya* (*GB*).

6 See the *Vedānta-dīpa* and *Vedānta-sāra*, which are two smaller commentaries on the *Brahma-sūtras*; the *Gadyatraya* (devotional songs) and *Nityagrantha* (manual for worship).

7 For an outline of the main philosophical schools concerned, see E. J. Lott, *God and the Universe in the Vedāntic Theology of Rāmānuja: a Study in his use of the Self–Body Analogy* (Madras: Rāmānuja Research Society, 1976). They include Śaṃkara's *Advaita*, Bhāskara's *Bhedābheda*, *Pūrva-mīmāṃsā*, *Sāṃkhya* and *Nyāya-vaiśeṣika*.

8 J. B. Carman, *The Theology of Rāmānuja: an Essay in Interreligious Understanding* (New Haven and London: Yale University Press, 1974), p. 28.

9 See Rāmānuja, *VS*(R), para. 47, p. 41.

10 *Ṛg-Veda*, 10.90, *The Hymns of the Ṛgveda* II, 4th edn, trans. and with a popular commentary by R. T. H. Griffith, The Chowkhamba Sanskrit Studies, vol. 35 (Varanasi: Chowkhamba Sanskrit Series Office, 1963), p. 517. For the Sanskrit text, see *Original Sanskrit Texts on the Origin and History of the People of India, their Religion and Institutions* V, collected and trans. J. Muir (London, 1874; 3rd edn reprint, Amsterdam: Oriental Press, 1967), pp. 367–8. (Rāmānuja refers to the *Ṛg-veda* ten times in his *Śrībhāṣya* and five times in his *Gītābhāṣya*.)

11 For the 'enigmatic' nature of the metaphors in the *Ṛg-veda*, see Willard Johnson, *Poetry and Speculation of the Ṛg Veda* (Berkeley and London: University of California Press, 1980). His argument is that these 'enigmatizing images' lead to an 'awakening of insight'.

12 *Ṛg-veda*, 10.130.

13 Ibid., 10.131.

14 In chapter 5, *antaryāmin* is actually discussed in terms of a chariot simile.

15 *Śatapatha-brāhmaṇa in Mādhyandina-śākhā with extracts from the commentaries of Sāyaṇa, Harisvāmin and Dvivedaganga*, ed. A. Weber (Varanasi: Chowkhamba Sanskrit Series Office, 1964), p. 294; here trans. Julius Eggeling, Sacred Books of the East 43, Part 4 (Clarendon Press, 1897; reprinted 2nd edn, Delhi: Motilal Banarsidass, 1966), p. 366.

16 Eggeling translation, pp. 367–8.

17 Cf. *Atharva-veda*, 10, 28–31 in J. Muir, *Original Sanskrit Texts* V, pp. 376–7 (where *puruṣa* is depicted as the *pur* (city) of Brahmā, containing 'a golden receptacle, celestial, invested with light'); also the *Vajasaneyi Saṃhitā*, 31.18, p. 373 ('I know this great *Puruṣa*, resplendent as the sun, above the darkness').

18 The relationship between *puruṣa* and the individual self is portrayed in the *Śatapatha-brāhmaṇa* in terms of sacrifice, and that which is offered is identified with that to which the offering is made. This, I suggest, anticipates Rāmānuja's theory of co-ordinate predication in which individuals are ultimately shown to denote Brahman. See *Śatapatha-brāhmaṇa*, 10: 6.2.1 in Sacred Books of the East 43, Part 4, pp. 398–9.

19 Ibid., 10: 6.3.1–2, p. 400 (cf. *Chāndogya Upaniṣad* 3.14).

20 See Walter Neevel, *Yāmuna's Vedānta and Pāñcarātra: Integrating the Classical and the Popular*, Harvard Dissertations in Religion, no. 10

(Missoula, Montana: Scholars Press, 1977), p. 4; also Christopher Duraisingh, who argues that Rāmānuja was brought up in an 'already integrated religious world' in 'Towards an Indian–Christian Theology', p. 69.

21 *Viṣṇu-purāṇa*, I.2.5; VI.8.59, trans. H. H. Wilson (London, 1840; Calcutta: Punthi Pustak, 3rd edn, 1961, reprinted 1979), pp. 7; 519–20 (cf. *VS*(R), para. 149, pp. 119–20).

22 This should not be confused with Viṣṇu's four divine forms of manifestation, namely, *puruṣa*, *pradhāna*, *vyakta* and *kāla*. These four forms, developed from Sāṃkhyan cosmology, bring about the creation, preservation and destruction of matter. Text, I.2 (trans., pp. 9f.).

23 See text, I.22.55–6 (trans., pp. 128–9).

24 Text, III.17.14 (trans., p. 268).

25 Text, I.22.16 (trans., p. 126). Cf. the discussion of Rāmānuja's concept of *vibhūti* and *svarūpa* or the 'proper form' of the Lord in Chapter 4.

26 It is unique and 'detached from all qualities', is composed of wisdom, and pervades all things. See text, I.22.42.

27 Ibid., IV.2.126f. (trans., p. 294); VI.7.73 (trans., p. 513).

28 Text, VI.7.69.

29 Ibid., VI.7.80–3a (trans., p. 514). Cf. Rāmānuja, *Gītābhāṣya*, trans. M. R. Sampatkumaran (Madras: Prof. M. Rangacharya Memorial Trust, 1969) (henceforth *GB*(S)), 9.34, p. 274. It should be mentioned in passing that the *avatāras* or 'descent forms' of Viṣṇu are also focused upon and worshipped as means to release, revealing the Lord's grace, and this Rāmānuja also develops, especially in his commentary on the *Bhagavad-gītā*, where Arjuna attains a vision of Kṛṣṇa, Viṣṇu's most popular descent form.

30 For the *Viṣṇu-purāṇa* equating Brahman with Viṣṇu, see I.2.13 (trans., pp. 7–8); I.14.38 (trans., pp. 90–1); V.18.53 (trans., p. 435). It is generally accepted that the *Viṣṇu-purāṇa* influenced Rāmānuja's understanding of the divine as Person: see Carman, *The Theology of Rāmānuja*, pp. 164–5; J. B. Chettimattam, *Consciousness and Reality: an Indian Approach to Metaphysics* (London: Chapman, 1971), p. 29; Lott, *God and the Universe*, pp. 30–1.

31 J. B. Carman claims that it is one of Rāmānuja's 'major polemical objectives to prove that it is Nārāyaṇa, synonymous with Viṣṇu, who is the Supreme Lord'. *The Theology of Rāmānuja*, p. 164.

32 Consider *Viṣṇu-purāṇa*, I.22.38 (trans., p. 129): 'The supreme condition of Brahman, which is meditated by the Yogis in the commencement of their abstraction, as invested with form, is Viṣṇu, composed of all the divine energies, and the essence of Brahman, with whom the mystic union is sought...This Hari, who is the most immediate of all the energies of Brahman, is his embodied shape, composed entirely of his essence; and in him therefore, is the whole world interwoven; and from him, and in him, is the universe...'

33 See Friedhelm Hardy, *Viraha-bhakti: the Early History of Kṛṣṇa Devotion in South India* (Oxford, Delhi and New York: Oxford University Press,

1983), p. 250, where he discusses the etymological origins of the term *āḻvār*.

34 See Hardy's maps in *Viraha-bhakti*, pp. 256–61.

35 It may be the case that they wanted to establish a *paramparā*, or direct line of guru lineage, as Hardy claims. In any case, it seems likely that the *Āḻvārs* played a role in the emergence of the Śrīvaiṣṇavite tradition.

36 This influence is illustrated in Śrīvaiṣṇava hagiographical literature about the *Āḻvārs*, and more especially in certain features of the content and style of writing by Yāmuna and Rāmānuja. With regard to style, there is a clear imitation of the *Āḻvār stotra* (hymn) in Yāmuna's *Stotraratna* ('Jewel of Hymns') – which even opens by tracing Nāthamuni's descent from Nammāḻvār – and in Rāmānuja's *Gadyas*. (See *Stotramālā*, ed. P. B. Annangarācārya (Kāñcīpuram: Granthamālā Office, 1958); also *Jitantā Stotra*, with Periya Āccān Pillai's commentary (Kāñcīpuram: Śrīvaiṣṇavagrantha Mudrāpaka Sabhai, 1919).) In fact there are divergent views on this question of *Āḻvār* influence. Bharatan Kumarappa, for example, finds considerable parallels between themes in the *Āḻvār* songs and Rāmānuja's *Gītābhāṣya* (*The Hindu Conception of the Deity as Culminating in Rāmānuja* (London: Luzac, 1934), pp. 294; 306; 314; 328), whereas Eric Lott finds no reflection of the *Āḻvārs* in Rāmānuja at all (*God and the Universe*, p. 26).

37 *Tiruvāymoḻi*, 6.9.5, in *Hymns for Drowning: Poems for Viṣṇu by Nammāḻvār*, trans. A. K. Ramanujan (Princeton, N.J.: Princeton University Press, 1981), p. 21. Friedhelm Hardy suggests that 'seeing Kṛṣṇa's body' is Nammāḻvār's most important religious attitude and 'method': 'We have arrived here at the centre of Nammāḻvār's mysticism, metaphorically styled "to see his body".' To 'see', he explains, 'stands for a complete experience involving all the senses (and satisfying them)', while 'body' 'suggests Kṛṣṇa's nature'. *Viraha-bhakti*, p. 312.

38 *Tiruvāymoḻi*, 4.4.1, in *Āḻvārs of South India*, trans. K. C. Varadachari (Chowpatty, Bombay: Bharatiya Vidya Bhavan, 1966), p. 189.

39 Text, 3.1.2 (trans., p. 186).

40 See Rāmānuja, 'Śaraṇāgati-gadya', trans. S. V. Srinivasan, in *Viśishtādvaita: Philosophy and Religion*, ed. V. S. Raghavan (Madras: Rāmānuja Research Society, 1974), p. 69. It is also clear that there is a shared heritage of spiritual language: compare Nammāḻvār, *Tiruvāymoḻi*, 1.1.1–3 (*Āḻvārs of South India*, pp. 178–9) with Rāmānuja, 'Śaraṇāgati-gadya' (*Viśishtādvaita: Philosophy and Religion*, p. 65). For further reflection on this, see Chapter 7 below. NB: there is debate about the authenticity of the *gadyas*, but J. B. Carman argues persuasively that Rāmānuja was their author, and suggests that they enshrine his teaching on the *Prabandham*.

41 Friedhelm Hardy categorises this concept as 'intellectual' in his distinction between 'emotional *bhakti*' (i.e. of the *Āḻvārs*) and 'intellectual *bhakti*' (of, for example, the *Gītā*). In fact, *antaryāmin* is associated with the heart, the centre of body and mind and therefore of emotion and intellect.

42 The term occurs in the *Upaniṣads* and *Pāñcarātra* literature also.

43 For a good introduction to the subject, see F. Otto Schrader, *Introduction to the Pāñcarātra and the Ahirbudhnya Saṃhitā* (Madras: Adyar Library & Research Centre, 1916; reprint 2nd edn, 1973).

44 V. Rangacharya, 'Historical Evolution of Śrī-Vaiṣṇavism in South India', in *The Cultural Heritage of India* IV, ed. Haridas Bhattacharya (Calcutta: Ramakrishna Mission Institute of Culture, 1937; reprint, 1969), p. 171.

45 Namely, the *Parama-*, *Pauṣkara-* and *Sāttvata-saṃhitās* (*SB*(T), 2.2.40; pp. 524–5). It must be pointed out that in fact it was Rāmānuja's commentators who referred more extensively to *Pāñcarātra* texts: Vedāntadeśika, for example, in his *Pāñcarātrarakṣā*, makes the earliest known reference to the *Lakṣmī-tantra*.

46 *The Theology of Rāmānuja*, p. 43.

47 For interpretations of the meanings of these terms see Schrader, *Introduction to the Pāñcarātra* and Carman, *The Theology of Rāmānuja*. In the context of Rāmānuja, the latter translates: *jñāna* ('knowledge'); *bala* ('untiring strength'); *aiśvarya* ('sovereignty'); *vīrya* ('immutability'); *śakti* ('creative power'); and *tejas* ('splendour').

48 Carman suggests that Rāmānuja is more concerned with their collective testimony to the 'lordship and supremacy of the Lord' than with their individual meanings (p. 163). Perhaps it is their function in meditation and worship which is their particular collective value to Rāmānuja.

49 See *SB*(T), 1.1.1 (p. 87).

50 The *Lakṣmī-tantra* had made the same point previously: '(Absolute) knowledge is the essence of Brahman Itself, which is omniscient and untainted. The essence of I-hood is also knowledge, which is all-knowing and all-seeing. The absolute state (literally 'form') of both myself and Brahman is identical with knowledge. The other attributes...are the ever-present attributes of knowledge; whereas knowledge is reputed to be the primary expression of "I".' *The Lakṣmī-tantra: a Pāñcaratrā Text*, trans. with notes by Sanjukta Gupta (Leiden: E. J. Brill, 1972), p. 10. Cf. Rāmānuja's definition of the *svarūpa* ('essential nature') of Brahman.

51 Lott asks whether this (i.e. the 'continual representation of the "body" of God before the devotee') could be the 'hidden spring' behind Rāmānuja's teaching on the universe as God's body, and his *aprakṛta* body (*God and the Universe*, p. 36).

52 The *Pādma-tantra* says: 'Scripture emphasizes the oneness of the highest Self and the one called *kṣetrajña*; [but] the plurality of the *kṣetrajña* is proved by the diversity of bodies.' Schrader, *Introduction to the Pāñcarātra*, p. 106.

53 The others are the *para*, *vyūha*, *vibhava* and *arcā* forms. Rāmānuja refers to these, but only in modified form: *SB*(T), 2.2.41 (p. 525). He only speaks of the *sūkṣma* ('subtle form'), *vyūha* and *vibhava*. In the *Pāñcarātra* tradition these forms of the divine are linked with a particular

understanding of creation according to stages with respective forms of the divine. Since Rāmānuja refuted this theory, it will not be dealt with here.

54 There are nine references in the *Śrībhāṣya*, eight of which are associated with the *Antaryāmī-brāhmaṇa*.

55 Carman, *The Theology of Rāmānuja*, p. 52; S. S. Raghavachar, *Śrī Rāmānuja on the Upaniṣads* (Madras: Prof. M. Rangacharya Memorial Trust, 1972; reprint, 1982), p. 5. Raghavachar quotes one of Rāmānuja's most famous commentators, Sudarśana Sūri, who claims that the *Vedārthasaṃgraha* extracts the 'nectar' of the *Vedānta* (i.e. the *Upaniṣads*). Rāmānuja's *Śrībhāṣya* refers to the *Upaniṣads* 433 times (compared, for example, with 72 references to the *Brahma-sūtras*); and in the *Gītābhāṣya* there are 125 references (compared with 129 references to the *Gītā*).

56 Hajime Nakamura considers this, together with the *Chāndogya Upaniṣad*, to be the earliest of the *Upaniṣads* (*A History of Early Vedānta Philosophy*, Religions of Asia 1 (Delhi: Motilal Banarsidass, 1983), p. 42), pre-dating the Buddha by one or two centuries. (See *The Principal Upaniṣads*, ed. and trans. S. Radhakrishnan (London: Allen & Unwin, 1953), p. 22.)

57 Cf. *Ṛg-veda*, 10.131, where *puruṣa* is depicted as extending and unbinding the threads drawn from the sacrifice.

58 *The Principal Upaniṣads*, trans. S. Radhakrishnan, pp. 224–30. Lott suggests that Rāmānuja's *śarīra-śarīrī-bhāva* may well have derived from this important *śruti* text (*God and the Universe*, p. 30).

59 It is not surprising, then, that Rāmānuja refers to the *Bṛhad-āranyaka Upaniṣad* no fewer than 151 times out of a total of 433 times in his *Śrībhāṣya* (and to this particular extract eight times).

60 See *SB*(T), 4.1.3 (p. 717). NB: The Upaniṣadic teaching on Brahman as Self integrates texts implying a Brahman–*ātman* identity with those implying a difference: 'He who dwelling within the understanding is different from the understanding, whom the understanding does not know, of whom the understanding is the body, who rules the understanding from within; he is thy self, the inner ruler, the immortal one' (*Bṛhad-āranyaka Upaniṣad*, 3.7.22 (*The Principal Upaniṣads*, p. 229)).

61 Raghavachar takes this to be the main theme of the *Vedārthasaṃgraha*: 'We may argue that Rāmānuja undertook to defend his philosophy as the import of this *vidyā*', he says, and in so doing, to disprove the advaitic interpretation of Śaṃkara (*Śrī Rāmānuja on the Upaniṣads*, p. 39). See also *GB*(S), 13.2 (p. 361).

62 *The Principal Upaniṣads*, p. 458.

63 Van Buitenen translates, 'the One who commands... the Commander' (p. 190); while Raghavachar translates, 'that principle which is the commanding spirit...' (p. 9).

64 See *VS*(R), para. 12, p. 15.

65 Ibid., para. 14, pp. 17–18. We shall be looking at Rāmānuja's explanation of this later.

66 See the *Dahara-vidyā*, for example, in the Chāndogya Upaniṣad 8 (*The Principal Upaniṣads*, pp. 491–6).

67 See *VS*(R), para. 222, p. 174, and compare with Chāndogya Upaniṣad 1.6.6–8 (*The Principal Upaniṣads*, p. 348).

68 In his book *Quest for the Original Gītā* (Bombay: Samaiya Publications, 1969), Gajanan Shripat Khair lists the different dates ascribed to the Great War (p. 13).

69 Scholars make differing claims for its influence. Bharatan Kumarappa implies in his book *The Hindu Conception of the Deity* that Rāmānuja's understanding of the divine was drawn directly from the *Gītā* (p. 84); Eric Lott claims that Rāmānuja reads *śruti* in the light of the *Gītā* (*God and the Universe*, p. 24); and van Buitenen argues more cautiously that it was the popular *bhakti* tradition (lying behind the *Gītā*) which influenced Rāmānuja more than the *Gītā* text itself (*Rāmānuja on the Bhagavadgītā: a Condensed Rendering of his Gītābhāṣya* (Delhi: Motilal Banarsidass, 2nd edn, 1968; reprint, 1974) (henceforth *GB*(VB)), p. 7). The reader is referred to S. Radhakrishnan's translation of the *Gītā*, notes and introductory essay (London: Allen & Unwin, 1948; reprint, 1949); and R. C. Zaehner's translation and commentary (Oxford: Oxford University Press, 1969; reprint, 1979).

70 Van Buitenen's study persuades him that there is hardly a word of the *Gītārthasaṃgraha* which is not included in Rāmānuja's own commentary in the same or slightly different form (*GB*(VB), p. 11).

71 The root meaning of *bhaj* is 'to share in, participate in'; it came to mean 'to share or participate in through affection'. Zaehner points out that it also refers to the Lord's love of mankind (p. 26).

72 Radhakrishnan, p. 372; Zaehner, p. 398.

73 To clarify the notion of *upeya* ('goal'): prosperity in the world (*aiśvarya*) is to be distinguished from the self's isolation from matter (*kaivalya*); and both of these from *bhakti-yoga* ('the way of loving devotion'), which is, for Rāmānuja, the highest goal and true meaning of *mokṣa* ('release'), resulting in the attainment of the Lord.

74 This *śloka* has become significant for understanding the role of the Lord's grace in attaining *mokṣa* ('release'). Historically, there was a split, several centuries after Rāmānuja, among his followers over this question. The Tengalai (southern school), represented by Periya Āccān Piḷḷai, maintains that the Lord's role is all-important (symbolised by the way a cat carries her kittens in her mouth); the Vaḍagalai (northern school), represented by Vedānta Deśika, claims that the devotee also contributes to his own release (as a monkey clings to its mother's back). *Prapatti* or total self-surrender is considered by the Tengalai to be separate from *bhakti* and the more important; the Vaḍagalai deny this separation. See *GB*(VB), p. 24; Carman, *The Theology of Rāmānuja*, p. 214; E. J. Lott, *Vedāntic Approaches to God* (London: Macmillan Press, 1980), p. 158.

75 See Rāmānuja's commentary on 18.65: *GB*(S), pp. 524–5 (cf. *VS*(VB), para. 92, p. 250).

76 It has been argued that since Rāmānuja uses this concept as a tool of interpretation for the *Gītā*, he must have formulated it before reading the *Gītā*. Such an idea would be almost impossible to prove, since *Gītā* and *śruti* themes are so closely intertwined.
77 Radhakrishnan, p. 333; Zaehner, p. 368.
78 *GB*(S), p. 435.
79 Radhakrishnan, p. 300; Zaehner, p. 333.
80 See *GB*(S), 13, p. 354 (cf. 10.20, p. 293).
81 Traditionally believed to have lived between CE 916 and 1036/8; scholars agree that such a long life may have been attributed to him to preserve his link both with Nāthamuni and Rāmānuja. Probably he lived in the early part of the eleventh century.
82 The *Siddhi-traya* comprises three doctrinal works: *Ātmā-siddhi*, *Īśvara-siddhi* and *Saṃvit-siddhi* (all of which are incomplete today); his *Āgāma-prāmāṇya* defends the *Pāñcarātra* tradition; the *Gītārthasaṃgraha* is a brief summary of the *Gītā*; and his *Stotraratna* and *Catuśśloki* (or *Śrī-stuti*) reveal *Ālvār* influences.
83 His *Vedārthasaṃgraha*, *Gītābhāṣya* and *Vaikuṇṭhagadya* all begin by paying tribute to Yāmuna.
84 *Ātmā-siddhi*, trans. Neevel, *Yāmuna's Vedānta and Pāñcarātra* p. 166 (cf. *Gītārthasaṃgraha* in *GB*(VB), p. 182).
85 Rāmānuja's *Vaikuṇṭhagadya* opens with the words: 'Having dived into Śrī Yāmunacharya's ocean of ambrosia to the best of my understanding, I have brought up (from the bottom) the gem called *bhaktiyoga* and am holding it up to view.' Trans. Carman, *The Theology of Rāmānuja*, p. 219.
86 This is clear from the opening *śloka* of his *Stotraratna* (on which Rāmānuja's *Vaikuṇṭhagadya* was possibly modelled). See Swami Adidevanananda's translation (Mylapore, Madras: Śrī Ramakrishna Math, 1950, reprint, 1951), p. 5.
87 See *SB*(T), p. 422.
88 See Neevel, *Yāmuna's Vedānta and Pāñcarātra*, p. 159.
89 Ibid., p. 161.
90 *Ātmā-siddhi 2*, trans. Neevel, *Yāmuna's Vedānta and Pāñcarātra*, p. 153. He translates *svarūpa* and *svabhāva* as 'own form' and 'own nature' (p. 182). See also *Siddhi-traya*, ed. U. T. Viraraghavacharya, trans. R. Ramanujacharya and K. Srinivasacharya (Madras: Ubhaya Vedānta Granthamālā Book Trust, reprint, 1972). Cf. Rāmānuja, *SB*(T), 1.1.1, p. 58.
91 *Svarūpa-upādhi-svabhāva*.
92 *Aṃśa-aṃśi-bhāvan*.
93 *Śeṣa-śeṣi*.
94 For *aṃśa-aṃśi* see *SB*(T), pp. 88, 191, 559, 619; *GB*(VB), p. 152. For *śeṣa-śeṣi* see *VS*(VB), pp. 183, 274; *SB*(T), pp. 153, 421.
95 Neevel refers in particular to the phrase *viśiṣṭa-svarūpa-bhāva* (qualified *svarūpa*) – *Yāmuna's Vedānta and Pāñcarātra*, p. 282 n. 71. In relation to this it is interesting to note that in his *Saṃvit-siddhi*, when discussing the *sadvidyā*, Yāmuna uses the term *prakāra* ('mode') when referring to the world in relation to Brahman, its *ātman*. Cf. *SB*(T), pp. 457–8.

96 Van Buitenen goes so far as to suggest that Yāmuna preceded Rāmānuja in elucidating a concept of *śarīra-śarīrī-bhāva* (body–self doctrine). See his introduction to Rāmānuja's *Vedārthasaṃgraha*.

3 THE BODY OF CHRIST IN THE WRITINGS OF TEILHARD DE CHARDIN

1 *SC*, pp. 11–13 (*Oeuvres* 9, pp. 33–5).
2 *Oeuvres* 9, p. 34; the translation is my own.
3 In 'Esquisse d'un univers personnel' (1936), Teilhard affirms that God is spirit in order to argue for his immanence in the world, and hence his inseparability from it. *HE*, p. 67 (*Oeuvres* 6, p. 85). It is interesting to note that on the same page, he describes the term 'God' as 'the name given by Man to consummated Being' ('Le nom donné par l'Homme à l'Etre consommé'). We can already see, therefore, that Teilhard refers to 'spirit' in terms of a relationship to the world.
4 'Le Phénomène spirituel' (1937). The translation is my own; cf. trans. in *HE*, p. 94 (*Oeuvres* 6, p. 118).
5 See his paper of this title (1953), in *AE*, pp. 375ff. (*Oeuvres* 7, pp. 397ff.).
6 In his article 'Are Spirits Bodiless Persons?', Patrick Sherry suggests certain distinguishing characteristics of the Spirit of God (or the Holy Spirit), one of which is that it is seen as a *power*. He refers to Geoffrey Lampe's book *God as Spirit*, in which he argues that 'spirit' properly refers to God's activity and not his essence; in other words, to the divine creativity (*Neue Zeitschrift für systematische Theologie und Religionsphilosophie* 24 (Berlin and New York: Walter de Gruyter), 1982, Part 1, 37–52). Teilhard is drawing upon the biblical notion of the divine Word in which and through which the world is created, which was developed in some of the Patristic writers in connection with the Spirit. In Irenaeus, for example, God is described as creating all things through the Word and adorning them in the Spirit (which, for him, is the Wisdom of God); it is the Spirit that fashions us in the likeness of God (*Adv. haer.*, IV.xx.1–2; *Demonstration of the Apostolic Preaching*, ch. 5).
7 'Le Phénomène spirituel', in *HE*, pp. 96–7 (*Oeuvres* 6, p. 121).
8 'L'Union créatrice', in *WTW*, p. 154 (*Oeuvres* 12, p. 199).
9 'L'Union créatrice', in *WTW*, p. 154 (*Oeuvres* 12, p. 199).
10 'L'Union créatrice', in *WTW*, p. 154 (*Oeuvres* 12, p. 200).
11 *WTW*, p. 155 (*Oeuvres* 12, p. 201).
12 E.g. 'Comment je vois' (1948), 'My Fundamental Vision', *TF*, p. 196 (*Oeuvres* 11, p. 211). Cf. 'L'Energie humaine', in *HE*, p. 141 (*Oeuvres* 6, p. 175): 'To act is to create and creating is continuous.'
13 'L'Union créatrice', in *WTW*, p. 155 (*Oeuvres* 12, p. 201). NB: The given translation, 'animation is proportionate to union', does not bring out the emphasis of 'bringing to life' which *l'animation* infers. Teilhard is referring to the quality of life rather than to the amount of movement.
14 'La Centrologie', in *AE*, p. 102 (*Oeuvres* 7, p. 107).
15 Ibid.; *AE*, p. 101.

16 'Le Phénomène spirituel', in *HE*, pp. 94–5 (*Oeuvres* 6, p. 119).
17 See 'La Centrologie', in *AE*, pp. 105ff. (*Oeuvres* 7, pp. 110ff.).
18 Teilhard makes the point that the term 'spiritualisation' is more accurate than 'spirit' for denoting the life-process. 'Le Phénomène spirituel', in *HE*, p. 96 (*Oeuvres* 6, p. 121).
19 For a fuller account of his evolutionary theory see *PM* (*Oeuvres* 1). Also *Man's Place in Nature* (*Oeuvres* 8). For a summary see 'La Centrologie', in *AE* (*Oeuvres* 7).
20 'L'Etoffe de l'univers', in *AE*, p. 378 (*Oeuvres* 7, p. 401). Cf. a letter of 1929 to Léontine Zanta in which he wrote: 'In a rather odd way the "Spirit" has now become an entirely real thing for me, the only real thing, not as the result of a sort of 'metaphysicisation' (!?) of matter, but as the result of a 'physicisation' of the Spirit. I see all the attributes that science has accumulated round matter in the last one hundred and fifty years, whether as regards energy or history, transposing themselves and passing over onto Spirit. As I see things, the universe, through all its experimental organisation... is not descending towards the homogeneous and the most probable: its equilibrium lies in falling laboriously, if the phrase may be permitted, onto the personal, the differentiated, the conscious. "Consciousness", that is to say the tension of union and desire, has in my eyes become the "fundamental element, the very stuff of the real".' *Letters to Léontine Zanta*, trans. Wall, pp. 86–7 (*Lettres à Léontine Zanta*, p. 97).
21 See 'Note sur l'Union physique entre l'humanité du Christ et les fidèles au cours de la sanctification' (1919), in *CE*, pp. 15–20 (*Oeuvres* 10, pp. 21–6).
22 *La Consistance* is an important term for Teilhard, designating the durability (perhaps the eternity) of a thing. Spirit, he writes, 'est plus primitif et consistant que la Matière' ('L'Esprit de la Terre' (1931), in *HE*, pp. 38–9 (*Oeuvres* 6, p. 47)). In 'Science et Christ' (1921) he writes: 'The only consistence beings have comes to them from their *synthetic element*, in other words from what, at a more perfect or less perfect degree, is their soul, their spirit', *SC*, p. 29 (*Oeuvres* 9, p. 55).
23 For a helpful summary of Teilhard's position with regard to the evolution of spirit or consciousness, see two short papers he wrote: 'Ma Position intellectuelle' (1948), in *HM*, pp. 143–4 (*Oeuvres* 13, pp. 173–4); and 'Esquisse d'une dialectique de l'esprit', in *AE*, pp. 144ff. (*Oeuvres* 7, pp. 147ff.).
24 'L'Atomisme de l'esprit: un essai pour comprendre la structure de l'étoffe de l'univers', in *AE*, p. 30 (*Oeuvres* 7, p. 37).
25 Ibid.
26 'La Centrologie', in *AE*, p. 119 (*Oeuvres* 7, p. 126).
27 'Esquisse d'un univers personnel', in *HE*, p. 55 (*Oeuvres* 6, p. 72).
28 See 'L'Union créatrice', in *WTW*, p. 157 (*Oeuvres* 12, p. 203).
29 Teilhard sees unification occurring through differentiation. See 'Le Phénomène spirituel', in *HE*, p. 103 (*Oeuvres* 6, p. 129).
30 See 'Le Phénomène spirituel', in *HE*, pp. 100ff. (*Oeuvres* 6, pp. 125ff.).

Cf. 'L'Atomisme de l'esprit', in *AE*, p. 44 (*Oeuvres* 7, p. 51), where he says that the only way he can see the 'spirit of the earth' coming to an end without perishing is by disappearing *in depth* through an 'excess of centration upon itself'. It should be noted that although Teilhard sought to prove his theory of evolving consciousness through his analysis of the past and in particular of man, nevertheless, his claims for the future were of a different order: they were unsubstantiated hypothesis – what he called 'scientific thought in action'. See 'Sur les degrés de certitude scientifique de l'idée d'evolution' (1946), in *SC*, p. 194 (*Oeuvres* 9, p. 247).

31 See 'L'Union créatrice', in *WTW*, p. 175 (*Oeuvres* 12, p. 223).
32 'L'Atomisme de l'esprit', in *AE*, p. 31 (*Oeuvres* 7, pp. 37–8).
33 See 'La Centrologie', in *AE*, pp. 104ff. (*Oeuvres* 7, pp. 109ff.).
34 'Esquisse d'un univers personnel', in *HE*, p. 57 (*Oeuvres* 6, p. 73).
35 'Le Phénomène spirituel', in *HE*, p. 103 (*Oeuvres* 6, p. 128).
36 'Esquisse d'un univers personnel', in *HE*, p. 68 (*Oeuvres* 6, p. 86).
37 See 'L'Energie humaine', in *HE*, pp. 145ff. (*Oeuvres* 6, pp. 180ff.).
38 Ibid.
39 'L'Energie humaine', in *HE*, p. 159 (*Oeuvres* 6, pp. 196–7).
40 'Le Cœur de la matière', in *HM*, p. 50 (*Oeuvres* 13, pp. 61–2).
41 'Esquisse d'un univers personnel'; the translation is my own. Cf. trans. *HE*, p. 89 (*Oeuvres* 6, p. 111).
42 Foreword, *PM*, p. 36 (*Oeuvres* 1, p. 30).
43 'L'Union créatrice', in *WTW*, p. 159 (*Oeuvres* 12, p. 205).
44 See 'La Centrologie', in *AE*, pp. 111ff. (*Oeuvres* 7, pp. 117ff.).
45 *MD*, pp. 123–5 (*Oeuvres* 4, pp. 137–41).
46 'Note sur "l'élément universel" du monde' (1918), in *WTW*, p. 275 (*Oeuvres* 12, p. 393).
47 *WTW*, p. 274 (*Oeuvres* 12, p. 392).
48 Ibid.
49 *WTW*, p. 275 (*Oeuvres* 12, p. 393).
50 'Note sur "l'élément universel" du Monde', in *WTW*, p. 274 (*Oeuvres* 12, pp. 391–2).
51 'Forma Christi'; the translation is my own. Cf. *WTW*, p. 266 (*Oeuvres* 12, p. 383).
52 'L'Elément universel', in *WTW*, p. 298 (*Oeuvres* 12, p. 440).
53 'Forma Christi', in *WTW*, pp. 253–4 (*Oeuvres* 12, pp. 369–70).
54 *WTW*, p. 268 (*Oeuvres* 12, p. 385).
55 Teilhard does not discuss God 'in himself', apart from the world.
56 'Esquisse d'un univers personnel'; the translation is my own. Cf. trans. *HE*, p. 58 (*Oeuvres* 6, p. 75).
57 See 'La Centrologie', in *AE*, p. 125 (*Oeuvres* 7, p. 131). (Here Teilhard is discussing centro-complexity in relation to 'l'Un' (spirit) and 'le Multiple' (matter).)
58 'L'Energie humaine', in *HE*, p. 148 (*Oeuvres* 6, p. 184).
59 See *PM*, p. 165 (*Oeuvres* 1, p. 181).

60 I.e. each person radiates over the past, present and future of the world around it. 'Pour y voir clair: réflexions sur deux formes inverses d'esprit' (1950), in *AE*, p. 218 (*Oeuvres* 7, p. 226).
61 *MD*, p. 60 (*Oeuvres* 4, p. 39). NB: the published translation misleadingly translates *pour devenir esprit* as 'to reach the level of spirit'.
62 Teilhard refers to this as 'Christifying matter': 'Le Cœur de la matière', in *HM*, p. 47 (*Oeuvres* 13, p. 58).
63 *HM*, p. 47 (*Oeuvres* 13, p. 58).
64 'L'Esprit de la Terre', in *HE*, p. 29 (*Oeuvres* 6, p. 36).
65 'Le Prêtre' (1918), in *WTW*, p. 219 (*Oeuvres* 12, p. 329).
66 See 'Le Cœur de la matière' (1950), in *HM*, pp. 52–3 (*Oeuvres* 13, p. 64).
67 Letter of 8 September, in *MM*, p. 126 (*Genèse d'une pensée*, p. 161).
68 'La Vie cosmique' (1916), in *WTW*, p. 16 (*Oeuvres* 12, p. 21).
69 'L'Esprit de la Terre', in *HE*, pp. 43ff. (*Oeuvres* 6, pp. 52ff.).
70 'Le Christ dans la matière' (1916), Appendix, in *HM*, p. 66 (*Oeuvres* 13, p. 80). (This paper is also in *HU*, pp. 66ff. (*Hymne de l'univers*, pp. 39ff.).)
71 'La Vie cosmique', in *WTW*, pp. 57–8 (*Oeuvres* 12, p. 67). In 'Forma Christi', Teilhard writes, 'If things are to find their coherence *in Christo*, we must ultimately admit that there is *in natura Christi*... some *universal physical reality*, a certain cosmic extension of his body and soul.' *WTW*, p. 252 (*Oeuvres* 12, p. 368). Cf. 'La Vie cosmique', in *WTW*, p. 51 (*Oeuvres* 12, p. 59).
72 'L'Esprit de la Terre', in *HE*, p. 44 (*Oeuvres* 6, p. 54).
73 See 'Le Prêtre', in *WTW*, p. 219 (*Oeuvres* 12, p. 329): 'I would wish, through my meditations, speech and the practice of my whole life, to disclose and preach the bonds of continuity which make the Cosmos, with which we are involved, a milieu divinized through the Incarnation, divinizing through Communion, and divinizable through our co-operation.'
74 See 'L'Union créatrice', in *WTW*, p. 175 (*Oeuvres* 12, p. 223). Here, Teilhard equates Christ's body with *le milieu mystique* (the term he used before 'the divine milieu'). Cf. 'Mon univers' (1924), in *SC*, p. 59 (n.) (*Oeuvres* 9, p. 88 (n.)): 'In short, Christ, understood in this sense, is the milieu in which and through which the (abstract) attribute of the *divine immensity* is concretely realised for us.'
75 See 'La Foi qui opère' (1918), in *WTW*, pp. 238–9 (*Oeuvres* 12, pp. 851–2). He argues that there are as many 'independent providences' as there are souls in the world, each person having his or her own centre and sphere of influence in proportion to faith. (This idea is behind his use of the term 'My universe' as a title for papers written in 1918 and 1924.)
76 See 'Le Christique', in *HM*, p. 96 (*Oeuvres* 13, p. 110).
77 'L'Etoffe de l'univers', in *WTW*, p. 381 (*Oeuvres* 12, p. 404).
78 'Le Milieu mystique' (1917), in *WTW*, p. 148 (*Oeuvres* 12, p. 191 (n.)).
79 'Le Christique', in *HM*, p. 96 (*Oeuvres* 13, p. 110).

80 'Le Milieu mystique', in *WTW*, p. 137 (*Oeuvres* 12, p. 179).
81 Ibid.
82 *MD*, p. 114 (*Oeuvres* 4, p. 124).
83 'Le Christique', in *HM*, p. 95 (*Oeuvres* 13, p. 110).
84 Ibid.
85 See 'L'Evolution de la responsabilité dans le monde' (1950), in *AE*, pp. 207ff. (*Oeuvres* 7, pp. 211ff.).
86 See 'L'Esprit de la Terre', in *HE*, pp. 32ff. (*Oeuvres* 6, pp. 40ff.).
87 'L'Atomisme de l'esprit', in *AE*, p. 47 (*Oeuvres* 7, p. 54).
88 In 'Le Cœur de la matière', Teilhard speaks of loving God 'not only with "all one's body and all one's soul" but with the whole Universe-in-evolution'. *HM*, p. 101 (*Oeuvres* 13, p. 116).
89 For Teilhard, therefore, matter was supremely worthy of praise and blessing for its divine potentiality and power. See 'Hymne à la matière' in 'La Puissance spirituelle de la matière', in *HU*, pp. 64–5 (*Hymne de l'univers*, pp. 72–3). See also 'Les Noms de la matière' (1919), in *HM*, pp. 225–39 (*Oeuvres* 12, pp. 449–64).
90 'L'Energie humaine', in *HE*, p. 145 (*Oeuvres* 6, p. 180).
91 Ibid.
92 *WTW*, p. 51 (*Oeuvres* 12, p. 59).
93 Even today, he points out, Christ the king is worshipped as the God of progress and evolution. 'Esquisse d'un univers personnel' (1936), in *HE*, p. 92 (*Oeuvres* 6, p. 113).
94 *HU*, pp. 13–38; also *HM*, pp. 119–34 (*Hymne de l'univers*, pp. 11–37).
95 *HU*, p. 34; also *HM*, p. 131 (*Hymne de l'univers*, p. 34).
96 See 'Le Cœur de la matière', in *HM*, pp. 57–8 (*Oeuvres* 13, p. 70).
97 *SC*, pp. 151–73 (*Oeuvres* 9, pp. 193–218).
98 *SC*, p. 166 (*Oeuvres* 9, p. 211).
99 *SC*, p. 166 (*Oeuvres* 9, p. 211).
100 See *MD*, p. 114 (*Oeuvres* 4, p. 124). Here Teilhard, when speaking of the attributes of the divine milieu, says that it is 'precisely because [God] is the centre that he fills the whole sphere [i.e. the universe]'.
101 The term 'consummate' refers to the Pauline term *plērōma*, which means 'fullness'. Teilhard interprets this in terms of the world's integration into God through Christ. See his second paper to Auguste Valensin (December 1919), in *Correspondence*, p. 46 (*Blondel et Teilhard de Chardin*, pp. 42ff.); also 'La Parole attendue' (1940), in which Teilhard refers to the *plērōma* as an 'internal sovereignty that, inaugurated in matter and culminating in grace, operates on us by and through all the organic foundations of the evolving world'. *Cahiers Pierre Teilhard de Chardin* 4, p. 427; trans. E. Rideau, *Teilhard de Chardin: a Guide to his Thought* (London: Collins, 1967), p. 61 (n. 80).
102 For 'consistency' see "Panthéisme et christianisme' (1923), in *CE*, p. 71 (*Oeuvres* 10, p. 87). Basically Teilhard is interpreting Col. 1:17 ('In him all things hold together'). Also 'La Route de l'Ouest: vers une mystique nouvelle', in *TF*, p. 55 (*Oeuvres* 11, p. 60), where he

translates the same text loosely to mean 'in whom all things find the consistence of their being'.

103 'Le Milieu mystique', in *WTW*, p. 123 (*Oeuvres* 12, p. 164).

104 'L'Elément universel', in *WTW*, p. 296 (*Oeuvres* 12, p. 438).

105 *WTW*, p. 302 (*Oeuvres* 12, p. 445).

106 *WTW*, p. 301 (*Oeuvres* 12, p. 444). See also 'Note sur "l'Elément universel" du monde', in *WTW*, pp. 272–6 (*Oeuvres* 12, pp. 387–93).

107 'Super-humanité – Super-Christ – Super-charité: de nouvelles dimensions pour l'avenir', in *SC*, p. 167 (*Oeuvres* 9, p. 212). Teilhard is not suggesting here that Christ or God is limited to the boundaries of the physical universe, but rather that the dimensions of the cosmos are as limitless as the divine nature. He writes: 'There is indeed no exaggeration in using the term Super-Christ to express that "excess" of greatness assumed in our consciousness by the Person of Jesus in step with the awakening of our minds to the super-dimensions of the world and of mankind' (*SC*, p. 167 (*Oeuvres* 9, pp. 211–12)).

108 'Esquisse d'un univers personnel', in *HE*, p. 91 (*Oeuvres* 6, p. 113).

109 The concept of 'sur-animation' balances the claim for the world's infinity: Christ and the cosmos are not equal, although they evolve as one, because as Centre, Christ is the primary principle, the animating spirit bringing creation to fulfilment in him.

110 'Esquisse d'un univers personnel', in *HE*, p. 91 (*Oeuvres* 6, p. 113).

111 Letter to E. Mounier (November 1947), Appendix, in *SC*, p. 222 (*Oeuvres* 9, p. 292).

112 See 'Mon univers' (1924), in *SC*, p. 57 (*Oeuvres* 9, pp. 85–6): 'Since Christ is Omega, the universe is physically impregnated to the very core of its matter by the influence of his super-human nature. The presence of the Incarnate Word penetrates everything, as a universal element. It shines at the common heart of things, as a centre that is infinitely intimate to them and at the same time (since it coincides with universal fulfilment) infinitely distant.'

113 By 'grace' Teilhard means the 'vital, organising influence of the universe'. In addition to 'Mon univers', see 'La Vie cosmique', in *WTW*, p. 50 (*Oeuvres* 12, p. 58).

114 Letter to Marguerite Teillard-Chambon, 1 January 1917, in *MM*, p. 160 (*Genèse d'une pensée*, p. 207).

115 Chastity and charity.

116 'L'Union créatrice' (1917), in *WTW*, p. 172 (*Oeuvres* 12, p. 220).

117 *WTW*, p. 173 (*Oeuvres* 12, p. 220).

118 Letter of 29 January 1917, in *MM*, p. 176 (*Genèse d'une pensée*, p. 228).

119 'Le Cœur de la matière', in *HM*, pp. 71–2 (*Oeuvres* 13, p. 86).

120 'Mon univers', in *SC*, p. 58 (*Oeuvres* 9, pp. 86–7).

121 See 'La Montée de l'autre' (1924), in *AE*, p. 70 (*Oeuvres* 7, p. 77).

122 Ibid.

123 See 'Esquisse d'un univers personnel', in *HE*, p. 72 (*Oeuvres* 6, p. 90). Here Teilhard defines love as the physico-moral energy of personal-

isation, to which all activities are reduced. It is, he says, *the physical structure of the universe.*

124 Teilhard discusses this in 'L'Atomisme de l'esprit', in *AE*, pp. 47ff. (*Oeuvres* 7, pp. 54ff.). In this context, he means by love, 'to relate to interiorly'.

125 This Teilhard sometimes called Christ's 'third' nature (i.e. in addition to his divine and human natures).

126 'Comment je vois' (1948), in *TF*, pp. 198–9 (*Oeuvres* 11, p. 214).

127 As René Hague points out in his translation of 'L'Union créatrice', Teilhard uses the term 'physical' in its original Greek sense of 'natural' or 'organic' (*WTW*, p. 171). C. F. Mooney reminds us that this is in contradistinction to the terms 'juridical' or 'abstract' (*Teilhard de Chardin and the Mystery of Christ* (New York: Harper & Row, 1966), p. 85). He suggests 'ontological' as a more appropriate contemporary term, but this is misleading in view of Teilhard's expressed realism in Christology. Mooney draws on 'Mon univers' (1924), where Teilhard refers to the 'physicalist' and the 'juridicist' (*SC*, p. 55; *Oeuvres* 9, pp. 83–4). For an evaluation of this see Lyons, *The Cosmic Christ in Origen and Teilhard de Chardin*, pp. 180–2.

128 In 'La Vie cosmique' he writes: '[The body of Christ] constitutes an organism that is animate and in motion, one in which we are all united, physically and *biologically*.' *WTW*, p. 50 (*Oeuvres* 12, p. 58).

129 See 'Forma Christi', in *WTW*, p. 252 (*Oeuvres* 12, p. 368).

130 See 'L'Union créatrice', in *WTW*, p. 175 (*Oeuvres* 12, p. 223).

131 Traditionally known as omnipotence and omnipresence.

132 See 'L'Etoffe de l'univers', in *AE*, pp. 375ff. (*Oeuvres* 7, pp. 397ff.).

133 This is somewhat akin to the relationship of a 'within' to a 'without'. See Pensée 8, in *HU*, p. 76 (*Hymne de l'univers*, p. 88): 'In all things there is a Within, co-extensive with their Without.'

134 See 'L'Energie humaine', in *HE*, p. 143 (*Oeuvres* 6, p. 178): 'The totality of a sphere is just as present in its centre, which takes the form of a point, as spread over its whole surface; in fact it really lies only in that point.'

135 Ibid.

136 Pensée 15, in *HU*, p. 81 (*Hymne de l'univers*, p. 94). Cf. 'Le Cœur de la matière', in *HM*, p. 32 (*Oeuvres* 13, p. 42).

137 'Le Cœur de la matière', in *HM*, p. 19 (*Oeuvres* 13, p. 27).

138 *HM*, pp. 16–17 (*Oeuvres* 13, pp. 23–4).

139 'Le Prêtre', in *WTW*, p. 211 (*Oeuvres* 12, p. 320).

140 Pensée 2, in *HU*, p. 70 (*Hymne de l'univers*, p. 80). Cf. Letter to Victor Fontoynont, 15 March 1916, Appendix 1, de Lubac, *The Religion of Teilhard de Chardin*, p. 241.

141 *WTW*, p. 218 (*Oeuvres* 12, p. 328).

142 'Forma Christi', in *WTW*, p. 253 (*Oeuvres* 12, p. 369).

143 Ibid.

144 Ibid.

145 *LLZ*, p. 74 (*Lettres à Léontine Zanta*, p. 81).

146 Introduction to 'Le Cœur de la matière' (1950), in *HM*, p. 16 (*Oeuvres* 13, p. 22).
147 *AE*, p. 263 (*Oeuvres* 7, p. 272).
148 See 'Le Cœur de la matière', in *HM*, p. 44 (*Oeuvres* 13, p. 56).
149 'En quoi consiste le Corps humain?', in *SC*, p. 13 (*Oeuvres* 9, pp. 34–5).
150 *HE*, p. 54 (*Oeuvres* 6, p. 70). Cf. the Introduction to 'La Vie cosmique', in *WTW*, pp. 14–15 (*Oeuvres* 12, pp. 19–20).
151 In a letter to Marguerite Teillard-Chambon of 9 January 1917, Teilhard remarks when commenting on Newman's views in *He and I*: 'In a way, the whole universe [is] centred on me, *whose destiny* (in a very true sense) is *played out in me* [in God's eyes isn't every soul worth the whole world, isn't it the whole world?]...And so the fundamental primacy of individual salvation leaves the soul all its fullness, as far-reaching as the Universe.' *MM*, p. 167 (*Genèse d'une pensée*, p. 215). Teilhard repeatedly claims that our salvation is only attained in solidarity with the whole 'body of the elect' (the 'damned' are those who 'defect' from union with the mystical body): 'The only subject ultimately capable of mystical transfiguration is the whole group of mankind forming a single body and a single soul in charity.' *MD*, p. 144 (*Oeuvres* 4, p. 170). For the relationship between the world and the institutional Church, see 'Sur mon attitude vis-à-vis de l'Eglise Officielle' (1921), in *HM*, pp. 115–18 (*Oeuvres* 13, pp. 133–7); and 'Ce que le monde attend de l'Eglise de Dieu' (1952), in *CE*, pp. 212–20 (*Oeuvres* 10, pp. 251–61). Teilhard's fundamental position is that the historical Church serves to channel the spiritual energy of the universe, which stems from Christ. The different doctrines and formulas it propagates express an 'invariable basis of truth (summed up in the claim that Christ is the physical centre of the gathering together of souls in God) which will necessarily assume a continually new aspect...' *HM*, p. 117 (*Oeuvres* 13, p. 137).
152 *Correspondence*, p. 22 (*Blondel et Teilhard de Chardin*, p. 21). He goes on to say: 'It is precisely the feeling of this double reality, the singular and the universal, which led me to study Action, simultaneously the expression of a being's incommunicable originality and a factor within the Whole...The problem of the Incarnation [thus] seemed to me to be the touchstone of a true cosmology, a metaphysics complete within itself' (p. 23 (p. 21)).
153 'La Vie cosmique', in *WTW*, p. 15 (*Oeuvres* 12, p. 20).
154 'En quoi consiste le corps humain?', in *SC*, p. 13 (*Oeuvres* 9, p. 35).
155 Ibid.

4 THE BODY OF BRAHMAN IN THE WRITINGS OF RĀMĀNUJA

1 *SB*, 2.1.9: *Śrī Bhagavad Rāmānuja Granthamālā*, ed. Śrī Kanchi P. B. Annangaracharya Swamy (Kancheepuram: Granthamālā Office, 1956), p. 223. Unless otherwise indicated, the translation is my own.

For other translations see J. J. Lipner, 'The World as God's "Body": in pursuit of Dialogue with Rāmānuja', *Religious Studies* 20 (March 1984), 147; Carman, *The Theology of Rāmānuja*, p. 127; E. J. Lott, 'The Conceptual Dimensions of Bhakti in the Rāmānuja Tradition', *Scottish Journal of Religious Studies* 2 (Autumn 1981), 101; Thibaut, *The Vedāntā-sūtras*, Sacred Books of the East 48, p. 424. Henceforth *Granthamālā* (the complete works in Sanskrit) will be abbreviated to *GM*. Since it is not numbered consecutively throughout, but in sections, an indication will also be given of the text in question: e.g. (*GM*(*SB*)).

2 *GM*(*SB*), p. 224.

3 *SB*(T), 1.1.1, p. 4.

4 *SB*(T), 1.1.2, p. 156 (*GM*(*SB*), p. 105).

5 I.e. *puruṣottama*, with its historical and associated meanings (see Chapter 2 above).

6 *GB*(S), 15:17, p. 433 (*GM*(*GB*), p. 138).

7 *GB*(S), 15:19, p. 435 (*GM*(*GB*), p. 139).

8 *SB*(T), 1.1.1, p. 4.

9 Ibid.

10 For the concept of *mokṣa* see Chapter 2, nn. 74 and 75 above.

11 See Chapter 2, pp. 38–41 above.

12 See Chapter 2, pp. 33–5; 38 above.

13 *VS*(R), paras. 127–9, pp. 99–101.

14 *GB*(S), 18.65, p. 525.

15 *VS*(R), para. 219, p. 172.

16 *VS*(R), para. 126, p. 98. This subject will be dealt with in more detail in Chapter 7.

17 *GM*(*VS*), pp. 40–1 (cf. *GB*, 9.34; 11.15).

18 It is worth noting that Rāmānuja supports his position here by quoting *puruṣa* references in *smṛti* texts.

19 See p. 33 above.

20 See p. 34 above. In fact Rāmānuja quotes six different references to the *Viṣṇu-purāṇa* in the second paragraph preceding this extract.

21 E.g. *Bhagavad-gītā*, 11.12–11.20.

22 *GB*(S), 11.18, p. 314 (*VS*(*R*), para. 217, p. 171).

23 In the paragraph immediately preceding the *Vedārthasaṃgraha* passage above, Rāmānuja quotes from the *Viṣṇu-purāṇa* describing how Śrī, the 'Mother of the Universe', makes her form 'conform to the form of Viṣṇu'. See *VS*(R), para. 217, p. 171.

24 *GB*(S), 11.18, p. 314.

25 *GB*(S), 11.8, p. 309.

26 Rāmānuja's position here is made all the more obvious by his explicating the *Gītā* word *rūpa* (form) as *śarīra* (body) (11.16): 'O Lord of the universe, with the universe for Your form, *that is, O Ruler of the universe, having as Your body the universe*...' (my italics).

27 *GB*(S), pp. 313–14 (*GM*(*GB*), p. 100).

28 I am drawing, here, upon Lipner's distinction between the ontological

and epistemological aspects of *pṛthak-siddhy-anarha* ('incapable of being realised apart from'). See 'The World as God's "Body"', p. 149.

29 NB: finite selves and *prakṛti* ('primordial matter') are co-eternal with Brahman, so this does not refer to primary origination. As we shall see, selves and matter form part of Brahman (his 'body') in both states (see *SB*(*T*), 1.1.1, p. 142).

30 *VS*(VB), para. 74, p. 234 (*SB*(*T*), 1.1.1, p. 142).

31 *VS*(VB), para. 18, p. 194.

32 *VS*(R), para. 12, p. 15 (*GM*(*VS*), p. 4).

33 *Prakāra-prakārin*, in Rāmānuja, has been translated in a variety of ways: Kumarappa uses 'substance–mode'; van Buitenen, Carman and Thibaut use 'mode–modified'; Lott, 'prototype–ectype'; and Lipner, 'mode–mode-possessor'. Although 'mode–modified' is perhaps the most literal, 'mode–mode-possessor' is clearer.

34 'Class etc., constitute the generic structure (*saṃsthāna*) of a given thing and are, consequently, modifications of the thing; hence, as we have said before, the modifying attribute and the modified thing are different *padārthas*; the modifying attribute has no separate function and cannot be separately apprehended, and the same generic structure can appear as modification in more than one thing.' *VS*(VB), para. 62, p. 227 (*GM*(*VS*), p. 15).

35 The operative term here is *pṛthak-siddhy-anarha* ('incapable of being realised apart from').

36 There is a distinction between Brahman's manifest (*saguṇa*) and unmanifest (*nirguṇa*) forms. The relationship between these two forms may be likened to that between the individual's subtle or etheric and gross 'bodies' in Indian anthropology. On the other hand, of course, *nirguṇa* Brahman has no physical form of expression or projective image in the mind.

37 *VS*(VB), para. 65, p. 229.

38 *SB*(T), 1.1.1, p. 138 (*GM*(*SB*), p. 98).

39 *VS*(VB), para. 68, p. 230.

40 A preferable translation would incorporate the word 'self' rather than 'soul', but for convenience, 'ensouled' is used here. (Note: Thibaut's translation misleadingly translates *ātman* as 'soul' throughout.)

41 *VS*(VB), para. 69, p. 231.

42 *VS*(R), para. 9, p. 11.

43 *GB*, 10.20, trans. Carman, *The Theology of Rāmānuja*, p. 128 (*GM*(*GB*), p. 92). (Cf. *GB*(S), p. 293, where *śeṣi* is translated as 'the recipient of service'.)

44 The *ādhāra-ādheya* metaphor is noticeably impersonal, and is modified by other terms.

45 *SB*(T), 1.4.1, p. 355. It is interesting to note Rāmānuja's use of the chariot simile here, because *niyantṛ*, in its common usage, refers to a charioteer. This is particularly appropriate in view of Kṛṣṇa's role in the *Gītā* as Arjuna's charioteer.

46 *SB*(T), 1.4.1, p. 356 (*GM*(*SB*), p. 194). In choosing, as he often does, to use the term *antaryāmin*, Rāmānuja is drawing upon its Upaniṣadic meaning. See *Antaryāmī-brāhmaṇa*, BU 3.7.3.

47 *SB*(T), 1.3.8, p. 308; 4.1.3, p. 717.

48 Strictly speaking Brahman 'in-forms' the world with (i.e. manifests) *saccidānanda* ('truth', 'consciousness', 'bliss').

49 *VS*(R), para. 120, p. 92 (*GM*(*VS*), p. 21).

50 *SB*(T), 2.3.19, p. 544.

51 Ibid., p. 545.

52 See Chapters 6 and 7 below for an analysis of his use of the divine body as a model.

53 *GB*(S), 13.2, pp. 355–6 (*GM*(*GB*), p. 115).

54 *GB*(S), 13.6, p. 372 (*GM*(*GB*), p. 119).

55 *GB*(S), 13.18.

56 *SB*(T), 1.3.7, pp. 305–6 (*GM*(*SB*), p. 170).

57 See above, p. 34. Elsewhere, Rāmānuja clarifies his position by referring to the Lord's *vibhūti* in the context of the released self: for such an *ātman* he says, the object of consciousness is 'the highest Brahman, which is free from all change and of an absolutely perfect and blessed nature... together with the manifestation of its/his glory (*vibhūti*)'. *SB*(T), 4.4.19, p. 768. Cf. the *Śaraṇāgati-gadya*'s reference to 'Thou who possessest *mahāvibhūti* (the great realm manifesting Thy rule)' (quoted by Carman, *The Theology of Rāmānuja*, p. 143, in his study of Rāmānuja's use of *vibhūti*).

58 *GB*(S), pp. 277ff.

59 *Sūtra* 16: Sampatkumaran translates *vibhūti* here as 'will to rule' (compare van Buitenen's 'divine and personal dominion' – pp. 121ff.).

60 *Sūtra* 19.

61 *Sūtra* 20.

62 *Sūtra* 42.

63 *GB*(S), 10.3, p. 278.

64 *VS*(VB), para. 42, p. 213 (*GM*(*VS*), p. 10).

65 *SB*(T), 3.3.13, p. 638 (*GM*(*SB*), p. 323).

66 See *VS*(VB), para. 42, p. 213 (*GM*(*VS*), p. 10).

67 Carman claims that his *svarūpa* can be defined without reference to any other entity (*The Theology of Rāmānuja*, p. 97).

68 There are several current translations for Rāmānuja's use of *svarūpa*: van Buitenen translates 'proper form' (*VS*(VB), p. 184 n. 20); Carman uses 'essential nature' (*The Theology of Rāmānuja*, p. 70) and Neevel, when discussing Yāmuna's use of the term, translates as 'essential form' or 'own form'.

69 See *SB*(T), 3.3.12, p. 638.

70 *GB*(S), 18.55 p. 518 (*GM*(*GB*), p. 166). In this passage, Rāmānuja uses the term *guṇa* ('quality') to refer to the defining attributes (*kalyāṇaguṇas*) or to the noble qualities (*ṣaḍguṇas*). Note how he distinguishes these from the Lord's essential nature (*svarūpa*) and manifest nature (*svabhāva*).

One reason for this is that knowledge (*jñāna*) is both a defining attribute and, as a *ṣaḍguṇa*, one of the Lord's six 'noble qualities' proper to his *svabhāva*. Theoretically, then, knowledge (and, therefore, the *kalyāṇaguṇas* as a whole) could be included in both categories. In practice, Rāmānuja does include them in both categories, but often refers to them separately, possibly to avoid confusion. For a more detailed discussion of this issue see Carman, *The Theology of Rāmānuja*, pp. 88–98.

71 Van Buitenen allows for the inter-relatedness of the two terms by defining *svabhāva* as the *svarūpa* 'in the process of being and becoming with and through its essential qualities' (*VS*(*VB*), p. 185, n. 20). Carman's translation of the former as 'inherent nature' and *svarūpa* as 'essential nature' (p. 70) is confusing, although his concern to indicate the primacy of *svarūpa* is correct. I find 'manifest nature', although further from the literal meaning of *svabhāva*, nevertheless clearer in the context of Rāmānuja's usage.

72 J. B. Carman points out that this term originally meant 'remainder'; and in *Karma Mīmāṃsā* it denoted that part of the sacrifice which was subordinate to the principal purpose (*The Theology of Rāmānuja*, p. 147). Van Buitenen translates *śeṣa* as 'accessory' (*VS*(*VB*), p. 182 n. 3); Lott prefers 'subordinate entity'; Carman himself refers to 'servant' in relation to 'master' (pp. 147ff.), and in the context of Rāmānuja's usage this personalised translation is, perhaps, the most appropriate.

73 Rāmānuja brings out a double allusion here, previously used by Yāmuna (*Stotraratna*, 39–40): *śeṣa* is the name of the serpent on which Viṣṇu reclines, and also denotes the One who dwells in all beings as their inner Ruler. (See van Buitenen, p. 183 n. 4.)

74 *VS*(VB), p. 183 (*GM*(*VS*), p. 1). See also *GB*, 10.20, quoted on p. 69 above.

75 *VS*(VB), paras. 121–2, p. 275 (*GM*(*VS*), p. 34).

76 *SB*(T), 1.1.1, p. 153.

77 *GB*(VB), 11.2, p. 127.

78 J. B. Carman discusses the relation between the *ātman*'s 'metaphysical subordination or subservience (*śeṣatā*)' to Brahman and the concept of service to the Lord (*kainkarya*) in some detail (pp. 150, 292, n. 23). In particular he draws upon material in the *Gadyas* which speak of the *ātman* serving the Lord and surrendering to him in an act of faith.

79 *GB*(VB), 7.19, p. 104 (cf. *GB*, 9.27–8). This text also speaks of 'taking refuge' in the Lord (after 'acquiring knowledge of the real nature of the self') as finding 'sole joy' in dependence upon him (p. 212).

80 *Kleśas* are the five causes of misery: ignorance, egotism, preference, aversion and passion.

81 *GB*(VB), 18.54, p. 174 (*GM*(*GB*), p. 166).

82 *SB*(T), 2.2.3, p. 488 (*GM*(*SB*), p. 250).

83 *GB*, 6.30, trans. Carman, *The Theology of Rāmānuja*, p. 94 (*GM*(*GB*), pp. 57–8).

84 *SB*(T), 1.1.1, p. 4 (*GM*(*SB*), p. 49) (cf. *GB*, 18.73).

85 Rāmānuja's use of the term *līlā* ('sport') is defined by van Buitenen in contradistinction to karma: it contains 'a free action' (performed to no purpose). In relation to the world, Brahman has 'no cause to effectuate and no end to achieve' (*VS*(VB), para. 14, p. 192 n. 83).
86 *VS*(VB), para. 17b, p. 194 (*GM*(*VS*), p. 4).
87 *SB*(T), 1.1.1, pp. 127–8.
88 See *SB*(T), 1.1.1 (*GM*(*SB*), p. 94).
89 *SB*(T), 1.1.1, p. 60.
90 Ibid., p. 58.
91 Ibid., pp. 58–9 (*GM*(*SB*), p. 67).
92 See pp. 218–25.
93 *SB*(T), 2.1.9, p. 422.
94 Ibid., pp. 422–3.
95 '[These definitions] do not take in such things as earth and the like which the texts declare to be the body of the Lord. And further, they do not take in those bodily forms which the Lord assumes according to his wish, nor the bodily forms released forms may assume according to "He is One" etc. (Ch.Up. VII.26.2); for none of these embodiments subserve the fruition of the results of actions. And further, the bodily forms which the Supreme Person assumes at wish are not special combinations of earth and other elements; for *Smṛti* says, "The body of that highest Self is not made from a combination of the elements." It thus appears that it is also too narrow a definition to say that a body is a combination of the different elements. Again, to say that a body is that, the life of which depends on the vital breath with its five modifications, is also too narrow, viz. in respect of plants... Nor again does it answer to define a body as either the abode of the sense-organs or as the cause of pleasure and pain; for neither of these definitions takes in the bodies of stone and wood...' (*SB*(T), 2.1.9, pp. 423–4 (*GM*(*SB*), p. 223).
96 Ibid., p. 424.
97 *GB*(S), 10.39, p. 303 (*GM*(*GB*), p. 95).
98 *GB*(S), p. 251: 'The existence and activity of all beings arise from the will of the Lord (who is independent of all others).'
99 Ibid., 10.41, pp. 303–4. Here Rāmānuja is developing the *Viṣṇu-purāṇa* theme that only a fraction of the 'ten-thousandth part of a ten-thousandth part' of Brahman's power is used in relation to the universe.
100 *SB*(T), 1.1.23, p. 241.
101 *GB*(S), 11.7–15, pp. 309ff.

5 FUNCTIONS OF THE DIVINE BODY IN RĀMĀNUJA AND TEILHARD DE CHARDIN

1 Janet Martin Soskice, *Metaphor and Religious Language* (Oxford: Clarendon Press, 1985), p. 15.
2 For example, one could say that a root-metaphor in the religion of the

North American Indians is the 'sacred hoop': to them this is a defining characteristic of reality – their tepees are round, the earth is round, the seasons rotate etc.

3 For a recent analysis of the cognitive potentialities of metaphor, with particular reference to religious language, see Martin Soskice, *Metaphor and Religious Language*, and for a critique of the role of metaphor in theology (and especially Christian theology) see Sallie McFague, *Metaphorical Theology: Models of God in Religious Language* (London: SCM Press, 1983).

4 *GB*(S), 11.15–18, pp. 313–14 (*GM*(*GB*), pp. 99–100).

5 The three commonly accepted *pramāṇas* or means of valid knowledge include perception (*pratyakṣa*), inference (*anumāna*) and testimony (*śabda*). Rāmānuja, who adheres to a scriptural basis for knowledge of Brahman, argues that all perception, both 'indeterminate' and 'determinate', has a definite structure (*saṃsthāna*) and basis in reality, and that immediate perception attained through meditation (*yoga*) is self-validating.

6 Introduction to 'Le Cœur de la matière', in *HM*, p. 16 (*Oeuvres* 13, p. 22). The reader is referred back to p. 61.

7 Pensées 2, in *HU*, p. 7 (*Hymne de l'univers*, p. 80). The reader is referred back to p. 60.

8 'La Messe sur le monde', in *HU*, p. 34 (*Hymne de l'univers*, p. 34).

9 One wonders whether there is, in fact, a correlation in each case between intensity of experience and the degree of anthropomorphism.

10 'Le Christ dans la matière: trois histoires comme Benson', 'Christ in the World of Matter', in *HU*, pp. 39f. (*Hymne de l'univers*, pp. 39f.).

11 The only person who comes close to touching on this issue is Eric Lott in his book *God and the Universe*. He comments that Rāmānuja uses this 'bold analogy' in both a 'descriptive' and a 'determinative' sense (p. 1).

12 Chapters 6 and 7 below are devoted to developing this idea of the divine body as theological model.

13 *GB*(S), 18.65, p. 525; cf. *SB*(T), 3.4.26, p. 699. This subject will be dealt with in more depth in Chapter 7.

14 'La Messe sur le monde', in *HU*, p. 25 (*Hymne de l'univers*, p. 24).

15 *HU*, p. 36 (p. 36).

16 Teilhard concludes the Mass by dedicating all that he is and does to Christ's body, the world, which becomes 'through [Christ's] power and my faith the glorious living crucible in which everything melts away in order to be born anew' (*HU*, p. 37 (p. 37)). He adds, 'It is in this dedication, Lord Jesus, I desire to live, in this I desire to die.'

17 *Sāmānādhikaraṇya* ('co-ordinate predication').

18 *SB*(T), 1.1.13, p. 227 (*GM*(*SB*), p. 132).

19 'Note sur le Christ-Universel' (1920), in *SC*, p. 14 (*Oeuvres* 9, p. 39).

20 'L'Elément universel' (1919), in *WTW*, p. 297 (*Oeuvres* 12, pp. 439–40).

21 'L'Union créatrice' (1917), in *WTW*, p. 175 (*Oeuvres* 12, p. 223).

22 'Mon univers' (1924), in *SC*, p. 75 (*Oeuvres* 9, p. 104).

23 In other words, the macro form, Christ and his body the universe, indwells the micro form, the individual and his or her body, and the micro form indwells the macro form, the divine milieu. The determining element in each case is Christ as Centre and milieu.

24 For Rāmānuja, consciousness is an attribute of a self, and all selves are attributes of the Supreme Self. For Teilhard, consciousness is a molecular property present in all matter, and evolving towards self-realisation in Christ (Christ-consciousness).

25 'Body' being understood in the respective ways outlined above.

26 A conscious cultivation of devotion, for example, is part of that transformation (see pp. 103–4 above).

27 I.e. in Rāmānuja, the self's *svarūpa* is of uncontracted knowledge or consciousness; in Teilhard, each person or 'conscious centre' represents the cosmic nature of Christ.

6 THE DIVINE BODY AS MODEL OF THE INTEGRATION OF CONSCIOUSNESS

1 Janet Martin Soskice makes the distinction: 'When we use a model, we regard one thing or state of affairs in terms of another, and when we use a metaphor, we speak of one thing or state of affairs in language suggestive of another.' *Metaphor and Religious Language*, pp. 50–1.

2 Steven Katz, 'Models, Modeling and Mystical Training', *Religion* 12 (1982), 250. He is referring here to 'paradigmatic individuals' who become norms for their respective religious traditions. However, it also holds good for other aspects of religious traditions which fulfil the same role.

3 *Metaphor and Religious Language*, p. 101.

4 Ibid., pp. 102–3.

5 Ibid., pp. 109–12.

6 See Langer, *Philosophy in a New Key*. Here she refers to meaning in terms of symbolic logic: 'Meaning is not a quality, but a *function* of a term. A function is a *pattern* viewed with reference to one special term around which it centres; this pattern emerges when we look at the given term *in its total relation to the other terms* about it' (p. 55).

7 The 'model of' and 'model for' distinction is Clifford Geertz', although his social anthropological usage is in terms of the social and economic realities of a group, and ways in which individuals can respond to those realities. See 'Religion as a Cultural System', in *Anthropological Approaches to the Study of Religion*, ed. M. Banton, ASA Monographs 3 (New York: Tavistock Publications, 1966; Social Science Paperback, reprint, 1985), p. 7.

8 'The Metaphorical Process as Cognition, Imagination and Feeling', in *On Metaphor*, ed. Sheldon Sacks (Chicago and London: University of Chicago Press, 1978–9), p. 150.

9 For theological models see David Tracy, 'Metaphor and Religion: The Test Case of Christian Texts', in *On Metaphor*, ed. Sacks, pp. 89–105.
10 Lott, *Vedāntic Approaches to God*, pp. 27f.
11 In *Temple Art and Architecture*, Ananthacharya Indological Research Series 10, ed. K. K. A. Venkatachari (Bombay, 1981), p. 37.
12 'The World as God's "Body"', 145–61. See also *The Face of Truth* (Houndmills and London: Macmillan Press, 1986), chapter 7.
13 Ibid., p. 149.
14 The finite *ātman* and its body.
15 Brahman and his body.
16 Lipner, 'The World as God's "Body"', 147: 'Rāmānuja claims to have exposed the basic *literal* sense of "body"... This enables him to affirm as we shall see that created being is literally – not metaphorically – Brahman's body, yet not in any obvious sense.' His footnote at this juncture indicates that Rāmānuja never says the world is *like* Brahman's body (which would be the use of simile).
17 Hale, *Christ and the Universe*, pp. 1–17. He points to the 'bridging' role of such a model for Teilhard's scientific and theological concerns.
18 These qualities are found, he goes on to explain, in the 'body' model: the union of body with a person makes the Personhood of Christ accessible through the model of his body. Such a unitive model leaves it open to the description 'organic'.
19 *Christ and the Universe*, p. 7.
20 See chapter 4, 'Analogy of Selfhood', in Lott, *Vedāntic Approaches to God*, and his book *God and the Universe*. Also chapter 4, 'Dynamic Analogy', in Henri de Lubac, *The Eternal Feminine: a Study on the Text of Teilhard de Chardin* (London: Collins, 1971); chapter 17, 'Neologisms and Analogies', in his *Religion of Teilhard de Chardin*; and chapter 3, 'Faith and Analogy', in his *Faith of Teilhard de Chardin*.
21 Later Thomists called this an analogy of proper proportionality. For a clear presentation of classical understandings of analogy, see Patrick Sherry, 'Analogy Today', *Philosophy* 51 (1976), 431–46.
22 Martin Soskice, *Metaphor and Religious Language*, p. 64.
23 Ibid., p. 91.
24 Eric Lott suggests that the roots of *Vedānta*'s analogical method are 'probably to be found in the Vedic idea of the innate correspondence between ritual microcosmos and the macrocosmos of the wider non-sacred universe'. *Vedāntic Approaches to God*, pp. 27f.
25 Ninian Smart points out that analogical directions are not necessarily mutually exclusive in the way that their literal counterparts are (for example, transcendence and immanence may be located in one concept). 'Myth and Transcendence', *The Monist* 50 (1966), 487. (See also *Concept and Empathy: Essays in the Study of Religion*, ed. Donald Wiebe (London: Macmillan, 1986), in which this paper is reprinted.)
26 'The World as God's "Body"', 155.
27 NB: the Latin term *forma* refers primarily to shape, or configuration of

parts. The Sanskrit *rūpa* has the broader meaning of any outward appearance or phenomenon of colour (in addition to shape and figure). See *Compact Edition of the Oxford Dictionary* 1 (1979 edn), p. 1059; M. Monier-Williams, *A Sanskrit–English Dictionary*, rev. edn (Delhi: Motilal Banarsidass, repr. 1984), pp. 885–6.

28 *WTW*, p. 250 (*Oeuvres* 12, p. 363).

29 For a helpful discussion of Teilhard's understanding of causality in this context, see Hale, *Christ and the Universe*, pp. 87–8.

30 Or more accurately, 'quasi-Soul': a 'plasmatic or informing element, a force of determination' – 'L'Elément universel', in *WTW*, p. 299 (*Oeuvres* 12, p. 442).

31 'Forma Christi', in *WTW*, pp. 266–7 (*Oeuvres* 12, pp. 383–4).

32 Teilhard writes: 'If every collective soul is born in *our* world through the instrumentality of a body, then Christ can consummate our unity in the Centre *that stands firm above us* – the Centre, that is, which is his Spirit – only if he first encloses us in a material network *underlying* our "*esse corporeum*". If he is to be the soul of our souls, he must begin by being the flesh of our flesh.' *WTW*, p. 268 (*Oeuvres* 12, p. 385).

33 Light is a traditional metaphor for consciousness.

34 Lipner translates 'supernal form' in *The Face of Truth*, p. 94.

35 Rāmānuja speaks of Brahman's and the *ātman*'s *svarūpa* as infinite (*ananta*) knowledge or unlimited (*aparicchinna*) consciousness (see p. 78 above). Teilhard, in defining consciousness as the inner structure of matter (p. 47 above), claims that Christ-consciousness is 'universal' (i.e. illimitable).

36 'Integration' is here understood to mean wholeness or completeness; the act of integration being the bringing together as parts of a whole. The elements are, therefore, qualitatively distinguishable but apprehensible as one.

37 Teilhard's understanding of Christ is not limited to a concept of this planet only. See his letter to E. Mounier (November 1947), in which he discusses the 'modifications introduced by science' to an acceptable theology. *SC*, pp. 221–3 (*Oeuvres* 9, pp. 291–3).

38 *VS*(VB), para. 17b, p. 194 (*GM*(*VS*), p. 4).

39 *MD*, p. 56 (*Oeuvres* 4, p. 33).

40 In Rāmānuja's model, for example, non-conscious matter is distinguished from conscious matter, both of which comprise the body or 'field' of Brahman. In Teilhard's model, the different spheres (geosphere, biosphere and noosphere) comprise Christ's body or milieu. Consider also the way in which traditionally, Indian anthropology sees a person in terms of different 'sheaths' or layers of consciousness or energy.

41 'Everything that happens in the world, we would say, suggests that the unique centre of consciousness around which the universe is furling could only be formed gradually, by successive approximations, through a series of diminishing concentric spheres, each of which in turn

engenders the next; each sphere being moreover formed of elementary centres charged with a consciousness that increases as their radius decreases. By means of this mechanism each newly appearing sphere is charged in its turn with the consciousness developed in the preceding spheres, carries it a degree higher in each of the elementary centres that compose it, and transmits it a little further on towards the centre of total convergence... And the final centre of the whole system appears at the end both as the final sphere and as the Centre of all the centres spread over this final sphere.' 'Le Phénomène spirituel', in *HE*, p. 101 (*Oeuvres* 6, p. 126).

42 By 'symbolic structure' I mean that it manifests a structural form consistent with the (divine) consciousness it represents.

43 'Pour y voir clair: Réflexions sur deux formes inverses d'esprit', in *AE*, p. 220 (*Oeuvres* 7, p. 228).

44 *HE*, p. 160 (*Oeuvres* 6, p. 198). He explains how each individual comprises these two polarities and provides the *locus* for integration: 'Here a sphere calling for a centre. There a centre awaiting a sphere. Far from contradicting one another, as might be feared, the two stars of totality and personality attract one another within the human soul with all the force of cohesion that tends to close the universe on itself. A conjunction is therefore inevitable' (*HE*, p. 159 (*Oeuvres* 6, p. 197)).

45 It has been said that we, as humans, are symbolic beings. We create symbols in order to function as perceiving, thinking people. See Cassirer, *The Philosophy of Symbolic Forms* 1–3 and *Language and Myth*. Also Langer, *Philosophy in a New Key*.

46 Including: 'circular'; 'a circle'; 'a disc'; 'a globe'; 'circumference'; 'a wheel'; 'a halo'; 'a district' or 'province'; 'a corporate body'; 'a church assemblage'; 'a particular oblation' or 'sacrifice'; 'a mystical diagram formed in summoning a deity'; 'a division of the *Ṛg-veda*'.

47 The circle is a two-dimensional representation of a sphere. Often the sphere is 'squared', i.e. the outermost shape is a square, sometimes built up of many smaller squares.

48 For example, the famous *Śrī Cakra*, comprising a series of interlinked triangles representing the male and, more predominantly, the female aspects of the divine.

49 Trans. A. H. Brodrick (London: Rider & Co., 1969), pp. 21–5.

50 Ibid., p. 25.

51 Not to be confused with the ego.

52 'The Symbolism of the Mandala', in 'Dream Symbols of the Individuation Process', *Eranos Yearbooks* 4, ed. J. Campbell, Bollingen Series 30(4) (Princeton: Princeton University Press, 1960), p. 365.

53 Teilhard de Chardin, 'La Messe sur le monde', in *HU*, pp. 19ff. (*Hymne de l'univers*, pp. 17ff.).

54 Rāmānuja, *GB*(S), 11.20, p. 316.

55 Ed. J. Campbell, *Myths and Symbols in Indian Art and Civilization* (New York: Pantheon Books, 1946), p. 143, quoted by R. W. Fulcher,

'Mandala Symbolism and Christ-Mysticism', Ph.D. thesis, University of London, 1959, 179–80.

56 Ibid.

57 See 'Transformation et prolongements en l'homme du mécanisme de l'évolution', in *AE*, pp. 308–9 (*Oeuvres* 7, pp. 322–3).

58 See 'L'Atomisme de l'esprit: un essai pour comprendre la structure de l'étoffe de l'univers', in *AE*, pp. 44–6 (*Oeuvres* 7, pp. 51–3).

59 For a contemporary Hindu understanding of evolution in this context, see R. C. Zaehner, *Evolution in Religion: a Study in Sri Aurobindo and Pierre Teilhard de Chardin* (Oxford: Clarendon Press, 1971).

60 *VS*(R), para. 236, pp. 183–4.

61 See 'Le Milieu mystique', in *WTW*, pp. 115–49 (*Oeuvres* 12, pp. 155–92). The circles through which the mystic passes Teilhard describes as the circles of presence, consistence, energy, spirit, and person.

62 I have taken the term 'centroversion' from Gerhard Adler, *The Living Symbol: a Case Study in the Process of Individuation* (London: Routledge & Kegan Paul, 1961). Adler himself takes the term from Newman's *Origin and Development of Consciousness*, where it is defined as 'the innate tendency of a whole to create unity within its parts and to synthesize their differences in unified systems' (*Living Symbol*, p. 25).

7 THE DIVINE BODY AS MODEL FOR THE TRANSFORMATION OF CONSCIOUSNESS

1 *Religion: Truth and Language Games*, p. 112.

2 'La Messe sur le monde', in *HU*, pp. 34–7, or *HM*, pp. 131–3 (*Hymne de l'univers*, pp. 34–6).

3 *GM*(*VS*), pp. 40–1. Cf. trans., *VS*(R), para. 220, pp. 172–3.

4 *GB*(S), 11.14, p. 312 (*GM*(*GB*), p. 99).

5 *GB*(S), 11.15–18, p. 313–14 ((*GM*(*GB*), p. 100).

6 Cf. the '*Puruṣa-sūkta*' (*Ṛg-veda*, 10.90), where 'all creatures' comprise one-quarter of *puruṣa* (pp. 50–1).

7 Here R will stand for Rāmānuja and T for Teilhard.

8 This image is suggestive of the famous *puruṣa-sūkta* in the *Ṛg-veda*, where *puruṣa* is depicted as having a thousand heads, a thousand eyes and a thousand feet.

9 See *Viṣṇu-purāṇa*, VI.7. Here, the actions of the *yogi* ('adept of yoga') are said to be 'consumed by the fire of contemplative devotion'. Further on, it is explained that Viṣṇu, seated in the heart, 'consumes the sins of the sage' in the way that fire, blazing in the wind, burns dry grass.

10 In 'La Messe sur le monde', Teilhard explicitly refers to *le Feu* as the source of being. 'In the beginning', he writes, 'was *Power*, intelligent, loving, energizing. In the beginning was the *Word*, supremely capable of mastering and moulding whatever might come into being in the world of matter. In the beginning there was not coldness and darkness;

there was *Fire*. This is the truth.' *HU*, p. 21, or *HM*, pp. 121–2 (*Hymne de l'univers*, p. 20).

11 See Teilhard's second paper to Auguste Valensin (1919), in which he argues that 'For Grace [depicted by him as fire], consuming and transfiguring are one and the same process.' *Correspondence*, pp. 46–8 (p. 112 n. 12) (*Blondel et Teilhard de Chardin*, pp. 42–4 (p. 97 n. 12)).

12 *Correspondence*, p. 46 (*Blondel et Teilhard de Chardin*, p. 43).

13 J. Fitzer, 'Teilhard's Eucharist: A Reflection', *Theological Studies* 34 (Baltimore 1973), 253. The implication is that Christ as the universal Element is both the element [bread] to be consecrated and the consecrated Host effecting the gradual consecration ('divinisation') of the universe. (Cf. the Prajāpati concept in the *Ṛg-veda*: the divine Person whose self-immolation signifies the creation of the world.)

14 *Correspondence*, pp. 47–8 (*Blondel et Teilhard de Chardin*, pp. 43–4). Cf. 'To adore... that means... to offer oneself to the fire and the transparency, to annihilate oneself in proportion to one's becoming more deliberately conscious of oneself, and to give of one's deepest to that whose depth has no end'. *MD*, pp. 127–8 (*Oeuvres* 4, p. 144).

15 See 'Le Milieu mystique', in *WTW*, p. 144 (*Oeuvres* 12, pp. 186–7).

16 It may be of interest to note that Rāmānuja and Teilhard also allude to the same colours in their descriptions of the divine Person, although the colours are associated with different features: white, gold and possibly red. Teilhard speaks of the forehead of the Lord as having the 'whiteness of snow'; his eyes are 'of fire' (i.e. red) and his feet of molten gold. Rāmānuja refers to the Lord's 'lustre' as being of molten gold, his splendour being of many suns (i.e. red) and his eyes and feet as lotuses (i.e. pinkish white).

17 Structurally there is a parallelism in each writer's vision, between the eyes of the divine Person and his feet: Rāmānuja describes the Lord's eyes in terms of unfolding lotus blossom and his feet, of full-blown lotuses. Teilhard refers to the Lord's eyes as 'of fire' and his feet of molten (i.e. burning) gold. However, it is not possible to embark on a study of comparative mystical physiology at this point.

18 Cf. the claim of a contemporary Hindu, Paramhansa Yogananda, in his *Autobiography of a Yogi* (London: Rider, 3rd edn, 1953) that the cosmic 'essence' is light: 'Devotees of every age testify to the appearance of God as flame and light... St. John described his vision (Revelation I: 14–16) of the Lord: "His eyes were as a flame of fire... and his countenance was as the sun shineth in his strength"... A yogi who through perfect meditation has merged his consciousness in the Creator, perceives the cosmical essence as light; to him there is no difference between the light rays composing water and the light rays composing land... thenceforth he sees the universe as an essentially undifferentiated mass of light' (pp. 228–9).

19 See 'Le Milieu mystique', in *WTW*, pp. 117–49 (*Oeuvres* 12, pp. 153–92).

20 Cf. the Pauline notion of having 'the mind of Christ'.
21 See Lott, 'Iconic Vision and Cosmic Viewpoint in Rāmānuja's Vedānta', pp. 32–3.
22 The reader should, perhaps, be reminded that the transformed consciousness does, in each case, retain a relational element.
23 *Upāsana* is 'the act of sitting or being near at hand; serving, waiting upon, service, attendance, respect... homage, adoration, worship (with Rāmānuja's [tradition] consisting of five parts, viz. *Abhigamana* or approach, *Upādāna* or preparation of offering, *Ijyā* or oblation, *Svādhyāya* or recitation, and *Yoga* or devotion...'. Monier-Williams, *Sanskrit–English Dictionary*, p. 215.
24 More precisely, 'the means to attain the [religious] goal'.
25 See *VS*(R), para. 129, pp. 101–2.
26 'Only through intensive devotional love to Bhagavan Viṣṇu [can] a devotee realise the relation of part to whole (*aṃśāṃśibhāva saṃbandha*), between Jīvātman and Paramātman. The former completely depends on the latter.' Ramnarayan Vyas, *The Bhāgavata Bhakti Cult and three Advaita Ācāryas: Śankara, Rāmānuja and Vallabha* (Delhi: Nag Publishers, 1977), p. v.
27 *GB*(S), 7.27, pp. 218–19. Cf. Yāmuna's *Gītārthasaṃgraha*, 29 (p. 544).
28 *VS*(R), para. 126, pp. 97–8.
29 Ibid.
30 For an excellent analysis of Rāmānuja's *sādhana* see R. C. Lester, *Rāmānuja on the Yoga* (Madras: Adyar Library and Research Centre, 1976).
31 *GB*(S), 4.34, p. 137. Rāmānuja explains the *Gītā* text thus: 'The wise are those who have had direct vision of the essential nature of the self.'
32 Ibid., 4.35, p. 138. Here the *Gītā* refers to the 'equality' of all beings who comprise the 'form of knowledge'.
33 *GB*(S), 4.37, p. 139.
34 Ibid., 4.41, p. 141; 6.1, p. 164.
35 As does the *Srībhāṣya*, which provides several *brahma-vidyās* or meditations on Brahman.
36 It is important to note that Rāmānuja interprets 'equality' not in terms of causative identity (selves are *similar* to the Lord), but substantive identity (they share the same form). See Lott, 'Iconic Vision and Cosmic Viewpoint in Rāmānuja's Vedānta', p. 38, for an approach to understanding the former in terms of 'the relational act of worshipful meditation'.
37 *GB*(S), 5.19, p. 156. Such meditation, when applied to daily life, enables the knowledge attained to ripen 'in the form of equality of vision'.
38 Ibid., 6.20, p. 157.
39 See 5.21–4, pp. 186–7.
40 Rāmānuja, when commenting on this *Gītā* meditation, claims that one who is 'intent on the vision of his self... is a liberated person at all times' (*GB*(S), 5.28, pp. 161–2). The sage is 'liberated' in the sense that he has

already detached himself from *prakṛti*. The *Gītābhāṣya* refers to the vision of the self as *mokṣa* (6.3, p. 166) and here, to one 'intent on the vision of the self' as 'liberated'. However, this is but the prefiguring (*kaivalya*: literally 'aloneness') of a higher state referred to elsewhere as 'attaining the Lord'. (For *mokṣa* see p. 174, nn. 73; 74 above.)

41 See above, n. 36, and p. 78 for the ambiguity concerning the devotee's 'oneness' with and 'similarity' to the Lord.

42 I.e. the darkness of ignorance in the form of negative karma.

43 *GB*(S), 10.11, p. 286.

44 Ibid., 9.34, pp. 274–5. He then explains that worship takes the form of offering to the Lord. The context for this is Kṛṣṇa's earlier teaching that whatever the devotee does, thinks, eats etc. should be made into an offering to the Lord (see *GB*(S), 9.27, p. 268). Here, he treats more specifically of ritual offerings (such as lights, incense, sandalwood paste, flowers etc.) which, as Vedānta Deśika points out in his *Tātparyacandrikā* (one of the most famous commentaries on the *Gītābhāṣya*), refer primarily to *Pāñcarātra* practices. Vedānta Deśika, *Tātparyacandrikā*, ed. Śrī Prativādibhayaṅkara Aṇṇamgarācārya (Kāñcipuram: Śrīmad-vedāntadeśika-granthamālā, 1941), p. 269.

45 *GB*(S), 18.65, pp. 524–6. The following, controversial stanza advocates taking refuge in the Lord alone and renouncing all other *dharmas*. As indicated earlier (p. 42 above), this need not be an injunction separate from, and in addition to, the overall concern with *bhakti*. Indeed, in the context of the *Vedārthasaṃgraha* text (p. 219), where taking refuge is advocated at the beginning of the path, yet total self-surrender features also at the end of the *bhakta*'s path (line 26), it would appear that *prapatti* is part of *bhakti-yoga*, indeed its most essential part. (Cf. *SB*(T), 1.1.1, pp. 14–16.)

46 It may be that included in this form of objectification are iconographical representations of the Lord (p. 60).

47 Cf. *SB*(T), 1.1.1, p. 14: 'Meditation means steady remembrance, i.e. a continuity of steady remembrance, uninterrupted like the flow of oil...'

48 *SB*(T), 3.4.26, p. 699.

49 Ibid., 1.1.1, p. 15: 'This character of seeing consists in its possessing the character of immediate perception (*pratyakśatā*).'

50 Rāmānuja is insistent that this meditation is brought about through the grace of the Supreme Person (ibid., 3.4.26, p. 699): 'Whom the Self chooses, by him it may be gained; to him the Self reveals its being' (1.1.1, p. 15).

51 'By constant daily practice [it] becomes ever more perfect, and being duly continued up to death secures final Release' (3.4.26).

52 In the *Vedārthasaṃgraha* Rāmānuja refers to this state as *parabhakti* (*VS*(R), para. 238, p. 185), and he explains that this is an end in itself. It is, he says, a form of love, and should be understood as a special cognition or knowledge in which the object is experienced subjectively as 'infinite and abiding joy' or bliss. In other words, knowledge of

Brahman involves the realisation of the *svarūpa* of both the self (*ātman*) and Brahman (p. 135).

53 It is important to remember that the devotee is at all times aware of his or her dependence upon the Lord.

54 *SB*(T), 1.2.23, p. 284.

55 This is not to say she or he has attained release fully, since Rāmānuja claims that this is only possible after the death of the body.

56 See *VS*(R), para. 243, p. 187.

57 By which he means the fulfilling of all things through Christ (p. 95).

58 Whereas Rāmānuja conceives *mokṣa* as attainable after death, only by those (rare) individuals deserving of it.

59 For an explicit example of this identification of the pleroma and the body of Christ, see 'Panthéisme et christianisme' (1923), in *CE*, p. 69 (*Oeuvres* 10, p. 86).

60 I.e. the salvation of the world.

61 A. M. Buono explains: 'A superior being in this respect is one in which the millions of cells that make it up lose their individuality and enhance the unity of the whole. Starting from a single cell, we end up with a multicellular being by means of an affinity (whose physio-chemical basis is little known) which works to maintain the group of cells.' 'The Evolutionary Ecclesiology of Teilhard de Chardin', Ph.D. dissertation, Fordham University New York, 1982, 60. This perspective can be helpful, providing the absence of personal concepts together with the idea of 'losing individuality' do not mislead one into envisaging a mechanistic process.

62 In a letter to Victor Fontoynont (1916) Teilhard asks: 'Couldn't the *object* of our human passions, in fact, *their very substance*, undergo transformation, undergo mutation into the Absolute, the definitive, the divine?' *Correspondence*, p. 68 n. 18 (*Blondel et Teilhard de Chardin*, p. 60 n. 18). For Teilhard's use of 'transformation' see 'Un problème majeur pour l'anthropologie' (1951), in *AE*, pp. 313ff. (*Oeuvres* 7, pp. 325ff.).

63 See 'Introduction à la vie chrétienne' (1944), in *CE*, p. 170 (*Oeuvres* 10, pp. 198–9): 'The saint, the Christian saint, as we now understand him and look for him, will not be the man who is the most successful in escaping matter and mastering it completely; he will be the man who seeks to make all his powers – gold, love or freedom – transcend themselves and co-operate in the consummation of Christ, and who so realises for us the ideal of the faithful servant of evolution.'

64 'Panthéisme et christianisme', in *CE*, p. 73 (*Oeuvres* 10, p. 89).

65 C. F. Mooney interprets 'mystical' in this context to mean 'hyper-physical'. *Teilhard de Chardin and the Mystery of Christ*, p. 82. (See 'Mon univers' (1924), in *SC*, p. 65 (*Oeuvres* 9, p. 93).)

66 'Quelque remarques "pour y voir clair" sur l'essence du sentiment mystique', in *TF*, p. 209 (*Oeuvres* 11, p. 227).

67 See 'Le Milieu mystique', in *WTW*, pp. 115ff. (*Oeuvres* 12, pp. 153ff.).

68 The first and second ways he sees as alternative forms of mysticism: one

comprising an 'escape' from everyday reality into a divine 'beyond'; and the second, a 'dissolving' into an envisaged undifferentiated unity of all things.

69 'Le christique' (1955), in *HM*, p. 95 (*Oeuvres* 13, pp. 109–10). See King, *Towards a New Mysticism*.
70 *HM*, pp. 95–9 (*Oeuvres* 13, pp. 110–14).
71 *WTW*, pp. 115–49 (*Oeuvres* 12, pp. 155–92).
72 *HU*, pp. 19–37 (*Hymne de l'univers*, pp. 17–37).
73 *Oeuvres* 4.
74 Cf. the successive 'circles' representing different levels of consciousness in 'Le Milieu mystique' (p. 201).
75 *MD*, pp. 131–2 (*Oeuvres* 4, pp. 150–1).
76 This perception Teilhard refers to in 'Le Milieu mystique' as the 'circle of presence'. He goes on to say that the mystic is one who is 'born to give first place in his experience to that aureole'. *WTW*, p. 119 (*Oeuvres* 12, p. 159).
77 Ibid.
78 *WTW*, p. 123 (*Oeuvres* 12, p. 163).
79 'La Messe sur le monde', in *HU*, pp. 19–21 (*Hymne de l'univers*, pp. 17–19). Fire, of course, is a traditional symbol for the Holy Spirit. Here it is linked with the sun (dawn) and Christ's love (see pp. 91; 126 above).
80 *MD*, p. 132 (*Le Milieu divin*, p. 151). Teilhard identifies this gift as the Holy Spirit, for whom he then prays: '"*Spiritus principalis*", whose flaming action alone can operate the birth and achievement of the great metamorphosis which sums up all inward perfection and towards which your creation yearns...'.
81 'Le Milieu mystique', in *WTW*, p. 121 (*Oeuvres* 12, p. 162).
82 See *MD*, p. 134 (*Oeuvres* 4, pp. 154–5), where Teilhard speaks about the power of purity to bring the divine to birth among us. Cf. 'Le Milieu mystique': 'Nothing is more intensely alive and active than purity and prayer, which hang like an unmoving light between the universe and God. Through their serene transparency flow the waves of creative power charged with natural virtue and with grace. What else is this but the Virgin Mary?' *WTW*, p. 144 (*Oeuvres* 12, p. 187).
83 *MD*, p. 133 (*Oeuvres* 4, p. 153).
84 'Le Milieu mystique', in *WTW*, p. 123 (*Oeuvres* 12, p. 164).
85 *WTW*, p. 124 (*Oeuvres* 12, p. 165).
86 See *Le Milieu divin*: 'Each one of the elect is called to see God face to face. But his act of vision will be vitally inseparable from the elevating and illuminating action of Christ. In heaven we ourselves shall contemplate God, but, as it were, through the eyes of Christ.' *MD*, p. 143 (*Oeuvres* 4, p. 168).
87 In the consecration of Teilhard's 'La Messe sur le monde' he prays that the spirit of God ('Fire') transfigure all that is incomplete and remould it, so that it becomes the body of Christ. *HU*, pp. 121–3 (*Hymne de

l'univers, pp. 20–2). Teilhard's teachings show that he envisaged this transfiguration taking place through the purity of individual souls. See 'Mon univers' (1924), in *SC*, p. 77 (*Oeuvres* 9, p. 106).

88 'Le Milieu mystique', in *WTW*, p. 125 (*Oeuvres* 12, p. 166).

89 In 'Le Milieu mystique', Teilhard discusses the 'passivities' before 'creative action', whereas in *Le Milieu divin*, the 'activities' are treated first.

90 See *MD*, pp. 134–7 (*Oeuvres* 4, pp. 155–9).

91 'Le Milieu mystique', in *WTW*, p. 130 (*Oeuvres* 12, p. 171).

92 *WTW*, pp. 134–5 (*Oeuvres* 12, pp. 176–7).

93 *WTW*, p. 135 (*Oeuvres* 12, p. 177).

94 Ibid. Cf. 'La Messe sur le monde', in *HU*, p. 125 (*Hymne de l'univers*, p. 25): 'I can no longer see anything nor any longer breathe, outside that Milieu in which all is made One.'

95 'La Messe sur le monde', in *HU*, p. 127 (*Hymne de l'univers*, pp. 27–8). See J. Fitzer, 'Teilhard's Eucharist: a Reflection', in which he suggests that the function of the Eucharist is, for Teilhard, to communicate the world's identity as the body of Christ to human consciousness. Fitzer calls this a form of 'transignification'. He does not fully allow, however, for the biological implications of a transformed human consciousness for evolution. See 'Introduction à la Vie chrétienne', in *CE*, pp. 165–7 (*Oeuvres* 10, pp. 193–5); also *MD*, pp. 123–8 (*Oeuvres* 4, pp. 138–45).

96 *MD*, p. 138 (*Oeuvres* 4, p. 160).

97 Ibid.

98 'Le Milieu mystique', in *WTW*, p. 144 (*Oeuvres* 12, pp. 186–7).

99 *MD*, p. 144 (*Oeuvres* 4, p. 169).

100 *MD*, p. 144 (*Oeuvres* 4, pp. 169–70).

101 'Le Milieu mystique', in *WTW*, pp. 144–5 (*Oeuvres* 12, p. 188). Cf. the 'Prière' section of 'La Messe sur le monde', in *HU*, pp. 32–7 (*Hymne de l'univers*, pp. 32ff.). Teilhard's description of the relationship between the mystic's devotion and his transformed vision of the world as Person illustrates what I am referring to as the process of centring. He remarks cryptically in 'Le Milieu mystique' that the 'movement' which opened his eyes to the world as Person began at the 'point' of his own person. It then came to centre on a 'single point', which was the person of Christ. *WTW*, p. 145 (*Oeuvres* 12, p. 189). Cf. *Le Milieu divin*, where he argues that the divine milieu is a centre. *MD*, p. 144 (*Oeuvres* 4, p. 124).

102 For a succinct summary of Teilhard's understanding of Christ in the Eucharist, see Mooney, *Teilhard de Chardin and the Mystery of Christ*, pp. 84–5.

103 See Appendix II, 'Teilhard de Chardin on the Mass'.

104 Rāmānuja refers to this knowledge as a 'mental energy' (see p. 135 above), and a kind of seeing: 'Knowledge... [is] a mental energy different in character from the mere cognition of the sense of texts and more specifically denoted by such terms as *dhyāna* or *upāsana*, i.e.

meditation; which is of the nature of remembrance (i.e. representative thought), but in intuitive clearness is not inferior to the clearest presentative thought (*pratyakśa*)...' (*SB*(T), 3.4.26, p. 699). Teilhard refers to it in terms of consciousness and vision: 'Seeing. We might say that the whole of life lies in that verb if not ultimately, at least essentially. Fuller being in closer union...But let us emphasize the point: union increases only through an increase in consciousness, that is to say, in vision.' *PM*, p. 35 (*Oeuvres* 1, p. 25).

105 It is necessary to make a clarification here: seeing things as equal facets of one reality is not the same as maintaining that there is an ontological identity between the individual and the Lord. Rāmānuja and Teilhard are not claiming that the individual's consciousness is identical with divine consciousness. The experience of seeing the Lord in all things is certainly a transcendence of the subject–object, world–divine dichotomies, and a vision of unity. However, an awareness of relationship is still present: the individual is still in a dependent relationship with the whole. Though 'at one' with the divine presence, the person concerned does not identify him or herself with the illimitability and completeness that the divine represents in entirety. The transcendent Lord is always 'supreme'; he is 'Alpha' and 'Omega'.

106 See Mircea Eliade, 'Cosmical Homology and Yoga', *Journal of the Indian Society of Oriental Arts* 5 (1937), 196. Here there is a discussion of the contemplation of images and the 'assimilation' of iconographically expressed symbols as 'mystical techniques' through which the human condition is 'exceeded'.

107 Peter Moore, 'Mystical Experience, Mystical Doctrine, Mystical Technique', in *Mysticism and Philosophical Analysis*, ed. Steven Katz (London: Sheldon Press, 1978), p. 116.

108 This is not to argue, as Lorna McDougall does, that archetypes such as mandalas are *reducible* to the commonalities of the human body and its structures (she uses as an example the relationship between mandalas and phosphenes experienced in the brain): 'Symbols and Somatic Structures', in *The Anthropology of the Body*, ed. J. Blacking (London: Academic Press, 1977), p. 392.

109 The reader is referred, at this point, to the current debate between 'new' physics, biochemistry and eastern models of psychology. For example, see Renée Weber, *Dialogues with Scientists and Sages: The Search for Unity* (London: Routledge & Kegan Paul, 1986) and Ken Wilber (ed.), *The Holographic Paradigm and other Paradoxes* (Boston and London: New Science Library, Shambhala, 1985).

8 THE BODY DIVINE: PARADIGM OF A CONSCIOUS COSMOS

1 For example, see Renée Weber, *Dialogues with Scientists and Sages.*

2 See D. Bohm, *Wholeness and the Implicate Order* (London: Routledge &

Kegan Paul, 1980). For Renée Weber's 'Reflections on David Bohm's Holomovement: a Physicist's Model of Cosmos and Consciousness', see R. Valle and R. von Eckartsberg (eds.), *The Metaphors of Consciousness* (New York and London: Plenum Press, 1981), pp. 121–40.

3 This term is used by K. H. Pribam in his neurological theory based on research into brain function. Valle and von Eckartsberg (eds.), *The Metaphors of Consciousness*, p. 132.

4 Ibid., p. 134.

5 Ibid., pp. 136–7.

6 Ibid., p. 137.

7 Richard Moss, *How Shall I Live* (Berkeley: Celestial Arts, 1985), p. xiii.

8 Rāmānuja and Teilhard de Chardin speak of 'seeing' the Lord through perceiving the world imbued with the divine. It is as if, in their terms, the divine form 'in-forms' human consciousness. Things are no longer viewed from the perspective of a limited ego, but from eyes 'on all sides' (cf. the *puruṣa* image of a thousand eyes, p. 31 above), from a de-limited perspective.

9 It would, I think, be rewarding to look at Buddhist descriptions of consciousness in this context.

10 Teilhard writes: 'Each one of the elect is called to see God face to face. But his act of vision will be vitally inseparable from the elevating and illuminating action of Christ. In heaven we ourselves shall contemplate God, but, as it were, through the eyes of Christ.' *MD*, p. 143 (*Oeuvres* 4, p. 168). There is still a distinction, therefore, between the self/soul and Brahman/God.

11 Background to this idea can be found in the following articles: William J. Wainwright, 'God's Body', *American Academy of Religion Journal* 42 (September 1974), 470–81; John B. Bennett, 'Nature – God's Body? A Whiteheadian Perspective', *Philosophy Today* vol. 18 no. 3/4 (Fall 1974), 248–54; Ninian Smart, 'God's Body', *Union Seminary Quarterly Review* 37 (Fall/Winter 1981–2), 51–68.

12 The reader is referred here to the writings of Ken Wilber, and in this context particularly to *The Holographic Paradigm and other Paradoxes*, ed. Wilber.

13 See Caroline Mackenzie's article, 'A Wound in the Body of God', *The Newman Journal* 21 (September 1990), 11–14.

14 Grace Jantzen, *God's World, God's Body* (London: Darton, Longman & Todd, 1984), p. 156.

15 Bede Griffiths, *A New Vision of Reality* (London: Collins, 1989), p. 293.

16 See M. Wiles, 'Christian Theology in an Age of Religious Studies', in *Explorations in Theology* IV (London: SCM Press, 1979), p. 39.

17 Valle and von Eckartsberg (eds), *The Metaphors of Consciousness*, p. 135.

18 Ibid., p. 138.

Select bibliography

A PRIMARY SOURCES

(I) PUBLISHED WORKS OF TEILHARD DE CHARDIN

(This is not a complete bibliography of Teilhard de Chardin's works. See Joseph M. McCarthy, *Pierre Teilhard de Chardin: a Comprehensive Bibliography* (New York and London: Garland, 1981).)

Series *Oeuvres de Pierre Teilhard de Chardin*. Paris: Editions du Seuil

1 *Le Phénomène humain* (1955)
2 *L'Apparition de l'homme* (1956)
3 *La Vision du passé* (1957)
4 *Le Milieu divin: essai de vie intérieure* (1957)
5 *L'Avenir de l'homme* (1959)
6 *L'Energie humaine* (1962)
7 *L'Activation de l'energie* (1963)
8 *La Place de l'homme dans la nature* (1956)
9 *Science et Christ* (1965)
10 *Comment je crois* (1969)
11 *Les Directions de l'avenir* (1973)
12 *Ecrits du temps de la guerre* (1965)
13 *Le Cœur de la matière* (1976)

Series *Cahiers Pierre Teilhard de Chardin*. Paris: Editions du Seuil

1 *Construire la Terre* (1958)
2 *Réflexions sur la bonheur* (1960)
3 *Pierre Teilhard de Chardin et la politique africaine* (1962)
4 *La Parole attendue* (1963)
5 *Le Christ évoluteur: socialisation et religion* (1965)
6 *Le Dieu de l'évolution* (1968)
7 *Sens humain et sens divin* (1971)
8 *Terre promise* (1974)

Accomplir l'homme: lettres inédites (1926–1952). Paris: Bernard Grasset, 1968.

Blondel et Teilhard de Chardin : correspondance. Paris: Beauchesne, 1965.

Ecrits du temps de la guerre. Paris: Bernard Grasset, 1956.

Genèse d'une pensée: lettres (1914–1919). Paris: Bernard Grasset, 1961.

Hymne de l'univers. Paris: Editions du Seuil, 1961.

Journal, vol. 1. Paris: Librairie Arthème Fayard, 1975.
Lettres à Léontine Zanta. Paris: Desclée de Brouwer, 1965.
Lettres d'Hastings et de Paris. Paris: Aubier, 1965.
Lettres de l'Egypte. Paris: Aubier, 1963.
Lettres de voyage. Paris: Bernard Grasset, 1956.
Lettres familières de Pierre Teilhard de Chardin, mon ami. Edited by P. Leroy. Paris: Centurion, 1976.
Lettres intimes de Teilhard de Chardin à Auguste Valensin, Bruno Solages et Henri de Lubac. Paris: Aubier Montaigne, 1972; 2nd edn, 1974.

Translations

Series *Oeuvres de Pierre Teilhard de Chardin*
1 *The Phenomenon of Man*. London: Collins, 1959; Fontana, 1965
2 *The Appearance of Man*. London: Collins, 1965
3 *The Vision of the Past*. London: Collins, 1966
4 *Le Milieu divin: an Essay on the Interior Life*. London: Collins, 1960; Fount Paperbacks, 1978
5 *The Future of Man*. London: Collins, 1964; Fontana, 1969
6 *Human Energy*. London: Collins, 1969
7 *Activation of Energy*. London: Collins, 1970
8 *Man's Place in Nature*. London: Collins, 1966; Fontana, 1971
9 *Science and Christ*. London: Collins, 1968
10 *Christianity and Evolution*. London: Collins, 1971
11 *Toward the Future*. London: Collins, 1975
12 *Writings in Time of War*. London: Collins, 1968
13 *The Heart of Matter*. London: Collins, 1978
Hymn of the Universe. London: Collins, 1965; Fontana, 1970; reprint, 1971.
Letters from a Traveller. London: Collins, 1962; Fontana, 1967.
Letters from Egypt, 1905–8. New York: Herder & Herder, 1965.
Letters from Hastings (1908–1912). Letters from Paris (1912–1914). 2 vols. London: Burns & Oates, 1967–8.
Letters to Léontine Zanta, trans. Bernard Wall. London and New York: Collins, Harper & Row, 1969.
'Letter to Père Victor Fontoynont', 15 March 1916. In Henri de Lubac, *The Religion of Teilhard de Chardin*, 241–5.
Letters to Two Friends, 1926–1952. London: Collins Fontana Library of Theology and Philosophy, 1972.
Pierre Teilhard de Chardin, Maurice Blondel: Correspondence. New York: Herder & Herder, 1967.
The Making of a Mind: Letters from a Soldier-Priest, 1914–1919. London: Collins, 1965.
The Prayer of the Universe. London: Collins, 1968; Fontana, 1973.

(II) PUBLISHED WORKS OF RĀMĀNUJA

(This is not a complete bibliography of Rāmānuja's works. For a more comprehensive bibliography, see Carman, *The Theology of Rāmānuja*, pp. 317–19.)

Śrī Bhagavad Rāmānuja Granthamālā. Edited by Śrī Kanchi P. B. Annangaracharya Swamy. Kancheepuram: Granthamālā Office, 1956.

Translations

Buitenen, J. A. B. van. *Rāmānuja on the Bhagavadgītā: a Condensed Rendering of his Gītābhāsya with Copious Notes and an Introduction*. 2nd edn, reprint, 1974. Delhi: Motilal Banarsidass.

Rāmānuja's Vedārthasaṃgraha. Critical text and translation with notes. Poona: Deccan College Postgraduate and Research Institute, 1956.

Karmarkar, R. D. *Śrībhāṣya of Rāmānuja*. Part I. Poona: University of Poona, 1959.

Narasimha Ayyangar, M. B. *Vedāntasāra of Bhagavad Rāmānuja*. Edited by Pandit V. Krishnamacharya. The Adyar Library Series 83. Madras: Adyar Library and Research Centre, 1953; 2nd edn, 1979.

Raghavachar, S. S. *Vedārthasaṅgraha of Rāmānujāchārya*. Mysore: Śrī Ramakrishna Ashrama, 1978.

Rangacharya, M., and M. B. Varadaraja Aiyangar. *The Vedānta-sūtras with the Śrī-bhāshya of Rāmānujāchārya*. 3 vols. Madras: Educational Publishing Co., vol. I, 2nd edn, 1961; vols. II and III, 1964, 1965.

Sampatkumaran, M. R. *The Gītābhāṣhya of Rāmānuja*. Madras: Prof. M. Rangacharya Memorial Trust, 1969.

Srinivasan, Śrī S. V. *Rāmānuja's Saranagati Gadya*. Quoted in *Viśishtādvaita: Philosophy and Religion*. Edited by V. S. Raghavan. Madras: Rāmānuja Research Society, 1974.

Thibaut, G. *The Vedānta-sūtras with Commentary by Rāmānuja*. Sacred Books of the East 48. Edited by Max Müller. Oxford: Oxford University Press, 1904; reprint, Delhi: Motilal Banarsidass, 1976.

B SECONDARY WORKS

(I) WORKS RELATED TO TEILHARD DE CHARDIN

Armagnac, Christian d'. 'Le Premier Teilhard: le Christ et le monde', *Etudes* 109 (May 1965), 652–63.

Bilaniuk, Petro. 'The Christology of Teilhard de Chardin', in *Proceedings of the Teilhard Conference Fordham University*. New York: n.p., 1964.

Birx, H. J. *Pierre Teilhard de Chardin's Philosophy of Evolution*. American Lecture Series, no. 852. A Monograph in the Bannerstone Division of American Lectures in Philosophy. Illinois: Charles C. Thomas, 1972.

Blondel, Maurice, *L'Action*, 2 vols. Paris: Presses Universitaires de France, 1936–7; reprint, 1949–63.

'*The Letter on Apologetics*' *and* '*History and Dogma*'. Translated by A. Dru and I. Trethowan. London: Harvill Press, 1964.

'The Theory and Practice of Action' (translated by J. M. Somerville), *Cross Currents* (1951), 251–61.

Bruteau, B. *Evolution toward Divinity: Teilhard de Chardin and the Hindu Traditions*. Wheaton: The Theosophical Publishing House, 1974.

Buono, A. M. 'The Evolutionary Ecclesiology of Teilhard de Chardin'. Ph.D. dissertation, Fordham University New York, 1982.

Cairns, Hugh Campbell, 'The Identity and Originality of Teilhard de Chardin'. Ph.D. thesis, University of Edinburgh, 1971.

Copleston, F. *A History of Philosophy* 4. London: Burns & Oates, 1965.

Corbishley, Thomas. *The Spirituality of Teilhard de Chardin*. London: Collins Fontana Library, 1971.

Dai Sil, K. 'Irenaeus of Lyons and Teilhard de Chardin: a Comparative Study of "Recapitulation" and "Omega"', *Journal of Ecumenical Studies* 13 (Philadelphia, 1976), 69–93.

Daly, G. *Transcendence and Immanence: a Study in Catholic Modernism and Integralism*. Oxford: Clarendon Press, 1980.

Deckers, M. C. *Le Vocabulaire de Teilhard de Chardin*. Gembloux: J. Duculot, 1968.

Delfgaauw, B. *Evolution: the Theory of Teilhard de Chardin*. London: Collins Fontana, 1969.

Encyclical Letter '*Pascendi Gregis*' *of Our Most Holy Lord Pius X by Divine Providence Pope on the Doctrines of the Modernists*. London, 1907.

Faricy, Robert L. *All Things in Christ: Teilhard de Chardin's Spirituality*. London: Collins Fount Paperbacks, 1981.

'Teilhard de Chardin's Theology of Redemption', *Theological Studies* 27, 553–79.

Fawkes, Alfred. *Studies in Modernism*. London: Smith, 1913.

Fitzer, J. 'Teilhard's Eucharist: A Reflection', *Theological Studies* 34 (Baltimore, 1973), 251–64.

Foch, Germain. *La Vie intérieure*. 6th edn, Paris and Lyons: Librairie Catholique Emmanuel Vitte, 1919.

Gilby, Thomas (ed. and trans.). *St. Thomas Aquinas: Philosophical Texts*. London: Oxford University Press, 1951.

Gray, D. *The One and the Many: Teilhard de Chardin's Vision of Unity*. London: Burns & Oates, 1969.

Hale, R. *Christ and the Universe: Teilhard de Chardin and the Cosmos*. Chicago: Franciscan Herald Press, 1972.

Huby, J. (ed.). *Christus: Manuel d'histoire des religions*. Paris: Beauchesne, 1912.

Hunt, Anne. 'Rothe's Christology: a Study of "Sermons for the Christian year"'. B.A. dissertation, University of Cambridge, 1975.

Jones, D. Gareth. *Teilhard de Chardin: an Analysis and Assessment*. London: Tyndale Press, 1969.

King, Thomas M. *Teilhard's Mysticism of Knowing*. New York: Seabury Press, 1981.

King, U. *Towards a New Mysticism: Teilhard de Chardin and Eastern Religions.* London: Collins, 1980.

Klubertanz, G. P. *St. Thomas Aquinas on Analogy: a Textual Analysis and Systematic Synthesis.* Chicago: Loyola University Press, 1960.

Lacroix, J. *Maurice Blondel: an Introduction to the Man and his Philosophy.* London and New York: Sheed & Ward, 1968.

Linscott, Mary. *Teilhard Today.* Rome: Sisters of Notre-Dame, 1972.

Lubac, Henri de. *Teilhard Explained.* Translated by A. Buono. New York: Paulist Press, 1968.

The Eternal Feminine: a Study on the Text of Teilhard de Chardin. London: Collins, 1971.

The Faith of Teilhard de Chardin. London: Burns & Oates, 1965.

The Religion of Teilhard de Chardin. London: Collins, 1967.

Lukas, M., and E. *Teilhard: the Man, the Priest, the Scientist.* New York: Doubleday & Company Inc., 1977.

Lyons, J. A. *The Cosmic Christ in Origen and Teilhard de Chardin: a Comparative Study.* Oxford: University Press, 1982.

Lyttkens, H. *The Analogy between God and the World: an investigation of its background and interpretation of its use by Thomas of Aquino.* Uppsala: Almqvist & Wiksells Boktryckeri AB, 1952.

McCool, G. A. *Catholic Theology in the Nineteenth Century: the Quest for a Unitary Method.* New York: Seabury Press, 1977.

McInerny, R. M. *The Logic of Analogy: an Interpretation of St. Thomas.* The Hague: Martinus Nijhoff, 1961.

McNeill, J. J. *The Blondelian Synthesis: a Study of the Influence of German Philosophical Sources on the Formation of Blondel's Method and Thought.* Leiden: E. J. Brill, 1966.

Maloney, G. A. *The Cosmic Christ: from Paul to Teilhard.* New York: Sheed & Ward, 1968.

Marlé, René, SJ (ed.), *Au Cœur de la crise moderniste: le dossier inédit d'une controverse: lettres de Maurice Blondel, H. Bremond, Fr. von Hügel, Alfred Loisy, Fernand Mourret, J. Werlé...* Paris: Aubiers, Editions Montaigne, 1960.

Mersch, Emile. *The Whole Christ: the Historical Development of the Doctrine of the Mystical Body in Scripture and Tradition.* Translated by J. R. Kelly. London: Dennis Dobson, 1938.

Mooney, C. F. *Teilhard de Chardin and the Mystery of Christ.* New York: Harper & Row, 1966.

'The Body of Christ in the Writings of Teilhard de Chardin', *Theological Studies* 25 (1964), 576–610.

New Catholic Encyclopedia II, 1967 edn, s.v. 'Blondel, Maurice', by J. M. Somerville.

Ouince, René d'. 'Vivre dans la plénitude du Christ', *Christus* 9 (1962), 239–47.

Pannenberg, Wolfhart. *Jesus – God and Man.* London: SCM Press, 1968.

Pegis, Anton C. (ed.). *Basic Writings of St. Thomas Aquinas.* New York: Random House, 1944.

Raven, C. E. *Teilhard de Chardin: Scientist and Seer*. London: Collins, 1962.
Rideau, E. *Teilhard de Chardin: a Guide to his Thought*. London: Collins, 1967.
Robinson, J. A. T. *The Body: a Study in Pauline Theology*. London: SCM Press, 1952.
Rothe, Richard. *Dogmatik* 2. Heidelberg, 1870.
Sermons for the Christian Year. Translated by W. Clarke. Edinburgh, 1877.
Rousselot, Pierre. 'Les Yeux de la foi', in *Recherches de science religieuse* I (1910), pp. 241–59.
Pour l'histoire du problème de l'amour au Moyen Age. Münster: Druck und Verlag der Aschendorffschen Buchhandlung, 1908.
The Intellectualism of St Thomas. Translated by J. C. O'Mahony. London: Sheed & Ward, 1935.
Schott, E. 'Richard Rothe', in *Die Religion in Geschichte Gegenwart*, III (3rd edn, Tübingen, J. C. B. Mohr, 1961).
Smart, Ninian, John Clayton, Stephen T. Katz and Patrick Sherry (eds). *Nineteenth Century Religious Thought in the West*. Cambridge: Cambridge University Press, 1985.
Speaight, Robert. *Teilhard de Chardin: A Biography*. London: Collins, 1967.
Strange, Roderick. *Newman and the Gospel of Christ*. Oxford Theological Monographs. Oxford: University Press, 1981.
Szekeres, Attila (ed.). *Le Christ cosmique de Teilhard de Chardin*. Paris: Editions du Seuil, 1969.
Thacker, Eric. 'Teilhard in Ordos: a Mandala Mass', *CR* 299 (Christmas 1977), 15–19.
Vidler, Alec. *A Variety of Catholic Modernists: The Sarum Lectures in the University of Oxford for the year 1968–1969*. Cambridge: Cambridge University Press, 1970.
Welch, Claude. *God and Incarnation in Mid-nineteenth Century German Theology*. Oxford: Oxford University Press, 1965.
Zaehner, R. C. *Evolution in Religion: a Study in Sri Aurobindo and Pierre Teilhard de Chardin*. Oxford: Clarendon Press, 1971.

(II) WORKS RELATED TO RĀMĀNUJA'S 'BODY OF BRAHMAN'

Appasamy, A. J. 'Christological Reconstruction and Rāmānuja's Philosophy', *International Review of Missions* 41 (1952), 170–6.
Bhagavadgītā. Introduced and translated by S. Radhakrishnan. London: Allen & Unwin, 2nd edn, 1949.
Bhagavad-Gītā. Translated by R. C. Zaehner. Oxford: Oxford University Press, 1969; Oxford University Press paperback, 1973, reprint, 1979.
Bhatt, S. R. 'Bhakti as a Means of Emancipation in Rāmānuja', *The Vedānta Kesari* (January 1965), 470–2.
Studies in Rāmānuja Vedānta. New Delhi: Heritage Publishers, 1975.
Bowes, Pratima. *The Hindu Religious Tradition: a Philosophical Approach*. London: Routledge & Kegan Paul, 1977.

Carman, J. B. *The Theology of Rāmānuja: an Essay in Interreligious Understanding*. New Haven and London: Yale University Press, 1974.

Chettimattam, J. B. *Consciousness and Reality: an Indian Approach to Metaphysics*. London: Chapman, 1971.

Dasgupta, Surendranath. *A History of Indian Philosophy* 3. Cambridge: Cambridge University Press, 1961.

De, D. L. 'Pāñcarātra and the Upaniṣads', *Indian Historical Quarterly* 9(3) (1933), 645–62.

Duraisingh, Christopher. 'Towards an Indian–Christian Theology: Rāmānuja's Significance; a Study of the Significance of Rāmānuja's Theological Hermeneutics for an Indian–Christian Understanding of the Relation between God and All-else'. Ph.D. dissertation, Harvard University, 1979.

Ghate, V. S. *The Vedānta, a Study of the Brahma-Sūtras with the Bhāṣyas of Śaṃkara, Rāmānuja, Nimbārka, Madhva and Vallabha*. Government Oriental Series, Class c(1). Poona: Bhandarkar Oriental Research Institute, 1960.

Griffith, R. T. H. (ed. and trans.). *The Hymns of the Ṛgveda* II. The Chowkhamba Sanskrit Studies, vol. 35, Varanasi: Chowkhamba Sanskrit Series Office, 1963.

Hardy, Friedhelm. *Viraha-bhakti: the Early History of Kṛṣṇa Devotion in South India*. Oxford, Delhi and New York: Oxford University Press, 1983.

Hiriyanna, M. *Outlines of Indian Philosophy*. London: Allen & Unwin, 1932.

Johnson, Willard. *Poetry and Speculation of the Ṛg Veda*. Berkeley and London: University of California Press, 1980.

Khair, Gajanan Shripat. *Quest for the Original Gītā*. Bombay: Samaiya Publications, 1969.

Kumarappa, Bharatan. *The Hindu Conception of the Deity Culminating in Rāmānuja*. London: Luzac, 1934.

Lacombe, Olivier. 'The Notions of Soul and Body in Rāmānuja's Doctrine', *Proceedings of the Thirteenth All-India Oriental Conference* (1946), 292–8.

Lakṣmī-tantra: a Pāñcarātra Text. Translated by Sanjukta Gupta. Leiden: E. J. Brill, 1972.

Lester, R. C. *Rāmānuja on the Yoga*. Madras: Adyar Library and Research Centre, 1976.

Lipner, Julius. *The Face of Truth*. Houndmills & London: Macmillan Press, 1986.

'The World as God's "Body": in pursuit of Dialogue with Rāmānuja', *Religious Studies* 20 (March 1984), 145–61.

Lott, E. J. 'Finite Self and Supreme Being: Vedāntic Types of Analogical Method', *Bangalore Theological Forum* 11 (1) (1979), 2–35.

God and the Universe in the Vedāntic Theology of Rāmānuja: a Study in his use of the Self–Body Analogy. Madras: Rāmānuja Research Society, 1976.

'Iconic Vision and Cosmic Viewpoint in Rāmānuja's Vedānta'. In

Temple Art and Architecture. Edited by K. K. A. Venkatachari. Ananthacharya Indological Research Series 10. Bombay, 1981, pp. 30–46.
'Śrī Rāmānuja's Śarīra-Śarīrī-Bhāva: a Conceptual Analysis'. In *Studies in Rāmānuja: Papers Presented at the All-India Seminar on Śrī Rāmānuja and his Social Philosophy at Śrīperumbudur, July, 1979*. Madras: Śrī Rāmānuja Vedānta Centre, 1980, pp. 21–40.
'The Conceptual Dimensions of Bhakti in the Rāmānuja Tradition', *Scottish Journal of Religious Studies* 2 (Autumn 1981), 97–114.
'The Significance of Rāmānuja Darśana in the Vedāntic Debate', *Rāmānuja Vānī* (a Quarterly Journal of Viśishtādvaita Vedānta) 5 (3) (1982), 37–51.
Vedāntic Approaches to God. London: Macmillan Press, 1980.
Muir, J. (ed. and trans.). *Original Sanskrit Texts on the Origin and History of the People of India, their Religion and Institutions* v. London, 1874; 3rd edn reprint, Amsterdam: Oriental Press, 1967.
Müller, Max (gen. ed.). Sacred Books of the East. 50 vols. Vol. XLIII: *Śatapatha-brāhmaṇa*. Translated by Julius Eggeling. Clarendon Press, 1897; 2nd edn reprint, Delhi: Motilal Banarsidass, 1966.
Nakamura, Hajime. *A History of Early Vedānta Philosophy*, Religions of Asia 1. Delhi: Motilal Banarsidass, 1983.
Neevel, Walter. *Yāmuna's Vedānta and Pāñcarātra: Integrating the Classical and the Popular*. Harvard Dissertations in Religion no. 10. Missoula, Montana: Scholars Press, 1977.
Parthasarathy, M. N. 'The Gītārtha Saṇgraha of Śrī Yāmuna', *Śrī Rāmānuja Vānī: a Quarterly Journal of Viśishtādvaita Vedānta* (April 1984), 21–36.
Radhakrishnan, S. (trans.). *Gītā*. London: Allen & Unwin, 1948; reprint, 1949.
(ed. and trans.). *The Principal Upaniṣads*. London: Allen & Unwin, 1953.
Raghavachar, S. S. *Śrī Rāmānuja on The Gītā*. Mangalore: Śrī Ramakrishna Ashrama, 1969; reprint, 1979.
Śrī Rāmānuja on the Upaniṣads. Madras: Prof. M. Rangacharya Memorial Trust, 1972; reprint, 1982.
Raju, P. T. 'The Existential and the Phenomenological Consciousness in the Philosophy of Rāmānuja', *Journal of the American Oriental Society* 84 (4) (1964), 395–404.
Ramakrishnananda, Swami. *Life of Śrī Rāmānuja*. Madras: Śrī Ramakrishna Math, 1977.
Ramanujan, A. K. (trans.). *Hymns for Drowning: Poems for Viṣṇu by Nammāḻvār*. Princeton: Princeton University Press, 1981.
Rangacharya, V. 'Historical Evolution of Śrī-Vaiṣṇavism in South India'. In *The Cultural Heritage of India* IV. Edited by Haridas Bhattacharya. Calcutta: Ramakrishna Mission Institute of Culture, 1937; reprint, 1961.
Schrader, F. Otto. *Introduction to the Pāñcarātra and the Ahirbudhnya Saṃhitā*. Madras: Adyar Library & Research Centre, 1916; 2nd edn reprint, 1973.

Sen Gupta, Anima. *A Critical Study of the Philosophy of Rāmānuja*. Benares: Chowkhamba Sanskrit Series Office, 1967.

Srinivasacharya, P. N. 'Rāmānuja's Conception of Jiva as a Prakara of Isvara'. In *Visishtadvaita: Philosophy and Religion*. Edited by V. S. Raghavan. Madras: Rāmānuja Research Society, 1974, pp. 113–30.

Varadachari, K. C. (trans.). *Āḻvārs of South India*. Bombay: Bharatiya Vidya Bhavan, 1966.

Vedānta Deśika. *Tātparyacandrikā*. Edited by Śrī Prativādibhayaṅkara Aṇṇamgarācārya. Kāñcipuram: Śrīmadvedāntadeśika-granthamālā, 1941.

Vidyarthi, P. B. *Knowledge, Self and God in Rāmānuja*. New Delhi: Oriental Publishers, 1978.

Viṣṇu Purāṇa. Translated by H. H. Wilson. Calcutta: Punthi Pustak, 1979.

Viṣṇu purāṇa. Gorakhpur edition. Gita Press, n.d.

Vyas, Ramnarayan. *The Bhāgavata Bhakti Cult and three Advaita Ācāryas: Sankara, Rāmānuja and Vallabha*. Delhi: Nag Publishers, 1977.

Weber, A. (ed.). *Śatapatha-brāhmaṇa in Mādhyandina-śākhā with extracts from the commentaries of Sāyaṇa, Harisvāmin and Dvivedaganga*. Varanasi: Chowkhamba Sanskrit Series Office, 1964.

Yāmuna. *Siddhi-traya*. Edited by V. T. Viraraghavacharya. Translated by R. Ramanujacharya and K. Srinivasacharya. Madras: Ubhaya Vedānta Granthamālā Book Trust, reprint, 1972.

Stotraratna, Translated by Swami Adidevanananda. Mylapore, Madras: Śrī Ramakrishna Math, 1950; reprint, 1951.

Yāmunāchārya, Śrī. *The Gītārthasaṅgraha*. Translated by M. R. Sampatkumaran. In *The Gītābhāshya of Rāmānuja*. Madras: Prof. M. Rangacharya Memorial Trust, 1969, pp. 535–45.

(III) GENERAL WORKS

Adler, Gerhard. *The Living Symbol: a Case Study in the Process of Individuation*. London: Routledge & Kegan Paul, 1961.

Beatson, P. *The Eye in the Mandala; Patrick White: a Vision of Man and God*. London: Paul Elek Books, 1976.

Beck, Brenda E. F. 'The Symbolic Merger of Body, Space and Cosmos in Hindu Tamiland', *Contributions to Indian Sociology* 10 (2) (March 1981), 213–43.

Bennett, John B. 'Nature – God's Body? A Whiteheadian Perspective', *Philosophy Today* vol. 18 no. 3/4 (Fall 1974), 248–54.

Burrell, D. *Analogy and Philosophical Language*. New Haven: Yale University Press, 1973.

Dillistone, F. W. *Christianity and Symbolism*. London: Collins, 1955.

Eliade, Mircea. 'Cosmical Homology and Yoga', *Journal of the Indian Society of Oriental Arts* 5 (1937), 188–203.

'Methodological Remarks on the Study of Religious Symbolism'. In *The History of Religions: Essays in Methodology*. Edited by M. Eliade and J. M. Kitagawa. Chicago: Chicago University Press, 1959, pp. 86–107.

Encyclopedia of Philosophy I, 1967 edn, s.v. 'Analogy in Theology', by F. Ferré.

Fulcher, R. W. 'Mandala Symbolism and Christ-Mysticism', Ph.D. thesis, University of London, 1959.

Geertz, Clifford. 'Religion as a Cultural System'. In *Anthropological Approaches to the Study of Religion*. Edited by M. Banton. ASA Monographs 3. New York: Tavistock Publications, 1966; Social Science Paperback, reprint, 1985.

Goldammer, Kurt. 'Is there a Method of Symbol Research which offers Hermeneutic Access to Depth-Dimension of Religious Experience?' In *Science of Religion: Studies in Methodology*. Edited by L. Honko. The Hague: Mouton, 1979.

Goodman, Nelson. *Ways of Worldmaking*. Hassocks, Sussex: Harvester, 1978.

Griffiths, Bede. *A New Vision of Reality*. London: Collins, 1989.

Gyory, R. A. *The Emergence of Being: through Indian and Greek Thought*. Washington D.C.: University Press of America, 1978.

Hunt, Anne. 'The Mandala: a Consideration of its Usage as a Religious Symbol'. Dissertation for Post-graduate Diploma, United Theological College (Bangalore), 1977.

Jantzen, Grace. *God's World, God's Body*. London: Darton, Longman & Todd, 1984.

Jung, C. G. 'Concerning Mandala Symbolism' in *Collected Works* IX (i). London: Routledge & Kegan Paul, 2nd edn, reprint, 1975.

'Dream Symbols of the Individuation Process'. In *Eranos Yearbooks* 4. Edited by J. Campbell. Bollingen Series 30 (4). Princeton: University Press, 1960.

'The Symbolism of the Mandala', in *Collected Works* XII. London: Routledge & Kegan Paul, 2nd edn, reprint, 1974.

Katz, Steven. 'Models, Modeling and Mystical Training', *Religion* 12 (1982), 247–75.

Kitagawa, J. M., and C. H. Long (eds). *Myths and Symbols: Studies in honour of Mircea Eliade*. London: University of Chicago Press, 1969.

Langer, S. K. *Philosophical Sketches*. London: Oxford University Press, 1962.

Philosophy in a New Key: a Study in the Symbolism of Reason, Rite and Art. Cambridge, Mass.: Harvard University Press, 1960.

McDougall, Lorna. 'Symbols and Somatic Structures'. In *The Anthropology of the Body*. Edited by J. Blacking. London: Academic Press, 1977, pp. 391–403.

McFague, Sallie. *Metaphorical Theology: Models of God in Religious Language*. London: SCM Press, 1983.

Martin Soskice, Janet. *Metaphor and Religious Language*. Oxford: Clarendon Press, 1985.

Mascall, E. L. *Existence and Analogy*. London: Longmans, Green, 1949.

'The Doctrine of Analogy', *Cross Currents* (1951), 38–57.

Moore, Peter. 'Mystical Experience, Mystical Doctrine, Mystical Tech-

nique'. In *Mysticism and Philosophical Analysis*. Edited by Steven Katz. London: Sheldon Press, 1978, pp. 101–40.
Rahner, K. *Spirit in the World*. London: Sheed & Ward, 1968.
Ramsey, I. T. *Models and Mystery*. London: Oxford University Press, 1964.
Ricœur, Paul. *Hermeneutics and the Human Sciences*. Edited and translated by J. B. Thompson. Cambridge: Cambridge University Press, 1981.
Rule of Metaphor: Multi-Disciplinary Studies of the Creation of Meaning in Language. Translated by R. Czerny. Toronto and Buffalo: University of Toronto Press, 1977.
'The Metaphorical Process as Cognition, Imagination and Feeling'. In *On Metaphor*, pp. 141–57. Edited by Sheldon Sacks. Chicago and London: University of Chicago Press, 1978–9.
Sacks, Sheldon (ed.). *On Metaphor*. Chicago: Chicago University Press, 1978–9.
Sherry, Patrick. 'Analogy Today', *Philosophy* 51 (1976), 431–46.
'Are Spirits Bodiless Persons?', *Neue Zeitschrift für systematische Theologie und Religionsphilosophie* 24. Berlin and New York: Walter de Gruyter (1982, Part 1), 37–52.
Religion: Truth and Language Games. London: Macmillan Press, 1977.
Smart, Ninian. *Doctrine and Argument in Indian Philosophy*. London: Allen & Unwin, 1964.
'God's Body', *Union Seminary Quarterly Review* 37 (Fall/Winter 1981–2), 51–68.
'Myth and Transcendence', *The Monist* 50 (1966), 475–87.
Reasons and Faiths: an Investigation of Religious Discourse, Christian and non-Christian. London: Routledge & Kegan Paul, 1958; reprint, 1971.
'The Scientific Study of Religion in its Plurality', in *Contemporary Approaches to the Study of Religion* 1, ed. Frank Whaling, Religion and Reason 27 (Berlin: Mouton, 1984), pp. 365–78.
Worldviews: Crosscultural Explorations of Human Beliefs. New York: Charles Scribner's Sons, 1983.
Splett, Jörg. 'Body', *Sacramentum Mundi: an Encyclopaedia of Theology* 1. Edited by Karl Rahner et al. London: Burns & Oates, 1968.
Sprung, Mervyn (ed.). *The Question of Being: East–West Perspectives*. Pennsylvania State University Press, 1978.
Tracy, David. 'Metaphor and Religion: The Test Case of Christian Texts'. In *On Metaphor*. Edited by Sheldon Sacks. Chicago: University of Chicago Press, 1978–9.
The Analogical Imagination: Christian Theology and the Culture of Pluralism. London: SCM Press, 1981.
Tucci, Giuseppe. *The Theory and Practice of the Mandala: with special reference to the modern Psychology of the Subconscious*. Translated by A. H. Bodrick. London: Rider, 1969.
Valle, Ronald S., and Rolf von Eckartsberg (eds). *The Metaphors of Consciousness*. New York and London: Plenum Press, 1981.

Wainwright, William J. 'God's Body', *American Academy of Religion Journal* 42 (September 1974), 470–81.
Weber, Renée. *Dialogues with Scientists and Sages: The Search for Unity.* London: Routledge & Kegan Paul, 1986.
Wilber, Ken (ed.). *The Holographic Paradigm and other Paradoxes.* Boston and London: New Science Library, Shambhala, 1985.
Wiles, Maurice. 'Christian Theology in an Age of Religious Studies'. In *Explorations in Theology* IV. London: SCM Press, 1979.

Index

upāsana 35, 38, 65, 89, 95, 98, 134, 142

Vedānta 30, 39, 81
Vedāntin 30, 41
Vedas 30–3
vibhūti 34, 72–3, 77, 92, 102–3, 115, 120, 129
vinculum substantiale 27–8
vision of Christ, 11, 28–9, 126; of the Highest Person, 34; of Kṛṣṇa, 170 n. 29; of universe as organism, 163 n. 23; of Teilhard de Chardin, 45, 51–2, 56, 61, 87–8, 95, 98, 103, 126; of Rāmānuja, 66, 87–8, 127; of the Lord, 65, 126–7, 130, 147; of Lord's form/*vibhūti*, 73, 78, 89, 93; of divine–world integration, 74, 83, 102, 105, 124, 126–32, 147; as (self-)-knowledge, 94, 132–5
viśiṣṭādvaita 2, 40, 44, 76, 80
Viṣṇu 30, 34, 66, 76, 90
Viṣṇu purāṇa 34–5, 65–6, 72, 81

worldview in religion, 1; disclosed by symbols, 4; of organic universe, 15, 123; of Christ and the cosmos, 17–18; of Teilhard de Chardin, 29, 45; in Rāmānuja, 67, 114; in root-metaphor, 88, 96; and structure of reality, 96, 129; relational, 100, 123; and models, 107–8; and consciousness, 125

Yāmuna 3, 30, 35, 37, 41, 43–4, 67

Printed in the United Kingdom
by Lightning Source UK Ltd.
136391UK00002B/7-9/A

9 780521 046695